lost in space
25th Anniversary Tribute Book

BY JAMES VAN HISE

PIONEER BOOKS, INC.   LAS VEGAS, NEVADA

Designed and Edited by Hal Schuster

OTHER PIONEER BOOKS

•THE MAGICAL MICHAEL JACKSON
Edited by Hal Schuster. March, 1990. $9.95, ISBN#1-55698-235-6
•FISTS OF FURY: THE FILMS OF BRUCE LEE
Written by Edward Gross. March, 1990. $14.95, ISBN #1-55698-233-X
•WHO WAS THAT MASKED MAN?
Written by James Van Hise. March, 1990. $14.95, ISBN #1-55698-227-5
•PAUL MCCARTNEY: 20 YEARS ON HIS OWN
Written by Edward Gross. February, 1990. $9.95, ISBN #1-55698-263-1
•THE DARK SHADOWS TRIBUTE BOOK
Written by Edward Gross and James Van Hise. February, 1990. $14.95, ISBN#1-55698-234-8
•THE UNOFFICIAL TALE OF BEAUTY AND THE BEAST, 2nd Edition
Written by Edward Gross. $14.95, 164 pages, ISBN #1-55698-261-5
•TREK: THE LOST YEARS
Written by Edward Gross. $12.95, 128 pages, ISBN #1-55698-220-8
•THE TREK ENCYCLOPEDIA
Written by John Peel. $19.95, 368 pages, ISBN#1-55698-205-4
•HOW TO DRAW ART FOR COMIC BOOKS
Written by James Van Hise. $14.95, 160 pages, ISBN#1-55698-254-2
•THE TREK CREW BOOK
Written by James Van Hise. $9.95, 112 pages, ISBN#1-55698-256-9
•THE OFFICIAL PHANTOM SUNDAYS
Written by Lee Falk. $14.95, 128 pages, ISBN#1-55698-250-X
•BLONDIE & DAGWOOD: AMERICA'S FAVORITE FAMILY
Written by Dean Young. $6.95, 132 pages, ISBN#1-55698-222-4
•THE DOCTOR AND THE ENTERPRISE
Written by Jean Airey. $9.95, 136 pages, ISBN#1-55698-218-6
•THE MAKING OF THE NEXT GENERATION
Written by Edward Gross. $14.95, 128 pages, ISBN#1-55698-219-4
•THE MANDRAKE SUNDAYS
Written by Lee Falk. $12.95, 104 pages, ISBN#1-55698-216-X
•BATMANIA
Written by James Van Hise. $14.95, 176 pages, ISBN#1-55698-252-6
•GUNSMOKE
Written by John Peel. $14.95, 204 pages, ISBN#1-55698-221-6
•ELVIS-THE MOVIES: THE MAGIC LIVES ON
Written by Hal Schuster. $14.95, ISBN#1-55698-223-2
•STILL ODD AFTER ALL THESE YEARS: ODD COUPLE COMPANION.
Written by Edward Gross. $12.95, 132 pages, ISBN#1-55698-224-0
•SECRET FILE: THE UNOFFICIAL MAKING OF A WISEGUY
Written by Edward Gross. $14.95, 164 pages, ISBN#1-55698-261-5

ALL PHOTOS FROM THE MIKE SUSSEK ARCHIVES, COMPILED BY MKE SUSSEK

Library of Congress Cataloging-in-Publication Data
James Van Hise, 1949—
    Lost in Space 25th Anniversary Tribute Book

    1.   Lost in Space 25th Anniversary Tribute Book (television)
I. Title

Published by Pioneer Books, Inc., 5715 N. Balsam Rd., Las Vegas, NV, 89130.

First Printing, 1990

CONTENTS

INTRO: LOST IN SPACE

A year before STAR TREK was launched into science fiction history, a different kind of science fiction show debuted. LOST IN SPACE was a family show in which a family were the main characters. While it started out as an action adventure show, it turned into something which was often TV's first science fiction sitcom. After all, how worked up could get when Will and Dr. Smith were imperiled by monsters in such decidedly shabby costumes as the second season of LIS presented?

But LOST IN SPACE nonetheless had its charm. The first season, filmed in black and white, has some of the most striking cinematography done for television. The early episodes which had extensive outer space special effects took particular advantage of the black and white film to achieve remarkable depth and clarity of contrast. When it went to color, like many shows of the mid-Sixties, its palette was a touch on the garish side in order to indulge in the creative capabilities that having a color scheme provided.

For some years after its cancellation, LIS fell into disfavor and was largely forgotten or dismissed, but in recent years the fans of the series have gotten together to discuss their mutual admiration for the series and even produced fanzines devoted to the adventures of the crew of the Jupiter II. This recently got a shot in the arm when fans nationwide could tune in to daily reruns on the USA cable network, although true to form in this modern technicolor time, the color episodes were run first so as not to put off viewers by showing the supposedly ordinary and dated-looking black and white episodes. That the B&W's were what the fans wanted to see most no doubt escaped the notice of the programmer. That LOST IN SPACE being seen on a national channel is a welcome reprise was even echoed last fall in TV GUIDE, which referred to the show as being so bad that it's good.

So journey with us now as we go back to the future, to that fateful day in 1997 when the space family Robinson became LOST IN SPACE!

—-JAMES VAN HISE
December, 1989

THE BIRTH OF LOST IN SPACE

By Paul Monroe

In 1964, the name Irwin Allen was well established in the entertainment field. Throughout the two previous decades, Allen had hit big with his own radio program, a literary agency, and motion pictures for RKO, Warner Brothers and 20th Century Fox. His first series for television, VOYAGE TO THE BOTTOM OF THE SEA, based on his film of the same name, was sailing along smoothly on the ABC network when Allen began looking for a follow-up series.

In the mid 60's, America had become very space- minded. The late President Kennedy had set a goal of reaching the moon before the end of the decade and we were very close to realizing that goal. Meanwhile, the story of THE SWISS FAMILY ROBINSON was in the back of Allen's mind, but he realized that the children of the 1960's might not easily identify with the adventures of the 19th century family. He combined the family story with the space backdrop, and SPACE FAMILY ROBINSON, about a family leaving an overpopulated Earth to colonize another planet, was born. Allen took his idea to CBS, and they agreed to fund a pilot episode.

As pre-production was getting underway, Allen's legal people informed him that Walt Disney Studios was producing a film called SPACE FAMILY ROBINSON and already owned a patent on the title. Additionally, Disney had called in Gold Key Comics, who handled other Disney titles, to create a comic tie-in for the movie. Allen decided to change the name of his pilot to LOST IN SPACE and proceed as planned. Disney never did release their film version of SPACE FAMILY ROBINSON.

Allen's production crew included a number of people who had worked with him on past projects: long-time friend Paul Zastupnevich would design the costumes as well as act as Allen's personal assistant. Art direction would be handled by William Creber, who would finish the basic design of the Robinson's space ship, the Gemini XII, before moving on to Allen's pilot for THE TIME TUNNEL. Robert Kinoshita, who designed Robby the Robot for the 1956 film classic FORBIDDEN PLANET, would finalize the exterior and design the interior of the ship. The cinematographer would be Emmy winner Winton Hoch. L.B. Abbott and his special effects team would provide whatever optical magic was needed to get Allen's space family lost in space. Allen then hired Shimon Wincelberg to write the script.

By this point, it was very clear LOST IN SPACE was going to be a very expensive pilot. The blueprinting alone cost upwards of $100,000 which, for 1964, was a huge amount to be spent on a film which may never be sold. Thus a partnership was set up consisting of Allen, CBS Television, 20th Century Fox and Red Skelton (Operating under the name Van Bernard) to spread the risk.

Allen's Robinson family consisted of father John, as Astrophysicist, mother Maureen, a Bio-chemist, and children Judy, Penny and Will. Also with them is Dr. Donald West, the young scientist who selected the planet to be colonized. Since the roles of John and Maureen were to be the leads, Allen wanted faces familiar to the TV audience. Guy Williams of Disney's ZORRO was cast as John and June Lockhart of LASSIE fame took the part of Maureen. Portraying the Robinson children was Marta Kristen as Judy, Angela Cartwright as Penny, and Billy Mumy as Will. Mark Goddard, familiar for his roles in the series MANY HAPPY RETURNS and THE DETECTIVES, was cast as their assistant, Don West, completing the group which Allen would launch into the unknown.

Allen directed the pilot, titled "No Place To Hide," in December of 1964. The final tab of $600,000 made LOST IN SPACE the second most expensive pilot to date, coming in just behind STAR TREK's first pilot, "The Cage." The story involved the Robinson family and Dr. West leaving Earth in 1997 to begin colonization of a planet in the Alpha Centauri star system. Deep in space, the ship encounters a meteor storm which damages the craft, sending it far off course. The ship, dark and silent, drifts for many years until it falls into the attraction of a planet and crashes. Several months later, the family has set up camp, domesticated several local animals, and begun a small farm. Eventually, the cold climate forces the Robinsons to travel southward in their land rover, the Chariot. They battle a giant cyclops, are nearly drowned in a whirlpool, and finally reach the planet's tropical regions. The episode closes with the family giving thanks for a safe journey while two humanoid aliens watch them from behind some bushes.

In early 1965, a screening of "No Place To Hide" was held for CBS. Enthusiasm ran high, and Allen was given the green light to begin production. LOST IN SPACE had achieved series status. First, the good news was passed on to the cast, who were told to be ready for filming to begin in the summer.

Next, Allen and story editor Tony Wilson reviewed the pilot to see what improvements could be made. They agreed that, while the story was exciting, the character development was shallow and the series risked falling into a "monster of the week" format unless some other antagonist was added.

Enter Dr. Zachary Smith.

In 1965, America was competing in the space race, the Cold War risked becoming hot and sabotage was an underlying concern. Allen reasoned that international competition among space programs in the near future would be no different, and sabotage would provide a dramatic way for the Robinsons to become lost in space. Smith, working for a foreign power, would somehow stay aboard the ship after launch to become the added continuing irritant that Allen and Tony wanted.

Several actors, including Carroll O'Connor, were considered to play Dr. Smith, but it was Jonathan Harris who seemed best able to portray the villain. Jonathan was well known for his role in THE THIRD MAN and THE BILL DANA SHOW. However, since all

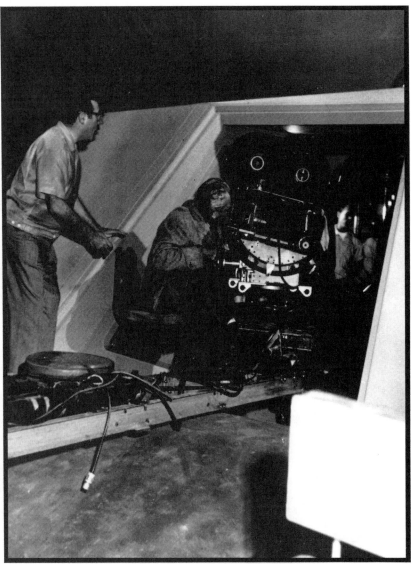

the other cast members had already signed series contracts, Jonathan's name would be listed last in the credits with one distinctive billing: Special Guest Star. LOST IN SPACE was the first show to use the guest title for a recurring character, and it was employed throughout the three seasons that the series ran. Today, Jonathan has commented that he has answered more interview questions about that one aspect of his Dr. Smith role than any other.

Changes were also being made to the Robinson's space ship. First, the name was changed from the Gemini XII to the Jupiter II, probably to avoid confusion with NASA's then current Gemini program. Next, landing gear was added and an electronic elevator now connected with a full lower deck. Art director Robert Kinoshita had designed this new level which included a computerized galley, a lab, an auxiliary control room (complete with crash couches), state rooms, a lavatory area (which we only see glimpses of in the series), and an engine room.

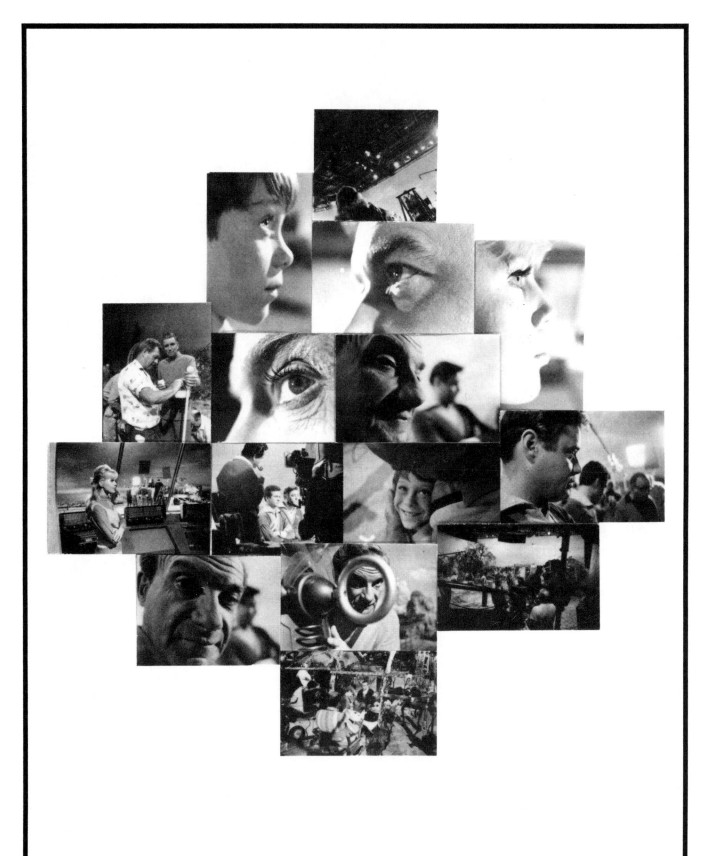

It was also during this time that Allen met with Kinoshita to discuss the design of one additional member of the Robinson expedition: an Environmental Control Robot. This machine would be part of the mission equipment capable of determining the suitability of the new planet. He would have a bubble head, a torso-shaped body and pleated arms and legs. He could analyze soil samples, discharge electricity from his claws, and when he spoke, his chest lit up.

The original plan was to build only the suit's upper half, support it by wires, and film it from the waist up, but eventually an entire suit was built for an actor to wear. Bob May, who had acted and stunted in various films and television programs, was at Fox auditioning for the remake of STAGECOACH when Allen asked him to play the robot. Bob accepted and, for three seasons, no one else ever appeared as the robot. In post-production, announcer Dick Tufeld dubbed in the robot's voice. As the series progressed, the robot would develop a personality of his own, eventually becoming one of the show's most popular characters.

The addition of Dr. Smith and the robot to LOST IN SPACE made it impossible to air "No Place To Hide" as episode number one, so Tony Leader directed the whole cast in new scenes written by Shimon Wincelberg which would be cleverly woven in between sequences from the pilot to form the basis of the first five episodes. Filming continued through the summer while the newspaper and radio ads announced the coming of a spectacular new series for the whole family. Fun adventure was the emphasis. The anticipation continued to build until September 15, 1965, when millions of American homes tuned in to get their first glimpse of LOST IN SPACE. The series begun as just an idea in creator Irwin Allen's mind was now a prime-time television series seen weekly across the country. What was to come in the next three years would challenge us, entertain us, and lay the foundation for the science fiction television which was to follow.

SHIMON WINCELBERG: FIRST CAME THE WORD

After Irwin Allen conceived the concept for LOST IN SPACE he had to film a pilot to convince CBS to back his new science fiction wonder.

First came the word, and the word came from Shimon Wincelberg, although he used his pen name S. Bar-David Before filming could begin, someone had to write the pilot. Wincelberg collaborated on it with Allen and the original pilot was filmed. It was shown to the network and became the series that we know and love today.

Wincelberg was one of the key people that brought LOST IN SPACE to the television screen.

Before there was the version of LOST IN SPACE that we're all familiar with, there had been an earlier version of the pilot which focused only on the Robinsons and did not include Dr. Smith or the robot. Writer Wincelberg, involved in developing the script for LIS from Irwin Allen's basic concept, worked on this initial version.

"I had a meeting with Irwin and I thought it was terrific," Wincelberg recalls, "because he had a wonderful enthusiasm and confidence. I could see that he would be just great fun working with. So many producers you work for are insecure and unsure of their own ideas, but he knew exactly what he wanted. He had an approximate storyline for LOST IN SPACE and he had the characters, all except Dr. Smith.

"The idea was that once you got them on the planet there would be plenty of stories. We didn't worry about it too much until we had the script in pretty good shape and the characters and their relationships worked out. We just assumed that there would be a monster-of-the-week and that we'd get our stories from that. It wasn't until later, when Story Editor Tony Wilson joined us, that we realized that we really needed that irritant within the family. Somebody who would get others into trouble, and that's where Dr. Smith came

in—a Long John Silver type. A loveable scoundrel. Then the relationship between him and the boy, and to some extent between the boy and the robot, is what really gave the story its fun. Otherwise it was a very square family where the father, mother and sister all behaved in a very nice and predictable way. They were good and the actors were excellent, but it didn't have the kind of verve that you got from Dr. Smith and the robot."

Since Wincelberg worked on the pilot, one wonders whether he might be considered the co-creator of LOST IN SPACE.

"The way they distinguish it today is that there is the creator of the show, who in this case is unquestionably Irwin Allen, and then there's a separate credit called 'developed by.' I suppose I was the one who took his storyline, his idea and basic premise and evolved it into a script with believable characters. But he came up with the idea that made it possible."

The ending of the unaired version of the pilot features two aliens peering menacingly around some bushes in a cliff-hanger which was never included in any series episode. While the two aliens looked similar to beings used in another LIS episode he wrote, "Invaders From The Fifth Dimension," Wincelberg doesn't recall that there was any connection.

"The similarity could be due to the art director who probably had an idea of what aliens should look like and whenever aliens were needed they looked pretty much the same."

During the period that he was involved with LOST IN SPACE, Wincelberg also wrote for STAR TREK and he has some interesting observations to make in comparing the two shows.

"STAR TREK was potentially more interesting, but it also took itself much more seriously. From a writer's point of view, it was much more fun to work on LOST IN SPACE. In fact, the people at STAR TREK sort of looked down at the LIS people and thought it was a kid's show. I suppose it was, but I certainly enjoyed working there more.

"Irwin really had a feeling for young people and what young people were doing. He was very much in touch with his own youth and he was one of the few people in this business at that time who could get away with it. Today we have Spielberg, but I think that Irwin Allen was the Spielberg of his time."

Registering an opinion that is common among writers of the time, Wincelberg is surprised that TV series such as LOST IN SPACE are still remembered twenty years later.

"At the time, I think that those of us who were fairly busy in television probably thought of it like writing on Kleenex—you use it once and then throw it away. The whole idea of something lasting all these years probably didn't enter our heads. Television was so young. Back in those days there weren't any classics yet and it's sometimes surprising which shows are totally forgotten. It's not a thing you can predict and not a thing you can consciously manipulate, because if you could then everybody'd be rich! Some things just reverberate in people's imaginations."

On the subject of whether or not he thinks that LOST IN SPACE could be re-launched in a successful revival, Wincelberg states, "It's hard

to tell. It depends on how badly Irwin wants to do it and how strong the demand is from the fans. It would probably have to be a great deal more sophisticated today, but certainly the idea of a family crash-landing on a planet and behaving like pioneers and trying to make a life for themselves is always a valid story going back to Robinson Crusoe and Swiss Family Robinson. I hadn't really thought about it. It would be in keeping with both the classic 19th century adventure stories as well as with what other people have done more recently with the science fiction idea of people being marooned in space."

Regarding which genre he prefers to write in, Wincelberg doesn't have a hard and fast reply.

"It really varies," he explains. "I had a wonderful time writing Westerns, especially for HAVE GUN WILL TRAVEL and GUNSMOKE. You could really deal with some very modern themes, which at that time you couldn't tackle in a modern story but you could deal with in a Western or a science fiction story. The networks weren't as nervous about dealing with something controversial if it were safely distant."

Carey Wilbur: Reforming Doctor Smith

After LOST IN SPACE was approved by CBS, Allen needed writers. These new writers had new ways of looking at the characters. For instance, Carey Wilbur completely revised the personality of Dr. Smith, from villain to cad.

Writing for television is a special art. Wilbur has been doing it for many years. Many of the best LOST IN SPACE episodes were written by him. Without his imagination, the show would not have been the same.

Wilbur was one of the first writers on LOST IN SPACE. "Tony Wilson, the story editor, called me in on a script ('There Were Giants In The Earth') because for some reason Shimon Wincelberg couldn't do the teleplay, so I was given the assignment, and from there we went on to others." Wilbur had worked with Tony Wilson before on LANCER and TWELVE O'CLOCK HIGH.

"I don't recall much about 'Giants In The Earth' other than that they were playing it straighter than the shows later on. Tony Wilson was an absolutely wonderful guy and with Irwin Allen producing he gave the writers so much leeway that it was really delightful to work on the show."

Wilbur's next episode for LIS was "The Sky Pirate." "That was about the time we started playing Dr. Smith as other than a straight villain and gave him the comedy bits. He became a funny character and was the kind of guy who would say, 'let's you and he fight—I'll hold your coat.' I guess you could say that I was the first writer to play Smith that way in the script and Tony and Irwin both seemed to like it. I was kind of basing him on a character I used to do on the old CAPTAIN VIDEO series which I'd written for three years. I shifted the Tucker name to the sky pirate character."

This was followed by "His Majesty Smith," which fell back on the formula

plot in which Smith's greed led him into trouble.

Then came "A Visit To Hades."

"Irwin Allen encouraged the use of rather wild imagination," Wilbur recalls. "We could bring in fantasy and old legends, which is what I did with this one that put Smith in Hell."

Another Wilbur script was for "The Questing Beast." "That was the one about the crazy knight errant who had been chasing this lady-like dragon. We certainly had a lot of fun with that one," he recalls. "The idea behind that was that it isn't the capture that counts, it's the pursuit. When the knight finally got the dragon at spear-point, he discovered that he really liked the old girl and the chase goes on. The last thing she does is go flirting off behind a rock saying, 'Ha, ha, ha! Can't catch me!' And he charges after her."

Then there followed a sequel to "The Sky Pirate" called "The Treasure of the Lost Planet."

"We brought Tucker back for that one. It may have been a story conference with Tony Wilson where we decided to bring him back."

Wilbur followed that up with "The Astral Traveller." "That was based on an old legend of the Glamous Castle where there is a monster supposedly hidden in the deepest dungeon."

Wilbur also wrote a script which didn't get filmed because of the show's cancellation.

"It was based on the Alice in Wonderland characters. I don't remember much about it other than the fact that Will, Dr. Smith and the robot stumbled on a cache of old books. The books had magical properties so that in reading them you were thrown into the story."

Wilbur also wrote the STAR TREK episode "Space Seed," which spawned THE WRATH OF KHAN. Even so,

LOST IN SPACE is the show he enjoyed writing for most.

"It was more fun writing on Irwin's shows, like LOST IN SPACE and TIME TUNNEL, because you could have a ball.

"STAR TREK was more straight science fiction—you couldn't bring monsters and such things into the stories. STAR TREK has a tremendously bright man in Gene Roddenberry, but LOST IN SPACE has a tender spot in my heart."

SEASON ONE

Introduction by Paul Monroe

The premiere episode of LOST IN SPACE, "The Reluctant Stowaway," reveals that the year is 1997 and that Earth is vastly overpopulated. Man is reaching out into space to find new worlds to colonize. When the Jupiter II lifts off carrying the Robinson family, Major Don West, Dr. Zachary Smith and their robot companion, the series first season is off to an exciting start. The next 28 episodes introduced us to alien worlds, monsters and futuristic equipment such as prime-time TV had never seen.

Year one's first five episodes contained most of the footage from LOST IN SPACE's original pilot filmed in December of 1964 plus new scenes shot to incorporate Smith and the robot (who weren't in the original pilot) into the story lines. Episode one launches the Robinson family on the way to the Alpha Centauri system only to be sent hopelessly off course by saboteur Dr. Smith. Episode two, "The Derelict," gives the Jupiter her first encounter with an alien race, and episode three, "Island In The Sky," sees the ship marooned on a desolate planet where it would stay for the rest of the season. From episode four on, each first season entry was a tale of survival and courage.

The series' first year differed from the second and third in several ways. First, it was filmed in black and white. At first thought, this may seem undesirable to watch, but the grays and shadings of these episodes actually let the alien visitors and monsters seem a bit more life-like and the set's panoramic desert backdrop more wistful and desolate. The early episodes were also more dramatic than the stories which followed. "The Sky Is Falling," in which the Robinsons try to co-exist with a visiting alien family whom they cannot talk to (as opposed to the many later aliens who speak English) and "The Raft," the story of the Robinsons's practical effort to build a craft and return to Earth, are fine examples of the survival theme that dominated the early entries. It was too soon abandoned.

Year one also gave us the most effective use of all the cast, something that would be lost as the series progressed. Stories like "My Friend, Mr. Nobody," in which we see Penny's compassion, and "The Keeper," where we witness the Robinsons' strong family devotion, helped to introduce us to the personalities, talents, likes and dislikes of the Robinsons, West and Smith.

John Robinson was the leader. Stories such as "The Reluctant Stowaway" and "One Of Our Dogs Is Missing" proved him not only able to make tough decisions, but to know his family well and respond accordingly.

Don West was a more fiery character than John, but also able to lead the group. Episodes like "The Hungry Sea" and "The Lost Civilization" showed us his technical skills with the mission equipment.

Other entries let us see Maureen's strength and undying support of her husband ("The Raft"), Judy's loyalty and wit ("The Magic Mirror"), Penny's love of classic literature and music ("Wish Upon A Star"), Will's electronic talents ("War Of The Robots"), and Dr. Smith's restless, scheming mind ("Island In The Sky") as well as his eventual fondness for the family ("The Raft").

The characters in LOST IN SPACE were written as real people with feelings and reactions that fitted the circumstances they found themselves in. By the fifth episode, "The Hungry Sea," the strain of survival has put tension on John and Don's relationship. Each has different ideas and, as in any group or family setting, discussions lead to arguments before a mutual agreement is reached. This riff not only allowed John and Don to understand one another a little better, but lent much more credibility to their characters, allowing us to better relate to them.

LOST IN SPACE employed a great deal of futuristic equipment during year one which often meant the difference between life and death for the castaways. Their ship was the Jupiter II, one of the simplest yet most dazzling crafts sci-fi television has yet produced. Taken along on the journey were the force field generator, laser rifles and pistols (the pilot's laser weapons, as well as a second laser rifle, were used throughout year one), Maureen's sonic washer, the Jet Pack, laser drilling gear used to extract the ores by which their fuel was made, farming equipment, heat shields, fatigues and parkas, and the Chariot, a solar-powered land rover.

The most important piece of equipment was the Robinson's Environmental Control Robot, designed to evaluate the new planet's conditions and help determine its suitability to support human life. In the beginning, the robot was just a machine, a tool to make survival easier just as the other Jupiter equipment was designed to do. Unfortunately, this machine fell into the secret hands of saboteur Dr. Smith, who programmed it as his evil tool.

Slowly the robot began developing a personality all his own. He was still a machine, but his voice took on a human quality and he began to think and converse more like a real person with each episode. Stories showcasing the robot included "The Space Trader," in which Smith trades the machine to the Trader for food, "The Lost Civilization," where we begin to see how much Will and the family mean to the robot, and "War Of The Robots," in which the robot tries to save the family from an evil robotoid played by Robby the Robot (Robby and the Robinson's robot were both designed by Robert Kinoshita). "War Of The Robots" is particularly important in the robot's evolution, for it is now clear that he is accepted by everyone as a member of the family. By the end of year one, the robot had become one of the program's most popular characters, and the network was requesting more stories centered around him.

High points in the first season included "The Derelict," featuring outstanding shots of the Jupiter orbiting the alien spaceship and the first use of the full Jupiter II mock-up. Included is the beautiful footage shot in Red Rock Canyon, for the pilot, of the ship slicing over the mountains.

"My Friend, Mr. Nobody" is a wonderful story of Penny's friendship with an ancient, alien life force. By listening to Penny talk, the being learns to communicate as well as what it means to care for something. Two of LOST IN SPACE's most atmospheric episodes are "Invaders From The Fifth Dimension," featuring the most unearthly designed craft the series ever produced, and "Ghost In Space," the tale of an invisible monster, using fog-lined bog sets and a very haunting score.

"The Keeper" is the series' only two-part episode and one of the finest produced. Guest star Michael Rennie (who co-starred with Jonathan Harris in the earlier THE THIRD MAN series) plays an alien who travels the universe collecting two of every species of animal in his mammoth ship. He sees the Robinsons as nothing more than just another species of animal and sets out to add Will and Penny to his collection.

"His Majesty Smith" features a wonderful performance by guest Kevin Hagen and employs some nice split-screened effects as Smith confronts his double, Daddy Zach. Will actually returns to Earth in "Return From Outer Space," although no one will believe his story. Child actor Kurt Russell competes against Will in "The Challenge." Will becomes a genius and Dr. Smith is turned into an old man in "A Change Of Space," and John falls into an ancient tomb and becomes possessed by an alien warrior's spirit in the season's finale "Follow The Leader."

In its first year, LOST IN SPACE began using two classic theatrical techniques which dated back to the movie serials of the 1940's: the narrator and the cliffhanger ending. At the end of each episode, the next story would actually begin. Then, at just the right climactic moment, the action would freeze and the words "To Be Continued Next Week, Same Time, Same Channel" would slide in. The following week, announcer Dick Tufeld (who also provided the robot's voice) would begin, "Last week as you recall. . . ," recapping the situation for us before we saw the res-

olution. Two of the most interesting cliffhangers, seen at the ends of "Return From Outer Space" and "The Challenge," instructed us to tune in "Two Weeks From To-night" due to network pre-emptions. The cliffhanger endings and narration be-ginnings were used in the first two seasons before being dropped in year three in favor of scenes from the next week's episode.

By the end of season one, it was clear that Will, Dr. Smith and the robot were the program's most popular characters and the majority of the scripts in year two would be centered around them. The first season gave us, with few exceptions, the best stories the series had to offer, and although the number of viewers increased in year two, season one stands unique for its blend of dramatic adventure, humor, a well-rounded use of the cast, and the theme of pioneer survival.

CAST AND CREDITS

CREATED AND PRODUCED BY: Irwin Allen
ASSOCIATE PRODUCER: Jerry Briskin
STORY EDITOR: Anthony Wilson
MUSIC SUPERVISION: Lionel Newman
THEME: Johnny Williams
DIRECTORS OF PHOTOGRAPHY: Gene Polito A.S.C., Charles Clarke A.S.C.
ART DIRECTORS: Jack Martin Smith, Robert Kinoshita, Carl Macauley
EXEC. IN CHARGE OF PROD. FOR VAN BERNARD PRODUCTIONS, INC. : Guy Della Cioppa
SPECIAL PHOTOGRAPHIC EFFECTS: L.B. Abbott A.S.C., Howard Lydecker
SOUND EDITOR: Don Hall, Jr.
MAKEUP SUPERVISION: Ben Nye
PRODUCTION MANAGER: Gaston Glass
UNIT PRODUCTION MANAGER: Hal Herman
ASSISTANT TO THE PRODUCER: Paul Zastupnevich

AN IRWIN ALLEN PRODUCTION IN ASSOCIATION WITH:
Jodi Productions, Inc.
Van Bernard Productions, Inc.
Twentieth Century Fox Television, Inc.
CBS Television Network

IN CHARGE OF PRODUCTION: William Self

REGULAR CAST

DR. JOHN ROBINSON: Guy Williams
MAUREEN ROBINSON: June Lockhart
MAJOR DON WEST: Mark Goddard
JUDY ROBINSON: Marta Kristen
WILL ROBINSON: Billy Mumy
PENNY ROBINSON: Angela Cartwright
DR. ZACHARY SMITH: Jonathan Harris
THE ROBOT: Bob May
THE VOICE OF THE ROBOT: Dick Tufeld

Episode commentaries by Mike Clark

EPISODE ONE:
"The Reluctant Stowaway"

First telecast: Sept. 15, 1965
Writer: S. Bar-David (Shimon Wincelberg)
Director: Tony Leader
Incidental Music: Johnny Williams
GUEST CAST: ALPHA CONTROL TECHNICIAN: Fred Crane, INSPECTOR: Tom Allen, TV COMMENTATOR: Don Forbes, THE GENERAL: Hal Tore, SECURITY GUARD: Brett Parker

The story opens on October 16, 1997 at Alpha Control where the Jupiter II sits ready and waiting on the launch pad. The Robinsons, the first family to ever be launched into space, are taking their final pre-launch tests. Their destination is a newly discovered planet orbiting the star-sun Alpha Centauri. The family will be placed in suspended animation for the five and one-half year voyage. We are taken on a tour of the Jupiter II and introduced to its wonders, including the robot.

While final preparations are being made, an enemy agent by the name of Zachary Smith is planning to sabotage the Jupiter II. Sneaking aboard the ship, he reprograms the robot to destroy the internal guidance system eight hours after liftoff, along with other vital ship functions such as the cabin control system.

When a soldier discovers Smith and attempts to arrest him, Smith knocks out the guard and dumps the body down a waste disposal chute. The soldier's body lands in a dumpster next to the spacecraft. Smith then reports the success of his mission to his superiors, whom he contacts by identifying as Aolus 14 Umbra.

Shortly after that, when the Robinsons are being given their final physicals, the Doctor on hand is none other than Zachary Smith. The family boards the Jupiter II and confers with their pilot, Don West, who is already aboard. Smith is among the staff members who come aboard to wish the Robinson's good luck on their voyage.

As everyone is leaving and the Robinson's are being put into suspended animation, Smith notices that the robot's power pack has been removed. Without it the robot will not be able to respond to his reprogrammed instructions. In attempting to find the power pack and reattach it to the robot, Smith delays to long and is locked on board when the hatches shut. Accepting his fate he straps himself in to one of the unused acceleration couches belowdecks.

Upon coming to after liftoff, Smith deactivates the robot to protect himself. Smith goes to the flight control deck but is unable to make contact with Alpha Control. Due to the excess weight of Smith on the ship, its flight path has altered and is heading directly into the path of a swarm of meteors. Alpha Control is unable to alter the path of the Jupiter II from Earth. When the meteors start bombarding the ship, Smith has no alternative but to awaken Don West from hypersleep in order to get the ship under control and out of harm's way. West accomplishes this and then awakens the rest of the family, due to the ship being off course.

Maureen Robinson collapses due to the aftereffects of the freezing process. Upon examining her, Smith observes that it might not be safe for her to undergo another exposure to the suspended animation process. On top of that, the ship has been damaged, including some vital tracking equipment.

In order to attempt to make necessary repairs, Major West temporarily turns off the artificial gravity, which Will and Penny take advantage of to full around. When

Will notices that the power pack has been removed from the robot, he reattaches it, unaware that this will activate the robot's deadly reprogramming.

The robot goes on its programmed rampage, smashing the astrogator and sending the ship into uncontrolled hyperflight. When the robot attempts to depressurize the ship, which would kill everyone aboard, Major West manages to remove the power pack from it, demobilizing the robot before it can break through the hull.

But now the Jupiter II is so far off course from its uncontrolled flight through hyperspace that it is beyond the limits of the galaxy and Alpha Control has lost all trace of it. The Robinsons cannot recognize any of the constellations they see.

Back at Alpha Control, they report to the President of the United States that the Jupiter II has passed the limits of the galaxy and must be presumed to be lost in space.

When John Robinson goes outside the Jupiter II to make a spacewalk to repair the scanner, his tether breaks. Don wants Smith to go out, but Smith claims he's not in condition for such a thing and his heart could go. Maureen suits up to go after him to rescue him before he floats too far away from the ship. She takes a rocket gun to shoot another line to him.

The Jupiter II miniature used here is the one created for the original pilot. It has extra-large view ports and almost no lower deck.

Since Jonathan Harris is prone to claustrophobia, his entrance on the hidden accelerator couch was accomplished by his double, Harry Carter.

Note that the robot actually "walks" towards the astrogator in the climactic battle with the Robinsons. And its chest light isn't functioning when it exits from the elevator.

The Alpha Control TV commentator is played by Don Forbes, who served similar duties on VOYAGE TO THE BOTTOM OF THE SEA in the feature and the series.

The President is portrayed by another Irwin Allen regular, Ford Rainey.

Dr. Smith shows what a bad guy he is by karate-chopping a security guard and dumping him into the garbage chute. Although some fans refer to Dr. Smith as having "killed" the guard, nothing in the episode indicates that the guard was any more than knocked out.

EPISODE TWO:
"The Derelict"

First telecast Sept. 22, 1965
Story: Shimon Wincelberg
Teleplay: Peter Packer
Director: Alex Singer
Incidental Music: Herman Stein
GUEST CAST: CREATURE: Dawson Palmer, TV COMMENTATOR: Don Forbes

John Robinson is drifting away from the Jupiter II, but Maureen finally manages to shoot a line to him. After she pulls him back to the ship she's told that a comet is approaching and that they only have four minutes before the heat outside the ship will become so great they'll burn up. But John decides that he still has enough time to repair the scanner. He makes the repairs, but when he tries to re-enter the ship, the heat has expanded the metal of the ship's hull so that the entranceway won't open. Don unsuccessfully tries to open the door from inside the airlock, but they're unsuccessful until Will suggests that a fire extinguisher might cool the metal enough to get the door open. Dr. Smith is sent to get the big fire extinguisher from below.

Back on Earth, Alpha Control announces that the Jupiter II is lost in space and that it may well have been due to sabotage by a foreign power.

The plan to cool the metal of the airlock is a success and John and Maureen are brought back into the ship just in time by Don. Maureen is unconscious and is carried in from the airlock, but she recovers.

Major West directs the Jupiter II away from the region occupied by the comet. Meanwhile, Dr. Smith is reprogramming the robot once again, this time so that it will only obey the commands of Dr. Smith's voice. When John discovers Smith tampering with the robot, he becomes very angry due to the havoc the robot has already wrought. He tells Smith that as far as he's concerned he's a stowaway and will be treated as such, and to leave the robot alone.

Just then the Jupiter II picks up a signal from an approaching spacecraft which is so gigantic it dwarfs the Jupiter II.

Smith secretly hopes that this is where his contact, Aolis 14 Umbra, originates even though the craft seems to definitely be alien to Earth. Smith tries to contact his superiors on his secret radio, but all he picks up is shrieking static.

Don doesn't want to approach the craft any closer, but John is curious to get a better look at the huge vessel. The front of the giant spacecraft opens and the Jupiter II is pulled inside. They're helpless to avoid the grip of whatever is pulling them inside.

Once safely inside the gigantic vessel, John Robinson, Major West and Dr. Smith decide to investigate who's operating it. They exit the Jupiter II and find crystalline cobwebs everywhere and everything seems run down, as though abandoned.

But they do find the apparent control room of the vessel and its star charts, which John and Major West study.

Meanwhile, Smith still hopes to find his secret contact here and goes looking for him.

Will wants to see what's going on but the robot won't allow the boy to pass until he does a successful imitation of Dr. Smith's voice ordering the robot to step forward, which allows the boy to slip past it and out the door. While Will is exploring, a slug-like creature encounters him. Will attempts to communicate with it, and it seems to mean no harm, but when Dr. Smith sees the thing, he tries to explain to the creature that he wants to return to Earth, but Will says they want to go to Alpha Centauri. Dr. Smith becomes annoyed when the creature won't respond to them and so he shoots at it. The creature reacts violently.

Don and John here Will calling for help and the four reunite and run back to the Jupiter II.

Major West prepares the ship for liftoff, using the ship's force field to hold the creature at bay. John Robinson uses his laser to blast an exit for them and the Jupiter II exits the giant alien spacecraft.

Deciding that the huge ship was a colony craft of some alien race, John suggests that the Jupiter II make for an Earth-like world he located on the star charts, which will allow them to hopefully make the rest of their needed repairs once they land.

They approach the planet, although Maureen thinks they should proceed to Alpha Centauri rather than stop on this world. But Don and John explain that they must land to make repairs. The Jupiter II approaches the planet, preparing to enter its atmosphere.

There are many good shots in this episode of the 15 inch Jupiter II miniature, which was controlled by horizontal guide wires. There's also an excellent angle of

the four foot Jupiter II miniature landing gear.
This episode also has a rare shot of the full-size Jupiter II mock-up showing the lower level with the landing gear extended.

EPISODE THREE:
"Island In The Sky"
First telecast Sept. 29, 1965
Story: Shimon Wincelberg
Teleplay: Norman Lessing
Director: Tony Leader
Incidental Music: Johnny Williams

The Jupiter II approaches the planet that John Robinson had discovered on the alien star charts. Not wanting to risk his family or the ship, he plans to send the robot down to scout the planet and determine whether it is safe, but Dr. Smith doesn't think too highly of this plan. Since Smith wants to keep the robot available for his own secret purposes, he has the robot fake a malfunction, thus making it unsuitable for the task of exploring the planet. In actuality, all Smith has done is reprogram the robot so that it will only respond to his voice, but John doesn't realize this yet.

John decides to go down himself, descending from the Jupiter II by means of parajet thrusters which will brake him from orbit and allow him to land safely on the planet's surface. But Smith has tampered with these, too! When John tries to activate the thrusters they fail to respond. John tumbles helplessly towards the planet's surface, disappearing through the clouds until radio contact with him is lost.

Dr. Smith is playing chess with the robot and is obviously waiting for something to happen. When John tries to activate the parajets and fails, Dr. Smith blithely tells the robot that it's time to give his condolences to the widow.

Although Smith believes that John Robinson must be dead, the others refuse to accept this. Major West decides that they should take the Jupiter II in as close as possible to John's projected landing site. Dr. Smith points out that with the loss of John Robinson's weight, they could possibly make their way back to Earth. When the others ignore him, Smith demands that they put it to a vote. When he's outvoted, Smith summons the robot. He has the robot crush a space helmet as a demonstration of its strength. He then insists that the Jupiter II return to Earth.

Smith attempts to use the robot to mutiny and gain control of the ship so that they'll be able to return to Earth. But Major West manages to upset the equilibrium of the ship using the stabilizers and grabs Smith in a neck hold. Forcing Smith to follow his orders or else, Smith sends the robot below decks, back to its compartment. Major West has had quite enough of Dr. Smith and puts him into a freezing tube to keep him from causing any more trouble. Smith tries to reveal the sabotage he's done in order to save himself, but Don won't let Smith finish talking before locking him in the tube.

But even out of commission, Smith's interference lives on as the ship's thrusters malfunction upon approaching the planet. The Jupiter II crash-lands on the planet's surface, burning up some more circuits but otherwise landing seemingly unscathed.

Observing the planet through the portal, they see a world which seems devoid of life. In order to determine just how safe it might be to exit the ship, Will once again successfully imitates Dr. Smith's voice and orders the robot to survey the area. The others are very surprised that Will is able to accomplish this. The robot deems the planet safe, if a bit frigid after testing the air and taking a soil sample. Atmospheric pressure 22 pounds per square inch. Temperature is 33 degrees. Major West supervises the assembly of the Chariot, a vehicle they can use to search the area themselves. Boarding the craft, they all begin to attempt to find some trace of John Robinson. Upon picking up a blip on their infra-red scan, they enter a small wooded area and discover a small chimp-like creature. Major West carries it back to the Chariot and it refuses to leave. Penny decides to adopt the creature and names it Debbie.

But there is still a blip on their scanner and following it they discover John trapped in a pit. While they're rescuing him, the robot returns to the Jupiter II, following preprogrammed instructions to check on Dr. Smith's welfare every hour.

The robot finds Dr. Smith in a suspended animation tube and awakens him. When Smith finds that he's aboard the Jupiter II alone, he plans to steal the ship and return to earth, but has to abandon this plan when the robot informs him that it cannot fly the ship by itself.

Smith decides on an alternative plan of having the robot dispose of everyone except Major West, the ship's pilot. When he's learned all he needs to know from Major West, he'll have Don eliminated as well. Smith doesn't want to be implicated and orders the robot to only kill the family members when they're alone, and by using an electrical discharge so that the deaths will look accidental.

The Robinsons and Major West decide to return to the Jupiter II, having noticed the inexplicable absence of the robot. But a large plant-thing absorbs the energy from the Chariot and strands them, forcing everyone to continue their return journey to the ship on foot. Will wants to fix the Chariot fuses, but John wants everyone back to the ship before nightfall.

Upon finally reaching the ship they find Smith out of the freezer tube and he's confronted by Don and John. Smith proclaims his innocence and insists that he's turned over a new leaf, but while the Doctor seems to be on good behavior for the moment, the others intend to be watchful. Dr. Smith sends the robot out to analyze the planet when night falls.

After dinner, Will goes out to try to repair the Chariot, even though John gave strict orders that no one is to leave the ship after dark. When Dr. Smith discovers this, he's very concerned because he knows that the robot is out there as well. Seeing young Will alone, the robot moves quitely towards him, planning to carry out Dr. Smith's command to kill the Robinsons whenever they are alone. Will starts talking to the robot, but it announces its intentions and starts sending out blasts of electricity. Will climbs to the top of the Chariot and orders the robot to keep back, but it keeps on coming.

This episode is directed by Tony Leader, who is also credited as director of "The Reluctant Stowaway" although people who worked on the show say that Irwin Allen actually directed the original pilot.

There's lots of footage in this episode from the original pilot including the spectacular crash of the Jupiter II. The miniature work was shot in California's Red Rock Canyon near the Mojave Desert.

When they decide to unload and assemble the Chariot, it all happens off-camera.

The Fox backlot with the concrete cliff was used in the scenes of the trapped Prof. Robinson. This setting was used again and again in LOST IN SPACE and VOYAGE TO THE BOTTOM OF THE SEA.

EPISODE FOUR:
"There Were Giants In The Earth"
First telecast October 6, 1965
Story: Shimon Wincelberg
Teleplay: Carey Wilber
Director: Leo Penn
Incidental Music: Herman Stein, Bernard Hermann (DAY THE EARTH STOOD STILL)
GUEST CAST: THE CYCLOPS: Dawson Palmer

Will is repairing The Chariot when he notices the robot approaching him. Will had decided that he couldn't repair the Chariot that night after all and was about to head back to the ship due to how cold it was, when the robot starts attacking him. He radios a distress call to his parents and then, by imitating Dr. Smith's voice, Will orders the robot to check its circuits. When the others see what the robot is doing, Don goes back to the ship and forces Dr. Smith to come with him and pull the robot's power pack.

While they're unsure about what happened and why, Smith is given a stern warning not to tamper with the robot's programming any further, although Smith proclaims that he's innocent of any wrong-doing.

The next day the crew of the Jupiter II begin erecting a permanent camp, re-signed to the fact that they are marooned on this planet, at least for the time being. John and Major West erect a force field generator to protect the encampment while Judy and Penny begin planting a garden to grow food. Will works on repairing the radio telescope and everyone pitches in to do something except for Dr. Smith who manages to avoid doing any work as much as possible.

Doctor Smith is told that it's not safe to use any of the native soil to plant in, but he dismisses the warning as being pointless. The seeds he plants near the ship are weirdly affected by the alien soil and within a day have grown into monstrous things with tentacles which menace everyone. Will uses a hand laser to dispose of the things, and when the pieces are examined they detect strange micro-organisms which clearly originated on the planet.

Will attempts to reprogram the robot, without a lot of success. In the middle of the night, when the robot hears a noise, it turns off the force field and rolls off by itself to investigate. John is annoyed with Will for tampering with the robot and sends him to bed. When it finally shows up again the next day the robot seems to be in bad shape as nothing it says about sixteen meter humanoids makes much sense.

John and Major West repair the Chariot and the following days pass peacefully enough until a frost starts to kill some of their plants. Upon checking their make-shift weather station, John and Major West learn that a bad cold spell is rolling in towards them and that the temperature will drop to a 150 degrees below zero with-in twenty-four hours.

The pair decide that they must relocate everyone to the planet's southern re-gions, but before they can return to the ship to warn the rest, Major West sees a gigantic footprint, and then they spot its owner--a sixteen meter tall cyclops! Now they know that the robot was not malfunctioning. The creature, although human-oid, is very primitive and attacks. John and Major West weren't carrying weapons and are forced to seek shelter in a cave.

In the Jupiter II, Will Robinson happens to witness the plight of his father and Major West on the ship's radio telescope. Grabbing one of the laser pistols, he runs off to help them. Just as the cyclops is attempting to force John and Major West out of their cave with a tree trunk, Will arrives on the scene and stuns the huge creature, allowing the men to escape.

Back at the Jupiter II, everyone is packing up and planning to head south, except Dr. Smith, who believes he can survive safely with the robot. The robot is too large to fit into the Chariot anyway, and so would have to either remain behind or follow the vehicle under its own power. Will says goodbye to the robot, which doesn't understand Will's sentiment over leaving, so the boy pulls its power pack.

Just as they're about to leave, Penny turns up missing. She was last seen playing with Debbie, the Bloop. John uses the rocket belt to search for her and finds her sitting on an alien turtle which had run away with her.

John returns with Penny just as the temperature hits ten below zero when Don was ordered to depart. Reunited, they pile into the Chariot and set off. But they haven't traveled far when they encounter the cyclops again, which hurls huge boulders at them. This time Major West uses a laser rifle on the creature, stunning it so that they can move safely past it and begin their journey south.

That night they camp under the stars and everyone relaxes, but Don and John have to work on the power unit which was damaged by the boulders. While Will plays the guitar to amuse everyone, Judy keeps Major West company while he works on the Chariot. Penny tells her mother that she saw Major West kissing Judy on the hand.

The next day they resume their journey, but when a huge electrical storm strikes, they have to stop and seek shelter in a large cavern to avoid the tremendous discharges of electricity from the sky. There they discover the remnants of a lost civilization. Everyone gets flashlights and starts exploring the ruins. When Debbie the Bloop wanders off, Will and Penny go looking for her. Will discovers a secret passage and accidentally locks himself and his sister, Penny, inside, where their only company an ancient mummified body. When Don and Judy attempt to rescue Will and Penny, they get trapped too when the door closes behind them. Then an earthquake starts to rock the cavern and everything starts to collapse around them.

Outside the sealed room, John Robinson uses his laser to try to blast his way in and free the others before it's too late.

The scenes with the giants also come from the original pilot. The giant's costume is actually made of dried palm fronds. It was designed and constructed by Paul Zasptupnevich.

When Maureen Robinson appears at the Jupiter II hatch holding laundry, inside the ship you can see the astrogator in its extended position, something never seen again. As she walks down the ramp, we see a rare shot of the upper hull. Catwalks for the crew were permanently placed atop the Jupiter II during the series.

Ostriches are seen in the background as Mrs. Robinson does her laundry. This is another carry over from the pilot where these bird-like creatures were dressed up by the art department. They were probably dropped from the series due to ostrich's bad temper and sharp claws.

As the Robinsons depart for the frozen sea, Dr. Smith and the robot remain behind at the Jupiter II mainly because they did not appear in the giant footage used to construct the episode.

The footage of the giant and the rocket belt was originally shot in color for use as stock footage.

Blooper: Robot's lights quit momentarily as he disables the force field.

This episode is directed by Leo Penn, the father of actor Sean Penn.

EPISODE FIVE:
"The Hungry Sea"
First telecast October 13, 1965
Story: Shimon Wincelberg
Teleplay: William Welch
Director: Sobey Martin
Incidental Music: Johnny Williams

John blasts his way into the passage so that the rest of the Robinsons and Major West and able to flee the cavern before it completely caves in. They clamber aboard The Chariot and exit the cave.

Dr. Smith and the robot are still back at the Jupiter II where the temperature is rapidly dropping. The robot reports observations it has made regarding the planets orbital trajectory, but Smith dismisses the robot's claims as ludicrous.

The Chariot arrives at an iced over inland sea. Outside the craft it is 125 degrees below zero. With the temperature so cold they feel that the ice should be safe enough to support their weight and they drive out onto it to search for land across the sea.

Meanwhile, the temperature back at the Jupiter II reverses and starts to rapidly increase. Smith wonders what this will mean for the Robinsons for if something should happen to them then he'll be stranded with only the robot for companionship. The impact of this realization causes Smith to countermand his previous order to the robot to kill the Robinson's and he actually contacts the Chariot to warn the Robinson's of their potential danger.

Major West thinks that Smith is just up to another trick and cuts off their radio contact. Smith is fit to be tied and sends the robot out to find the Chariot and convey his message to the Robinson's about the planet's extreme climatic changes and what they harbinger. But when the robot catches up to them, Major West sees it and believes they're under attack again, so he blasts the robot and disables it.

Will has always liked the robot and pleas with his father to get it working again. John Robinson finally relents, but they don't have much luck getting the robot in working order again. But they do manage to play the message which the robot had been instructed to give. Due to the weird orbit of the planet, it passes very close to its star-sun at one point while at the farthest point in its orbit it is very far away from its sun, thus causing massive temperature extremes. Thus the cold wave is about to be eclipsed by a heat wave.

Major West refuses to believe it but John doesn't feel that they can take the chance and has a protective reflective tent constructed over the Chariot. Just as they complete the shelter, the heat-wave rolls in.

Under their thermal blankets they're able to ride out the heat-storm which burns up the nearby vegetation. After the crest of the storm has passed over them, the Robinsons and Major West emerge and pack things up in preparation to return to the Jupiter II. But the sea they crossed is no longer covered with ice but is a maelstrom of raging waters.

Since the Chariot is amphibious they're able to cross the wide body of water, but as they near the opposite shore their solar battery conks out. Major West climbs up to the top of the Chariot to repair the damage but the fury of the storm tossed sea sweeps him off the craft. But he manages to get back to the Chariot, climb back to the top and complete the needed repairs.

The Chariot finishes crossing the sea and emerges on shore and into a huge jungle which has suddenly sprung up in the wave of the heart-storm. But they traverse it safely and return to the Jupiter II.

Back at the Jupiter II things have reached a stage of truce with Dr. Smith since his warning did save their lives. While Will is monitoring the radio and the robot is playing a guitar, Smith notices that the radar indicates that something is rapidly approaching them from space. Could it be that they're in . . . danger?

The cave sequence and the Chariot crossing the ocean is also from the original pilot, but this exhausts that footage for the rest of the series.

This episode is the first one showing genuine concern for the Robinsons on the part of Dr. Smith.

EPISODE SIX:
"Welcome Stranger"
First telecast October 20, 1965
Teleplay: Peter Packer
Director: Alvin Ganzer
Incidental Music: Herman Stein
GUEST STAR: JIMMY HAPGOOD: Warren Oates

Will's fussing with the radio and sending out signals has brought a response in the form of a strange space capsule which is approaching the planet. It lands nearby the Jupiter II and out steps Jimmy Hapgood, cowboy spaceman. He's from Earth, having left years before the Robinson's did. In fact Jimmy has been in space since June 18th, 1982. He was aiming for a soft landing on Saturn but sort of missed the planet entirely and has been on a gypsy course ever since.

Will likes Hapgood and helps Jimmy decontaminate his spacecraft. But they somehow miss a part of the rocket engines and space spores begin to reproduce and rapid grow as well as glow.

John Robinson thinks he can help Jimmy Hapgood return to Earth, but in exchange he'll want the cowboy to take Will and Penny, his two youngest children, back with him. Maureen isn't pleased with the idea but agrees that it might be better if they did. They decide to approach Hapgood with this plan.

But meanwhile Dr. Smith has been overhearing this discussion and is determined that if anyone returns to Earth with Hapgood, it will be Dr. Zachary Smith!

Dr. Smith tries to ingratiate himself with Hapgood and offers the robot's circuitry as replacement parts for Jimmy's capsule which will serve as a fine navigational aid. The parts in question are removed from the robot and given to Hapgood.

When John Robinson suggests that Hapgood could return his two children to Earth, the cowboy spaceman won't even consider it and thinks that John was an idiot for ever bringing children along on a spaceflight to begin with. This annoys Major West who gets into a slugfest with Hapgood which ends without resolving anything.

Encouraged by Hapgood's refusal to let the children aboard, Smith asks if he could return with Jimmy to Earth, but the cowboy isn't any more interested in that than he was in bringing the two kids back with him.

John and Don decide not to hold a grudge again Hapgood and continue to help Jimmy repair his ship for the return trip. They all go to check over the capsule and discover that the untreated spores have run wild, having grown into huge plants. Penny is captured by one of the alien plants but she's rescued by Hapgood. Will uses the decontaminant he used on the ship before to kill the space spores.

Hapgood is so grateful for what Will did to rescue his ship from the giant plants that he agrees to take Will and Penny back to Earth with him after all.

Smith is properly annoyed and tries to manipulate Will and Penny into wanting to stay behind so that they'll run away and keep from being taken home by Hapgood. Dr. Smith is certain that by the process of elimination Hapgood will agree to take Smith back instead.

When Will and Penny run off to hide, Hapgood starts having second thoughts about going home again after all his years roving in space. Earth would be dull in comparison and he'd never be allowed to journey into space again once he goes back to Earth.

When Hapgood leaves, the children are nowhere to be found and Smith isn't around either to hitch a ride and returns too late to accompany Hapgood, where ever he may be going. Hapgood has decided to continue to explore space rather than return to the comparatively dull life on Earth.

Guest star Warren Oates does a fine turn as astronaut Jimmy Hapgood. His spaceship and footage of liftoff would be reused numerous times in the series.
In this episode the robot is opened up and operated on by Dr. Smith!

EPISODE SEVEN:
"My Friend, Mr. Nobody"
First telecast: October 27, 1965
Writer: Jackson Gillis
Director: Paul Stanley
Incidental Music: Johnny Williams

Penny accidentally wanders into an area where her father and Major West have set a test explosion while drilling for possibly radioactive materials they can adapt as a fuel substitute. John Robinson barely rescues Penny in time and angrily orders her to leave the area.

The girl feels like nobody wants her and wanders off to a small pond where she decides to get a drink of water. But as she bends down the water seems to automatically rise to her lips, which frightens her. When she calls out in fear, a voice answers back like an echo from a nearby cave. As Penny enters the cave to investigate, a rocky door swings shut behind her.

When Penny returns to the Jupiter II and tells everyone what she's been up to, no one believes her, assuming that it's just some game she's playing to keep herself occupied, which annoys Penny to no end. Even Will claims that she's been talking to nobody.

The next day Penny returns to the cave and decides that she's going to try to teach her mysterious friend to talk. She dubs her friend "Mr. Nobody" and he gives her some crystals to play with. But later when she shows them to Dr. Smith, he immediately recognizes them as diamonds but keeps that knowledge to himself, believing that with enough of them he'll return to Earth a wealthy man. Dr. Smith acts very friendly towards Penny and says that he'd like to meet her "Mr. Nobody," but she refuses. Not to be outdone, Smith follows her and has the robot accompany him.

They observe Penny enter the cave and the rock swing shut behind her, but Smith is unable to gain entry the same way as the rock won't budge.

Inside the cave, Penny is conversing with Mr. Nobody and trying to learn more about him. The entity explains that he's existed for millions of years but is still learning and growing.

Outside, Dr. Smith finds a small opening but a rock suddenly slides over it, sealing the little opening. Still, Smith is certain now that he knows where the diamonds came from and plans to blast his way in using equipment from the Jupiter II.

Realizing that Major West has been searching for radioactive ores, Smith tricks Don into helping him set up the equipment for blasting into the cave.

Meanwhile, Maureen explains to Penny that when she was a little girl, she had an imaginary friend, too. Penny becomes angry at the suggestion that Mr. Nobody is imaginary. Then when she learns from Will that Major West and Dr. Smith have gone out to blast for ore, Penny realizes exactly what Smith's true intentions are.

Penny runs to warn Mr. Nobody but before she can the explosives are detonated, knocking Penny off her feet, dazing her. But Mr. Nobody believes that she must be dead and becomes angry and threatens vengeance. It pursues Major West and Dr. Smith, who have returned to the ship, unaware that Penny was knocked out by the blast.

Back at the Jupiter II the robot warns of something approaching which consists of pure force with an anti-matter nucleus. Somehow the robot knows that it is an angry intelligent entity with tremendous powers.

Major West and Dr. Smith make it back safely to the Jupiter II while the robot engages the entity with energy blasts, but the robot is defeated and blasted to pieces.

Penny comes running up, all upset, and manages to quiet Mr. Nobody down. The entity now realizes its mistake. The entity then changes form and becomes visible, taking on a form like a ball of energy filled with stars. Having transformed into its next stage in its metamorphosis, it leaves the planet and heads into space.

Dr. Smith manages to reassemble the robot and finally decides to just throw the diamonds away, believing that they'll never get off this planet anyway. But all of Dr. Smith's actions are being cooly observed by alien eyes on a strange view screen. . .

Dr. Smith portrayed as a greedy bastard for the first time, and certainly not the last.

The robot is torn apart into three pieces by a spectacular storm in this episode.

EPISODE EIGHT:
"Invaders From The Fifth Dimension"
First telecast November 3, 1965
Writer: Shimon Wincelberg
Director: Leonard Horn
GUEST STARS: THE ALIENS: Joe Ryan, Ted Lehmann

Judy detects someone on the radar screen, but it disappears before she can show it to Major West. Don decides that it was just a malfunction.

A short distance away, the alien spaceship which had briefly shown up on the Jupiter 2's radar lands behind some rocks. The craft is a globe-shaped ship with long landing legs.

The aliens within the craft see Dr. Smith, who tries to flee, but they stun him with a beam before he can escape. The aliens have landed because one of their guidance control circuits has burnt out and they need to repair it somehow. Since their entire computer needs to be replaced to accomplish the needed repairs, they've decided that the only available substitute would be a human brain. Although Dr. Smith's brain is primitive by their standards, they decide that it will have to do.

When they try to bring Dr. Smith aboard, they realize that he's too large and will have to be reduced in size through their powers to manipulate the fifth dimension. Dr. Smith thinks fast and suggests that they would do better to use a small Robinson whose brain would be much more to their liking. Since the aliens have found Smith's mind to be too treacherous for their scientific uses, they agree to this alternative. Knowing what Smith is capable of, they fit him with a control collar to strangle him should he try to betray them. This will insure that Smith will return with the "small Robinson" so that they'll remove the collar.

Dr. Smith finds Will rock-hunting in the lava beds and convinces the boy that only he can save them from the menace of these weird aliens and follows Smith.

John and Maureen are disturbed by the way Smith was acting when he came looking for Will and they decide to go out searching for him in the Chariot. They take the robot with them. They come upon the area where Will had been rock-hunting and finds his sample bag and Dr. Smith's flashlight, so they know that Smith found Will.

The aliens are observing this and the robot detects their presence. He announces that anti-humans are nearby, but cannot get a fix on their position.

Dr. Smith arrives back at the alien ship with Will, who is taken captive. The aliens are true to their word and free Dr. Smith from the control collar. The aliens explain to Will that they need his youth and energy because their own ancient minds have become weary with age.

When John and Maureen locate Smith, the craven cad immediately makes up a story and leads them to the alien ship. Major West soon arrives via the rocket belt.

When the aliens see the Robinsons approaching, they open fire on them, disabling the robot.

Will agrees to operate the alien computers so long as they do not harm his family. The aliens agree, but Will's mind cannot carry out its tasks because of the interference of his human emotions. When he sees his mother on the monitor screen, Will begins to cry. Unable to deal with the strain caused by this, the computers begin to overload. The aliens release Will as also being unsuitable for their task. But just as Will escapes from the craft, the power feedback from the malfunctioning computers blows it up, destroying the aliens.

After everything has returned to normal, a drought sets in caused by a massive heatwave. Don and Judy are working on one of the vital water conversion units when a quake shakes that area of the planet causing a rockfall which buries Major West!

The design of the alien ship is quite intriguing. The alien make-up reuses the skull caps created for the aliens which appeared in the original LIS pilot.

There's extensive use of helicopter footage in this episode showing the Chariot cruising through Red Rock Canyon.

Dr. Smith displays what is becoming his characteristic chicanery by making a deal with the aliens to provide them with one of the Robinson kids.

Blooper: The only time in the series that Bob May's legs are plainly visible at the bottom of the robot costume. In the finale, the robot walks past rocks and bushes towards the alien ship, revealing May's legs and a power cable.

EPISODE NINE:
"The Oasis"
First telecast November 10, 1965
Writer: Peter Packer
Director: Sutton Roley

A rockslide traps Major West, but he's quickly freed by John Robinson. What caused the quake which resulted in the rockslide is the planet's strange orbit which takes it very close to its sun at zenith and incredibly far from its sun at the apex of the orbit. The planet is once again approaching the star-sun and a heat wave is resulting.

The fuel cells in the vital water extractors are failing until only one remains in working order, but it can provide only about a pint a day of water, which results in severe rationing for the stranded crew of the Jupiter II. This is also because Dr. Smith took a shower, which depleted their reserve tank. Now they have to try and locate a natural supply of water on the planet by searching the dry river bed. They search the river bed but the only pool of water they find is stagnant. But the pool does contain a fruit-bearing plant, and John takes some samples back to camp to examine and analyze.

The fruit, if safe, could be eaten to provide a supply of liquid to help replace the needed water they must have daily to survive. Debbie, the little ape-thing, snatches one and eats it, not knowing any better. Smith, who should know better, is so thirsty that he steals a couple and eats them. When Maureen discovers what Smith has done and tries to explain it to him, Smith panics, thinking that John and Major West deliberately left the fruit for him to eat in revenge for Smith using up the reserve water supply. Smith abandons the encampment and steals the remaining working fuel cell in revenge for what he perceives as the Robinson's trickery. Without the fuel cell, the remaining water-extractor will not function at all.

Discovering Smith's theft, John and Major West go searching for him.

Back at the Jupiter II, Debbie has grown in size to the height of a normal man instead of her usual small chimp size. But Debbie remains docile and friendly.

When John and Major West find Dr. Smith, he's grown to a height of twenty feet, and angry about it. Smith wants them to leave him alone and he hurls a tree at them to force them to retreat. Strangely enough, not only has Smith grown in height, but his clothes have expanded as well and still fit him quite comfortably!

Will goes to try to reason with Dr. Smith, but with no avail.

But when Maureen Robinson goes to speak with him, she manages to convince Smith that he must have deliberately chosen to test the fruit on himself to see if it was safe in order to make up for using all the water. Now Smith thinks he's a hero and decides to return to the Jupiter II with the needed fuel cell for the water-extractor. But it will take time for the water to be extracted and everyone is suffering from the effects of water deprivation.

That night it rains for the first time in weeks and under its cool influence Debbie and Dr. Smith shrunk back to their normal sizes. With the heat wave past and their supply of water renewed, life returns to normal for them.

There are several split-screen shots of an enlarged Dr. Smith and regular-size Robinsons.

This is the first LIS directed by Sutton Roley. In one sequence, Maureen Robinson enters the elevator on the lower deck, and in apparently one take, rides it up to the upper level and walks out. Since the upper and lower decks were on separate soundstages, credit Roley's careful camera angle and tight editing.

EPISODE TEN:
"The Sky Is Falling"
First telecast November 17, 1965
Story: Herman Groves
Teleplay: Barney Slater and Herman Groves
Director: Sobey Martin
GUEST STARS: RETHSO: Don Matheson, MOELA: Francoise Ruggieri, ALIEN CHILD: Eddie Rosson

Dr. Smith is outside trying to take a nap when he's rudely interrupted by an alien device. Upon seeing the shell-like object, the cowardly Smith panics and flees to the Jupiter II. The device projects itself through the hull of the ship and then shuts down.

The Robinsons examine the device and determine that it is some kind of probe which is testing the environment, perhaps in advance of a forthcoming ship.

Later, Will witnesses the arrival of a transmission beam which brings a strange machine and a tall, male humanoid. The device transmits two more humanoids to the planet's surface, but these are a woman and a young boy.

Dr. Smith has meanwhile decided to follow the probe to see if it will lead to another spacecraft. When he encounters the newly arrived aliens he tries to talk them into returning him to Earth, but they ignore him. Smith doesn't know what to make of this and pulls his laser on them. When the alien male responds in kind, Smith panics and leaves.

The following day, Will tries to befriend the alien child while back at the Jupiter II, Dr. Smith is convinced that these aliens are the advance party for an entire horde of the beings who will come to colonize the planet. He's convinced that the aliens will want to get rid of the humans and tries to convince the Robinsons and Major West to go on the offensive. But luckily the Robinsons pay as little attention to this as they do to any of Dr. Smith's other usual wild fantasies.

Will meets with the alien boy again, who brings what appears to be a toy ball which returns to the owner when thrown. Then the alien child inexplicably collapses. Will takes the boy to a nearby shelter of rock and waits for his parents to come, not wanting to leave the child helpless and alone.

Maureen becomes worried over Will's absence and so John and Major West go out to search for the boy. The same scene is taking place at the alien encampment where the alien mother, Moela, is worried about the prolonged absence of her child. Rethso agrees to search for his son.

Smith tries to convince everyone that the aliens have taken Will, just as he predicted they would come after the humans. When neither search party locates the boys, trouble starts to brew in both encampments. The next morning John, Major West and Dr. Smith arm themselves and go to the alien encampment.

When the aliens see the armed men approaching they get out their own weapons. John Robinson puts down his laser and goes to talk with Rethso, but they don't get anywhere. Smith then makes the situation worse when he sees Moela with her gun and panics, convinced she's going to shoot him, but he fires first. Everyone takes cover. They are on the verge of warfare when Will arrives with the alien boy. John Robinson carries the child over to the alien encampment, but now the aliens think that the Robinsons had their child all along. Moela wants Rethso to shoot John down.

Will steps forward and convinces the aliens that he's the boy's friend, which ends hostilities. The Robinsons and the aliens then make peace. But the child collapsed because of the germs he contracted from his close contact with Will, which the aliens have no defense against.

The aliens manage to finally communicate with the Robinsons via radio waves, which is their normal mode of speech, and explain this. It's evident that the two races cannot live on the same world safely, and so the alien family uses the matter transmitter to leave again after giving Will the special alien toy ball as a token of friendship.

Future LAND OF THE GIANTS co-star Don Matheson is the mute alien, Reth-so.

EPISODE ELEVEN:
"Wish Upon A Star"
First telecast November 24, 1965
Writer: Barney Slater
Director: Sutton Roley

Dr. Smith is under foot and in trouble again, dropping things and breaking things. He's working on the Chariot with Will and Major West when Smith fumbles and drops a fuel cylinder which explodes. Although no one is hurt, since Smith just recently was also responsible for the destruction of their hydroponic gardens, this is pushing things to the limit. After getting chewed out by John and Major West, Dr. Smith decides that he's not wanted and packs his things and leaves.

That night he sleeps under the stars, terrified that there are things out in the dark waiting for him to fall asleep. Will finds Dr. Smith the next morning and agrees to help Smith find a decent place to make his camp and set up housekeeping.

When they come upon the wreck of a spacecraft, Smith agrees that this will serve as acceptable living quarters. While cleaning the place up, Will encounters a device which looks like a hat which he experimentally puts on. When he wishes out loud for some food, it miraculously appears out of thin air. When he asks for apples, a bunch fall from the ceiling.

Smith is fascinated by this device and wants to keep it a secret from the rest of the crew, but Will tells his father about it anyway.

Dr. Smith uses the device to create all the comforts of home, including wine and other luxuries. Will tells Dr. Smith how selfish he's being and finally Smith agrees to return to the Jupiter II with the wishing machine.

Smith attempts to use the machine to create a duplicate of the Jupiter II which they could use to return to Alpha Control, but such a demand is beyond the machine's humble capabilities. Instead the machine produces a Jupiter II the size of a toy. Smith then reveals that he'd discovered that the machine will only function twice a day.

Squabbles break out over who's turn it is to use the wish machine. Penny even cheats to get the machine to make some new music tapes for her. Judy uses the machine to create a new dress and John Robinson quickly realizes that they're becoming too dependant on it and wishing for frivolous things. The machine is also being used to do things they could do themselves, thus making most of them act as lazy as Dr. Smith is.

Finally John Robinson tells Dr. Smith to get rid of the machine, and so Smith takes it back to his domicile in the old spaceship hull. Smith returns to creating luxurious foods for himself to indulge in, but then he finally goes to far. He asks the machine to create a slave for him. Instead an alien who was a crewman on the ship is awakened and is furious with Smith for using its device for himself.

Dr. Smith panics and runs back to the Jupiter II with the machine, where all of the miraculous things the machine had created are starting to deteriorate as they were never permanent. Dr. Smith turns on the force field which holds back the alien, but all it wants is its machine.

John insists that Dr. Smith return the device to its rightful owner, and with great and painful reluctance, Smith agrees to do so.

The alien returns to its seemingly derelict ship and uses the device to take the ship back where it came from. But before it leaves, the alien leaves Will an apple as a parting gift.

Later, Will tries sending up a small rocket with a message in hopes that someone will pick it up, but the rocket malfunctions and starts to fall towards its launch point, only now it has burned up and turned into a ball of fire!

Terrific direction by Sutton Roley.
The 15 inch Jupiter II miniature appears when conjured up by Smith. It's handled briefly by Bill Mumy.

EPISODE TWELVE:
"The Raft"
First telecast Dec. 1, 1965
Writer: Peter Packer
Director: Sobey Martin

When Will's message rocket explodes and falls back towards them, they are protected by the Jupiter 2's force field. After the near disaster, John Robinson tells Will that he's not to send up any more rockets. Plus, Will's latest experiment has used up the last of the Jupiter 2's fuel.

John and Major West start to experiment with the possibility of using plasma motors to power the Jupiter II, and their experiment seems to be successful. But when they hook it into the ship's propulsion systems, the control box malfunctions and explodes.

Since they would need much more power to launch the Jupiter II, Will suggests that they build a smaller craft, which he calls a raft, to see if they have enough power available to launch it. Major West thinks that the idea just might work and he begins to build "The Raft."

The smaller craft will be lifted a thousand feet into the atmosphere and then its motors will be engaged. John Robinson programs the "raft" to home in on Procyon and from there it could navigate to earth. Being such a small craft, only one person could fit in it and Major West, their pilot, is the logical choice to make the journey to bring back help.

That evening Will sees Dr. Smith puttering around in the small craft and enters it to talk with him. But then the robot, acting on orders from Smith, activates the balloon which launches the craft into the sky, but Will is still aboard. The launch sequence is activated and Will and Dr. Smith begin the voyage aboard the small craft.

When they approach a planet which Smith thinks is Earth, Will takes the ship in for a landing. They emerge on a desert landscape and go in search of a road which would lead them to civilization.

Will leaves the radio on aboard the craft which is picked up by the Jupiter II, and the Robinsons attempt to home in on the signal.

Dr. Smith and Will encounter what at first glance appears to be a cactus, but it's a plant-creature which begins to follow them and corners them in a narrow canyon. The canyon is filled with plants and Will figures out that the plant-thing wants them to take care of the other plants, much to Dr. Smith's chagrin.

But Dr. Smith had brought a belt radio with him and Will uses it to contact the Jupiter II. They quickly discover that their craft never had enough lift to achieve escape velocity and they just landed back on the planet they took off from.

John and Major West track down "the raft" and from there follow their trail and track Will's radio signal to the valley. They arrive just as the plant-thing attack Will and Dr. Smith for refusing to obey it. John and Major West uses their lasers to blast the plant-creature. They all then return to the Jupiter II.

Some time later, John, Will and Major West go out in the Chariot to set up an antenna. Just as they drive off, the robot sets up its common warning cry of, "Danger! Danger!" But John and the others fail to hear it. When they are some distance away, a shower of meteorites crashes to the ground where the Chariot is, engulfing it.

The Jupiter 2's reactor chamber is used as an escape pod. Chamber is actually the Seaview's diving bell from VOYAGE TO THE BOTTOM OF THE SEA.

EPISODE THIRTEEN:
"One of our Dogs Is Missing"
First telecast December 8, 1965
Writer: William Welch
Director: Sutton Roley

When the meteorites strike the Chariot, its communications are knocked out so that they can't report back to the Jupiter II regarding their situation or location.

Meanwhile, back at the ship, Maureen and Judy become concerned over the prolonged absence of John and Major West. Dr. Smith panics as usual and starts raving about an alien invasion. Finally the Maureen, Judy and Penny go out in search of the missing men. Their first sign of trouble are the huge meteorite craters they discover. But finally John and Don re-establish communications and notify the three that they're fine and are continuing their mission.

While returning to the Jupiter II, Penny finds a small, empty space capsule, but there's no indication as to who or what might have been inside. But upon returning to the ship they discover that their food stores have been broken into and stolen. Although Smith is immediately suspect, he denies any knowledge of the crime. That night, they hear a ferocious howling coming out of the darkness and wonder what new menace they'll be faced with.

Since Dr. Smith always has a handy excuse not to do anything that's potentially dangerous, Maureen and Judy go out the next morning to search for any signs of what they heard howling the night before. But all they find is something which looks like a small dog, which they carry back to the Jupiter II. But as soon as they leave the area, there is movement in the bottom of one of the craters and a monstrous creature rises from the sand.

Penny takes to the dog right away and wants to keep it, but Dr. Smith is convinced that it's some sort of alien infiltrator that's plotting their destruction. Smith even attempts to communicate with it, assuring it that he's penetrated its disguise. But meanwhile Maureen finds a strange piece of fur, which convinces her all the more that what they're looking for is not the little dog they found. She wonders if it could be some sort of mutation.

When Penny playing with the dog, it manages to run off with the only working laser. Dr. Smith has disassembled the others to clean them but can't figure out how to put them back together again, leaving them defenseless until John and Major West return.

While Penny searches for the dog, the monster seen earlier is tracking Penny. But then the dog reappears and frightens away the monster!

When John Robinson contacts Maureen to check on them, she seems evasive when he asks her if everything is all right. That bothers John and he and Major West decide they'd better return to the Jupiter II to make sure that everything is under control.

Judy decides to look for the dog, and the same monster starts to trail her.

Arriving back at the ship, John and Major West learn what's been happening and they set out in search of Judy.

Meanwhile Will manages to reassemble to rest of the lasers and he sets off with Dr. Smith to hunt the dog, which he too now believes must be an alien spy since it stole one of their lasers, and the one which was the only working one at the time.

The monster starts chasing Judy but the dog finds John and Major West and leads them to it. John catches up to them and fights with the creature, which works John over pretty good before he can finally shoot it with his laser. Now all of them start looking for the mysterious and elusive dog.

But after they leave the scene, the monster wakes up as the laser only stunned it, and the thing sets off to return to its pit.

At the pit, Will and Dr. Smith have found the little dog, but in spite of Dr. Smith urgings, Will can't bring himself to shoot the little animal. Just as Don, Judy and Major West meet up with them at the pit, the monster reappears and attacks. Judy faints, John is knocked out of the way, but the little dog retrieves the dropped laser so that John can shoot the monster and force it back into the pit where they blast the pit and bury the thing.

Back at the camp, John Robinson and Dr. Smith have gone out to mine deutronium when the vine of some kind of plant-thing ensnares John's leg and drags him towards another sand pit while Dr. Smith screams helplessly. . .

A very strangely titled episode. A takeoff of an early 60's novel ONE OF OUR PLANES IS MISSING.

The dog never appears again after this episode.

EPISODE FOURTEEN:
"Attack of the Monster Plants"
First telecast December 15, 1965
Writer: William Read Woodfield and Allen Balter
Director: Justus Addis

John Robinson is attacked by the creeping tendril of some sort of carnivorous plant which starts dragging him towards a sand pit while Dr. Smith stands there screaming like a woman. Major West hears the commotion and runs to help John, but then he becomes trapped just as surely. Dr. Smith is too frightened to help either of them and so he runs to the Jupiter II to get help. He has Will run to help them with a rope. By this time John and Major West have been pulled into the sand pit, but with the help of the rope Will brings them, they're able to clamber out to safety.

Due to Smith's cowardly performance in the face of danger, he's kicked out of the camp and forced to find somewhere else to set up housekeeping.

John and Major West continue drilling for Deutronium to use for fuel for the Jupiter II, but the vein of ore they're mining becomes exhausted when they get only enough to supply them with minimal liftoff power. Smith learns of this and is terrified that everyone is so angry with him that they'll strand him there on the planet all alone. He's certain that if he can find some more of the ore that he'll be able to use it to bargain his way back into their good graces.

Talking Will into coming out to his humble abode. Smith has discovered some cyclamens; plants which can duplicate the appearance of something, although internally they'll still be plants. Smith uses the cyclamens to duplicate a canister of Deutronium and then switches the fake for the real one. But before Smith can use the real deutronium to bargain his way back aboard the Jupiter II, the cyclamens consume the deutronium, leaving Smith not only empty handed, but now he's responsible for the destruction of some of the precious substance, and Will Robinson soon discovers the ruse.

Back at the Jupiter II they're preparing for departure. Since they're going to be taking Debbie the Bloop, Will is constructing a suspension chamber for her. It's apparent that their intention is to leave Dr. Smith behind, much to his chagrin.

Smith observes Judy out near some huge plants and sees her captured by them and stunned into immobility. Deciding to use this to his advantage, Smith goes to the Robinsons and states that he won't reveal where Judy is unless Major West and Dr. Smith are the only ones to take off in the Jupiter II and return to Earth. Major West isn't having any of this and is on the verge of beating the truth out of Dr. Smith when Judy comes strolling into camp. She seems a little spacey from her ordeal and keeps to herself.

That night, when the rest of the family are asleep, Judy steals the supply of deutronium and walks out into the darkness. She is observed by Dr. Smith and he sees her take the material to the plants and feed it to them, whereupon he realizes that this isn't Judy at all, but just a duplicate created by the cyclamens.

Smith talks "Judy" out of some of the deutronium, convincing her that the Robinsons will be able to manufacture more, even though this is a lie. Smith makes off with just enough deutronium for two people to lift off in the Jupiter II.

The next morning the Jupiter II is overrun with the plants and the Robinsons and Major West attack the things and drive them back using the Chariot and the neutron gun. When Judy tries to stop them, she's revealed as a duplicate.

Smith is forced to reveal where the real Judy is and Will suggests that they can get to her by using the tanks from the freezing unit since the plants will freeze at 44 degrees. This plan is successful and Judy is rescued from the plant-things. But now they're short of the deutronium again and will have to continue their mining expeditions.

While Smith is out with Will and Penny exploring, Penny finds a strange sort of egg, which Dr. Smith carries back to the Jupiter II. Nearby they find the machines left behind by the alien family (from "The Sky Is Falling"), and Debbie the Bloop accidentally switches one one, causing Penny and her Bloop to vanish into a light beam.

This is a rare storyline which prominently features the Judy Robinson character.

EPISODE FIFTEEN:
"Return From Outer Space"
First telecast December 29, 1965
Writer: Peter Packer
Director: Nathan Juran
GUEST CAST: AUNT CLARE: Reta Shaw, SHERIFF BAXENDALE: Walter Sande, DAVEY SIMS: Donald Loseby, RUTH TEMPLETON: Sheila Matthews, THEODORE: Keith Taylor, LACY: Robert Easton, GROVER: Harry Harvey, Sr., PHONE OPERATOR: Helen Kleeb, FIRST SELECTMAN: Ann Dore, FIRST BOY: Johnny Tuohy

Penny and the Bloop are zapped by a beam of light when Debbie accidentally activates the matter transporter left behind by the Taurons (in episode 10). When Will arrives at the device with Dr. Smith and the robot, Dr. Smith hopes that the device can transport him to earth and he has the robot activate it. But Smith's hope is shattered, although the robot is able to bring back Penny and the Bloop from where ever they were transported to.

They return to the Jupiter II, where the food preserver is malfunctioning because they're running out of carbon tetrachloride. When Will tells his parents about the matter transporter, they forbid him to go anywhere near it. Fearing a repeat of what happened to Penny, John and Major West plan to dismantle it to insure that no more accidents can happen.

But Will decides to take the chance and has the robot program the matter transporter to project him to Earth and return him at twelve o'clock.

The device works and Will appears in the Vermont town of Hatfield Four Corners, where they're celebrating Christmas. Will meets Davey Sims, but the boy and his Aunt Clara don't take Will's story seriously. Everyone on Earth believes that the Robinson's were lost in space, never to return.

Will is taken to the sheriff, where he's treated like a runaway. But Will has a supporter in the person of a local reporter, Lacey, who thinks there might be something to the boy's story. Lacey decides to contact Alpha Control, while the sheriff decides to have Will placed in the local boy's home.

Meanwhile, John and Major West are searching for Will, and Dr. Smith has ordered the robot to accompany him, thus leaving the matter transmitter unattended.

On Earth, Theodore and some of the other local boys provoke Will into a fight. Branded a troublemaker, Will is taken before the town council, but they find his story preposterous. Will flees the disbelieving adults, and while trying to elude recapture he ducks into a hardware store where he sees a bottle of carbon tetrachloride. But Will is found by the sheriff and taken back to Aunt Clara, who wants to adopt the boy. Will has had about all he can take of this.

Back on the planet, the robot finally returns to the matter transmitter and prepares the device to return Will to Earth, provided Will is at the same point where the beam originally deposited him.

Will finally convinces Davey Sims that his story is true and the boy helps Will to escape again, this time with the needed carbon tetrachloride. Will returns to the roof where he landed, but the sheriff is hot on his heels. The beam appears, snatching Will up just in the neck of time to elude the hands of the well-meaning townspeople and the boy is returned to the planet.

Upon rematerializing on the planet, the machine malfunctions, never to work again. No one believes his claim until, he hands them the bottle of carbon tetrachloride, which he couldn't have obtained by any other means.

Later, Will is out with Dr. Smith digging a new irrigation ditch when Smith suddenly wanders off as though in a trance. Dr. Smith enters a cage and a horned monster appears which makes threatening moves towards Will.

The Earth city "Hatfield Four Corners" is actually a side street on the Fox lot.
Although LIS is set in 1997, Hatfield resembles a New England town with mid-Sixties school buses, telephones, cameras and clothing.
Aunt Clara is played by veteran actress Reta Shaw, who often portrayed domestics for Disney films. Shaw co-starred in the Fox series THE GHOST AND MRS. MUIR.
Newspaper photographer is played by Robert Easton, who was "Sparks" in the VOYAGE feature and the voice of "Phones" from STINGRAY.
The overweight bully is played by Keith Taylor, who returns in a third season episode.

EPISODE SIXTEEN:
"The Keeper" (Part One)
First telecast January 12, 1966
Writer: Barney Slater
Director: Sobey Martin
GUEST STARS: THE KEEPER: Michael Rennie, ALIEN LEADER: Wilbur Evans

While working on a new irrigation project, Smith suddenly wanders off as though hypnotized and states that he has been summoned. Will follows Dr. Smith, trying to discover what is happening, but for his trouble he is menaced by a horned monster while Dr. Smith obediently enters a cage.

Suddenly a strange humanoid being who calls himself The Keeper appears and uses his staff of power to subdue the horned monster and protect Will Robinson. The horned creature is itself placed into another cage, which promptly vanishes.

Will gets his father and Major West and they return to the site and secure the release of Dr. Smith by breaking into his cage.

While examining a cage containing a lizard, the robot explains that the cage lures a prisoner and then provides all of its needs.

The Keeper appears again, disturbed at these beings who are interfering with its trapping expedition. The Keeper collects two specimens of every type of animal and views the humans as primitive, despite what they may think of themselves. The Keeper retrieves the small cage containing the lizard and vanishes, returning to his spacecraft.

Aboard his ship, The Keeper contacts the Alien Leader, and it's suggested that the humans would make interesting specimens to add to their zoo.

The Keeper visit Major West and Judy Robinson, offering them the opportunity to join his menagerie as pampered pets who will receive their every desire while in his care. But Don and Judy aren't interested in being zoo specimens.

Meanwhile, Dr. Smith suggests that were they to steal The Keeper's spacecraft they could all return to Earth, but the others refuse to use violence to achieve their goals.

Later, The Keeper appears to Will and Penny and lures them into visiting his zoo. The Keeper explains that his staff is charged with cosmic energy and he entertains Penny by summoning up a miniature unicorn for her amusement. While visiting the Keeper's menagerie, the humanoid attempts to lure them into a cage.

Will and Penny attempt to flee, but the Keeper uses his cosmic staff to force them to return. But since Dr. Smith is also particularly susceptible to the summons, he also arrives in response to the staff's cosmic urging. Dr. Smith, in his usual bumbling way, manages to knock the staff from the Keeper's hand and breaks it, which shatters his control.

While Will and Penny flee back to the Jupiter II, Smith apologizes profusely and offers to help him if The Keeper will return him to Earth, where he will find many more unusual specimens to add to his collection. The Keeper could go to Earth, but he doubts Dr. Smith's claims at how worthwhile the flight would be.

The Robinson's use the robot to guard the children, but they trick the machine, responding to The Keeper's call, and return to the Keeper's ship. Smith is un-affected by the summons this time due to the earplugs he's wearing.

Major West and John Robinson make Dr. Smith show them where the ship is so that they can go and rescue the children. They confront The Keeper and use their laser to attack him, but his cosmic staff protects him from the assault. But when Major West uses a simple slingshot, the stone shatters the head of the staff and the Keeper's power is neutralized.

With Will and Penny once more rescued and everyone gone back to the Jupiter II, The Keeper decides that he's had enough and decides to leave and search for new specimens elsewhere.

Dr. Smith sneaks back aboard The Keeper's ship with the robot. Eager to take off, Smith starts pressing buttons on the control panel and inadvertently opens all the cages in the menagerie, freeing a variety of dangerous animals on the surface of the planet. Knowing he's really done it this time, Dr. Smith flees from The Keeper's ship before he can be discovered and punished.

EPISODE SEVENTEEN:
"The Keeper" (Part Two)
First telecast January 19, 1966
Writer: Barney Slater
Director: Harry Harris
GUEST STARS: THE KEEPER: Michael Rennie, ALIEN LEADER: Wilbur Evans

In attempting to escape in The Keeper's spacecraft, Dr. Smith has pushed the wrong buttons and pulled the wrong switches and instead released all of the animals in the Keeper's zoo, and some of them are quite deadly. The animals have escaped to the planet's surface, as has Smith, fearing The Keeper's wrath.

The Robinsons discover that something is very wrong when John and Major West encounter a monstrous lizard and are forced to flee for safety to the Jupiter II.

The Keeper appears, revealing that his menagerie has escaped and the animals are taking over that section of the planet, which will make life especially hazardous for the humans. The Keeper reveals that he can use his cosmic staff to recall the creatures, but in payment he wants Will and Penny. The Robinson's refuse The Keeper's extortion demand.

When The Keeper discovers that Dr. Smith was responsible for this fiasco, he confronts Smith and forces him to help him get the children or he'll feed Smith to his menagerie.

Meanwhile, Judy and Major West discuss the situation and decide to offer themselves to The Keeper in place of Will and Penny in hopes that this will ap ase the alien. Elsewhere, John and Maureen Robinson have made the same decision in regards to offering themselves to The Keeper in place of the children.

When the two couples independently approach The Keeper with their offers, he refuses them all, believing that they wouldn't adjust as well to captivity as the children would. As John and Maureen leave, John accidentally knocks over the cosmic staff, causing its power to drain. Thus when one of The Keeper's creatures confronts him, he's helpless against it when attacked and is left unconscious.

Dr. Smith has his own plan and reveals to Will and Penny what the others are doing, telling them that they should go to The Keeper to try to talk the alien out of his demands.

When the others discover that Will and Penny are missing, they immediately launch a search using the Chariot to protect them from marauding monsters. Major West finds the children but they barely make the safety of The Chariot when a huge spider monster attacks.

Meanwhile, Maureen has arrived at The Keeper's ship and found him unconscious. The Keeper is amazed when Maureen helps him as it is a trait he never expected from the humans. When Maureen explains that Will and Penny are missing, The Keeper agrees to help her find them as he never intended to harm the children, he just wanted them for his zoo.

John Robinson arrives to try to help the others in the Chariot, but he's unable to defeat the spider monster. Things are looking pretty grim when The Keeper arrives and uses his recharged cosmic staff to recall the creature and send it back to his ship.

The following day, all of the escaped animals have been recalled by The Keeper, who plans to leave the planet. The humans have proven to be much too much trouble and he won't even take the one human specimen he does have. When The Keeper takes off, he leaves Dr. Smith behind, in a cage.

That evening, another unidentified flying object enters the planet's atmosphere and is detected by the robot, which reports that there are two life forms aboard. While investigating the landing area the following day, a huge shadow approaches Dr. Smith. . .

This is the only two-part episode of LIS.

Michael Rennie (The Keeper) co-starred with Jonathan Harris in the Fifties series THE THIRD MAN.

The more extensive use of special effects in this story can be attributed to the higher budget available for a two-part story.

Blooper: In Part one, as Smith is locked inside the glass cage, the camera dollys in for a closeup and the reflection of a crew man in visible.

The props inside the Keeper's ship include the Derelict model from episode two and the glassy control knobs from the "5th Dimension" episode.

The full range of Irwin Allen monsters are seen in this episode. The big escape scene has them repeated over and over to generate the idea of scores of rampaging aliens.

The finale involves a giant spider attack on the Chariot. The spider was used again underwater in an episode of VOYAGE TO THE BOTTOM OF THE SEA.

EPISODE EIGHTEEN:
"The Sky Pirate"
First telecast January 26, 1966
Writer: Carey Wilber
Director: Sobey Martin
GUEST STAR: CAPTAIN ALONZO P. TUCKER: Albert Salmi

When the robot reports that a UFO has landed with two life forms aboard, John and Major West investigate. They find a spacecraft shaped like an inverted cone, but no one is aboard. They do find a few items on the craft which have the name A.P. Tucker on them. But while they are rummaging through the belongings, the spacecraft's door seals behind them, preventing their escape.

Outside a man dressed like an old Earth-style pirate approaches Dr. Smith. We learn that this is one Captain Tucker. He has a mechanical, mind-reading parrot and uses it to help him capture Will.

Tucker explains that he's lost and short on provisions and forces Will and Smith to take him to the Jupiter II. Once at the encampment, Smith orders the robot to attack Tucker, but the mechanical parrot snatches the robot's power pack, thus disabling him.

Using Will as a hostage, Tucker is given some food. Then Tucker takes the boy with him when he retreats to a cave he's using as a hideout. But even though Tucker is holding Will prisoner, he decides that the pirate isn't really a bad guy and they become friends. Will is amused by the pirate stories Tucker tells. They become friends and while Will takes a watered down version of the pirate oath, Tucker accompanies Will at night when the boy says his prayers.

But things are more complicated than they seem, and the following day a robotic eye arrives on the planet, searching for Tucker. Tucker sees it, claiming that the robot is after his treasure. When Will manages to distract the robot hunter, Tucker is able to get the drop on it and destroy the device.

John and Major West have finally escaped Tucker's ship, and when Tucker visits the Jupiter II he announces that he's release Will in exchange for repairs being made to his ship so that he can escape again.

It turns out that the reason that Tucker acts like a terrestrial pirate is that he was kidnapped by Tellurians in 1876 who were on Earth collecting specimens. Tucker was kept in suspended animation and brought out only for occasional study. The pirate doesn't understand the ship he landed in or how to repair it himself. Tucker agrees to return Will and stay at the Jupiter II until the repairs on his own ship are completed.

John and Major West are impressed with the ship that Tucker had stolen as it contains a faster than light hyper-drive system. They want Tucker to return them all to Earth in his ship so that it can be studied and duplicated, but Tucker isn't too keen on going back to Earth now, over a hundred years after he'd left.

Suddenly another spacecraft arrives. It's huge and spherical and Tucker is frightened so much by it that upon seeing it he flees for his hideaway. Will, who has become quite friendly with Tucker, follows after him.

Tucker reveals that he's being tracked by creatures from Signet IV, but since he doesn't even know how to work his ray gun, he can't defend himself from them. While the blob-like creature is hunting elsewhere, Tucker and Will return to the Jupiter II where the boy figures out how to make the gun work.

The gun isn't a weapon at all, but is a mind-reading device which can show the intentions of anyone the person holding the gun is thinking of. For instance, when Will thinks of Dr. Smith, they see that Smith intends to steal Tucker's spacecraft.

When the creature comes to the Jupiter II, Tucker grabs the device and runs, knowing that the thing will leave everyone else alone. While trying to elude the monster, Tucker drops the device, which the monster grabs and leaves with. It had never been after Tucker at all, just the thought-projector.

Tucker's ship is repaired, and before he leaves he reveals to Will that he was never a pirate and he made up all of the wild adventures he related to the boy. Tucker leaves the planet, planning to go off on his own with no intentions of returning to Earth.

Later, John, Major West, Will, and Dr. Smith are out boring for more radioactive ore. John is placing warning signs about pockets of ionized has when one bursts, which overwhelms John, choking him. . .

This episode marks the first appearance of Albert Salmi in the role of Alonzo P. Tucker, whom we would meet again.

EPISODE NINETEEN:
"Ghost In Space"
First telecast February 2, 1966
Writer: Peter Packer
Director: Don Richardson

When John breaks into a pocket of has and is stunned, Major West happens on the scene just in time and rescues him. Major West orders Smith to go and place an explosive at another drilling site they'd charted, but Smith is too lazy and just tosses the device into the swamp. Not long after, an invisible presence emerges from the swamp and moves off heavily into the darkness.

Dr. Smith is finding new ways to waste his time back at the Jupiter II and is constructing a Ouija board to try and communicate with his great Uncle Thaddeus. Although the others dismiss Smith's attempts as foolishness, Penny is curious enough to participate in the game.

They attempt to activate the board and the glass they use to move around the board suddenly shatter and the board hurls itself to destruction against a rock.

Later, the invisible entity approaches the Jupiter II. Smith is convinced that he really did contact his Uncle Thaddeus and goes outside to see if he can contact him again somehow. He encounters the invisible menace which hurls a boulder at Smith, which just convinces him that he'd been right all along about the ghost of his uncle having returned.

John and Major West don't buy this theory and go out to search for clues as to what is really out there. They decide to search near the swamp where they've been working. Back at the ship, Dr. Smith talks Maureen and Judy into holding a seance with him to once more contact Uncle Thaddeus.

Out in the swamp, John and Major West observe trees being knocked aside by something unseen, but before they can get away, they're attacked by whatever is out there, and are forced to flee to the Jupiter II. The creature follows them back to the ship and starts absorbing their stores of energy, and it doesn't depart until dawn.

John and Major West spend the day constructing a trap to lure the creature in using energy. That night when the thing returns, they succeed in trapping it.

Smith is still convinced that ghosts are running loose and he has Will come with him to the swamp where Smith hopes to calm the angry spirits. Smith mistakes a strangely shaped tree for a spirit, and when Will goes to prove Smith wrong, he inexplicably disappears, leaving only one of his boots behind.

Meanwhile, the invisible entity has broken free, but it's now visible and encounters the craven Dr. Smith. Will has actually turned invisible and manages to battle the visible creature until at sunrise the creature vanishes under the sun's rays while Will returns to normal.

Later, when Will and Dr. Smith are returning home after a little fishing foray, they encounter an alien robot. . .

Belief in the supernatural is added to Smith's human failings.

EPISODE TWENTY:
"War Of The Robots"
First telecast February 9, 1966
Writer: Barney Slater
Director: Sobey Martin

Returning to camp from a fishing jaunt, Will backs into another robot. While at first Smith is petrified, Will quickly realizes that the robot is rusted and unmoving. Their own robot states that this alien robot poses dangers.

Will reports his find to his father, who thinks that the antique robot is beyond repair but allows Will to work on it in his spare time. Although the robot is in poor condition, Will's scientific expertise enables him to get it back into working order.

The Robinson's robot warns Will that this is a robotoid and that it will not restrict itself to programmed parameters and actually contains a free will. Will thinks that their robot is just jealous of the newcomer and his opinion seems to be justified when that night they catch their robot attempting to destroy the robotoid.

When the robotoid begins functioning, it reveals that it, too, has a voice and easily communicates with the Robinsons. It gets into their good graces through its almost uncanny ability to repair things.

But when the Robinsons are asleep, the robotoid sneaks out and communicates with the aliens who are its true masters, and reveals the presence of the humans on the planet. The aliens inform the robotoid that they want the humans for experimentation purposes, and the robotoid states that it will assist its masters by disabling the Robinsons for them.

When the robotoid is confronting by the Robinson's robot, the robotoid informs the other robot that it is obsolete and blasts it with a bolt of energy as a demonstration of its superiority.

The robotoid later offers to help the Robinsons repair the Chariot, which their robot had been unable to do. Feeling that it is being displaced, the robot becomes depressed, which Dr. Smith just intensifies with its insults. Finally the robot goes off by itself, leaving the Robinsons with the robotoid, which they seem to prefer.

When Will catches the robotoid near their lasers, he orders it away from them. The robotoid realizes by Will's stance that he is suspicious of it after all.

When Will discovers that their robot is gone, he goes after it. When he catches up to it, the robot states that the robotoid is evil, but is unable to provide any concrete examples to support this statement.

The next morning, the force field generator is discovered to be damaged. Even worse, their weapons are all missing and the Chariot has been sabotaged, and the missing parts cannot easily be replaced.

When confronted, the robotoid admits its guilt, but also announces that the humans are all now his prisoners, and he demonstrates his powers to insure they know the futility of resistance.

But Will refuses to accept defeat and flees into the rocks nearby, eluding the robotoids deadly energy bolts. Will finds the robot, which agrees to return and help them. But since the robotoid is more powerful than the robot, they must have a clever strategy to deal with this.

The robot returns to camp, announcing that he has decided to side with his metal brother. But the robotoid is suspicious of this sudden change and orders the robot to keep its distance. When the robot emits a smoke screen, it manages to sneak up behind the robotoid and use its electrical blasts to drain the robotoid of power so that it cannot menace anyone ever again. Without the robotoid to aid them, the aliens cannot come for the Robinsons.

The Robinsons realize now that there is more to the robot than they suspected, and believe that it has some sort of human spark within it. They ask it to forgive the way they treated it, and it agrees, on the condition that Smith polish the robot daily to make amends for his insults.

The alien robotoid is played by Robby the Robot, who first gained fame in FORBIDDEN PLANET and also appeared in the film THE INVISIBLE BOY as well as a couple episodes of the original TWILIGHT ZONE.

This episode marks the Robinsons sporting new outfits for the first time.

EPISODE TWENTY-ONE:
"The Magic Mirror"

First telecast February 16, 1966
Writer: Jackson Gillis
Director: Nathan Juran
GUEST STAR: THE BOY: Michael J. Pollard

A cosmic storm is detected approaching the planet, but while everyone else is warned in time and seeks shelter in the Jupiter II, Penny is out with Debbie the Bloop. She happens on a strange, full-length mirror with carved bulls' heads on it. When Smith finds her with the mirror, he, Penny and the Bloop manage to use the mirror as shelter from the cosmic storm. The mirror seems to respond with a life of its own as the eyes of the carvings on it light up.

Dr. Smith has recognized that the mirror is made of platinum and plans to salvage it for himself in the wake of the storm, but Penny and Judy beat him to it. The two girls stand up the mirror, and then start to argue when Judy remarks that it's time that Penny stop acting like a tom-boy, something that the younger girl doesn't think is any of Judy's business. Within the mirror a strange boy observes them. Finally Penny runs back to the ship and Judy follows.

Later, the Bloop steals some of Smith's tools and when he gives chase he sees the little creature walk directly into the mirror. Upon seeing this, Smith faints from the shock.

When the Bloop re-emerges from the mirror, it is carrying a little bell which it takes and shows to Penny. When Penny wants to know where Debbie got the bell, the Bloop leads her to the mirror, and then pushes her through it.

Penny tumbles to the floor in a huge, old room which is dusty with age and disuse. The room is filled with all kinds of strange things, which all look long aban doned. She doesn't understand where she is and when she tries to go back the way she came, she finds that she cannot.

When someone speaks to her she turns and finds a strange looking boy who explains that the mirror is a gateway to another dimension. He casually explains they they're trapped there, but they can still see into other worlds through any mirrors there. Since people in his dimension never grow old, he thinks that Penny will be the perfect friend for him there.

Meanwhile, Dr. Smith thinks he must have imagined what he saw and returns to the Jupiter II.

In the other dimension, the boy takes Penny to his home, which is filled with a variety of lost objects. He does nothing but play all day, and when Penny mentions that Debbie was able to pass in and out of the mirror, the boy explains that only animals can, not people.

In that dimension there's a strange lurking monster which the boy eludes, calling it all a part of his many games. When the monster approaches, he and Penny hide, and then the boy runs off. When Penny follows, she runs into Dr. Smith, who had returned to the mirror and fallen through. He thinks he's dreaming all this.

Suddenly the monster catches up with Penny and grabs Dr. Smith, who shrieks bloody murder. But when Penny finds a gun among all the junk lying around, she manages to shoot the beast and drive it off. Smith examines the gun, which actually seems useless, but when he points it at his reflection in the mirror and pulls the trigger, he disappears and reappears outside the mirror again.

Penny realizes that there is an escape from this dimension after all. The boy is upset and pleads with Penny to stay. But she's come to decide that perhaps it is time to grow up, and that she can't spend the rest of her life just playing. She points the gun at her reflection and reappears back on the other side of the mirror, after inviting the boy to follow her. But the boy can't follow Penny, because he doesn't have a reflection to point the gun at.

Dr. Smith doesn't believe that what happened is real and angrily smashes the mirror, claiming that it was all a dream, even though Penny and he both somehow had the same dream.

The alien boy is played by Michael J. Pollard, the future co-star of BONNIE AND CLYDE and currently turning up on SUPERBOY as Mr. Mxyzptlk.

EPISODE TWENTY-TWO:
"The Challenge"
First telecast March 2, 1966
Writer: Barney Slater
Director: Don Richardson
GUEST STARS: THE RULER: Michael Ansara, QUANO: Kurt Russell

When Major West's knife and various food items are missed, it's apparent that there is a thief on the loose. Dr. Smith rigs up a crude burglar alarm system and he and Will sit up that night to see if the thief returns. When he does they discover that it's a boy brandishing a spear who is trying to test his courage. When the Robinsons attempt to befriend him, the boy adopts a macho pose and looks down at the women.

The next day the boy returns, and it's revealed that his name is Quano, and his father is the ruler of his home world. On that planet, women are treated as being inferior to men. When Quano goes rock hunting with Will, the boy won't fight to ove himself and Quano calls the boy a coward. Quano explains that he's been sent to the planet as part of a test of manhood. Quano demonstrates this by taking Will to a cave wherein a monster dwells. Quano challenges the monster, but then trips over a rock and dazes himself. Will tries to help, but ultimately the boy's father appears and drives the monster off.

The ruler is impressed by Will's action to save Quano. But when the ruler meets Dr. Smith, he immediately recognizes the man for what he is. The ruler is impressed by John Robinson, though, and suggests that their sons engage in a contest of strength and skill. Although John doesn't think much of the idea, Quano taunts Will and the boy accepts. When Maureen tries to put a halt to this, the ruler dismisses her complaints since she's only a woman.

John decides that Will has to start making his own decisions some time and live with the consequences, but John doesn't believe that the contest will be dangerous. But when Dr. Smith overhears a private conversation between Quano and his father, he learns that this is not Quano's first challenge, and that he has lost his previous contests. The boy's father states that should the boy lose again, that just like before he'll destroy the winner and the witnesses to erase his shame from anyone else's knowledge.

The Robinson women are not allowed by the ruler to view the contest.

The first contest is one of strength and Quano and Will each hold a rod over their heads. A machine measures their strength and the one who holds the rod up the longest is the winner. Will is the loser of this first contest.

The test of fear comes next and the two boys each wear a helmet which creates hallucinations of danger and measures their response. This time Will emerges triumphant, much to the ruler's dismay.

The contests continue and first one boy wins, and then the other, using such things as power gloves and guns. They remain tied with only a single challenge remaining.

Uncertain of his son's victory, the ruler chooses to stand in for his son and challenges John Robinson to do the same. This test involves a battle of voltablades, which are swords charged with fifty thousand volts of electricity. The battle is intense, but finally John emerges as the victor.

When the dust clears, the ruler realizes that Quano has taken a spear and fled, having been shamed by his father by not being allowed to complete the challenges.

Quano has returned to the cave to face the monster he had to be rescued from before. The boy is followed to the cave and they arrive in time for the ruler to battle the monster alongside his son, and they defeat it together.

The ruler apologizes to Quano for his lack of faith in his boy, and accepts that when a person does their best, that should be accepted. They bid the Robinsons good-bye and return to their home world.

The alien boy, Quano, is played by future roughneck actor Kurt Russell. His "dad" is Michael Ansara, who also turned up on VOYAGE TO THE BOTTOM OF THE SEA as well as a lot of other Sixties TV shows.

EPISODE TWENTY-THREE:
"The Space Trader"
First telecast March 9, 1966
Writer: Barney Slater
Director: Nathan Juran
GUEST STAR: THE TRADER: Torin Thatcher

Dr. Smith is working on an Impressionist painting when a sudden storm sweeps in, dislodging a large tank which starts rolling straight for John Robinson and Dr. Smith. They manage to avoid it and return to the Jupiter II to take shelter from the storm.

An alien is watching all this transpire on a viewscreen, pleased by the effects of the storm he caused.

Following the storm, the Robinsons find that their water supply is running short and once again the condensation unit needs repairing. Since the food supply was spoiled and the hydroponic garden also needs repairing, they have to revert to the nutrition pills they brought on the ship.

When Will goes for a walk with Dr. Smith, they encounter the alien trader, who encampment is filled with food and other valuable supplies that he is willing to trade. Will doesn't trust the alien but Dr. Smith refuses to look a gift horse in the mouth.

When the Trader returns with Will and Smith to the Jupiter II, John Robinson finds the alien's arrival a bit too timely, and refuses to deal with him. John says they have all that's necessary for their survival.

Later, the Trader decides that the first storm he created wasn't enough, so he sends another one crashing down on the Robinson's encampment. When the Trader meets with Dr. Smith, the alien offers to trade a twelve day supply of food for the robot, which the self-centered Smith easily agrees to. What Smith doesn't realize is that the Trader's ultimate goal is to obtain him, as he knows he could trade Smith on a certain world and make quite a profit on the deal.

When Will finds that the robot is missing, he goes searching until he locates it chained up in the Trader's camp. When the Trader tells Will that Smith made the deal, Will goes to the others and reveals what has happened. Major West soon discovers Dr. Smith's secret stash of food.

From that moment on, Smith is ostracized by the others, much to his great dismay. Will suggests that were Smith to get the robot back, that all might be forgiven.

Smith goes to the Trader and they bargain over a price, finally agreeing that in exchange for the robot, the Trader will take possession of Smith. . . in two hundred years. Smith finds this an equitable arrangement and signs a contract with his hand print. But later, as the Trader is about to leave for the planet Tauron, he invokes his contract's fine print clause and states that he's taking possession of Dr. Smith immediately.

John Robinson objects to what on Earth would be termed slavery, but the Trader insists that he has a legally binding contract. Smith is hypnotized into returning with the Trader to his encampment where the human is place under the guard of two huge dogs. But Will intervenes, distracting the canines and helping Smith to escape.

The Trader is outraged and uses his guard dogs to track Smith back to the Jupiter II, where a confrontation takes place. The robot reveals that it was the Trader who caused the storms which wrecked so much damage, and when the alien waves his contract which he insists he can invoke, the robot zaps the paper with one of his bolts and disintegrates the document. The robot uses high-pitched electronics to drive off the dogs and the alien leaves, deciding that these humans are altogether too much trouble to cope with.

The trader is Torn Thatcher, a favorite of Irwin Allen who turns up sooner or later in all his series. Most fans recognize him as the evil wizard from the film THE SEVENTH VOYAGE OF SINBAD.

This episode marks the first time (but not the last) that Smith trades the robot for food.

EPISODE TWENTY-FOUR:
"His Majesty Smith"
First telecast March 16, 1966
Writer: Carey Wilbur
Director: Harry Harris
GUEST STARS: NEXXUS: Liam Sullivan, ALIEN: Kevin Hagen

Dr. Smith is out walking with Will when they see something which appears to be a crown sitting on a rock. When Smith admires it and places it on his head, there is an electrical reaction and Smith quickly removes it. But when Will tries on, the crown seems to respond well to him, even though it's a bit large for the boy.

Suddenly an alien called Nexus of Andronica appears and announces that the crown has chosen Will to be their new king. Their king is always an off-worlder chosen for the role, but Will isn't interested in the honor. After Will leaves to return to camp, Dr. Smith insists that he'll change the boy's mind so that the aliens will take him off the planet as well.

Later, Nexus reports to his superior (a hideous alien creature) that their trick seems to be working.

That night, Smith tries to sneak out of the Jupiter II, but Will is suspicious and follows him. Will overhears Smith tell Nexus that they have other potential kings--John Robinson and Major West--but that the alien would find them unsuitable. Nexus then suggests that Smith himself might be fit for the role, an observation that Smith readily agrees with.

Will is reporting all this to his family when Nexus suddenly appears and invites them to visit the camp of His Majesty Smith.

Upon arriving at the camp, Dr. Smith offers Will the position of Heir apparent, but Will still refuses to leave his family. Smith dismisses the others and has himself carried into the alien structure. But once inside, the aliens become immobile and the hideous alien appears. He is a true Andronican, as the others are merely androids created by him to trick some human into accepting the crown. The king is actually just chosen for ceremony and at the height of the coronation festivities the king is stuffed and mounted as a sacrifice to their gods.

In order to keep the Robinsons from interfering with his planes, the alien creates an android duplicate of Smith to keep them occupied.

Somehow the robot figures out the real reason the Andronican wanted a king, and informs the Robinsons. When John and Major West go to rescue Smith, sure enough, they return with the android double. But the duplicate is too perfect. It makes breakfast for the Robinsons and is eager to work. It even urges Will to call it "Daddy Zach."

The Andronican explains that on its world they only sacrifice useful people, and that the entire series of events, including the apparent rejection of Smith by the crown, was a ploy to make Smith eager for the opportunity to be chosen. Just then Smith bashes the alien over the head and flees to the Jupiter II, where he promptly encounters his double.

Smith tries to talk the android into taking Smith's place as the king. He has figured out that he could appeal to the androids sense of honor since the duplicate lacks all of Smith negative characteristics.

When Nexus and the other androids besiege the camp, Smith heroically gives himself up while the android Smith remains with the Robinsons, or so it appears. After the aliens have left, the "android" reveals that he is the real Smith after all. When they question the fairness of this, Smith points out that the Andronicans only sacrifice useless people, which means they'd free the android as soon as his true identity was revealed.

This is the first episode with Smith look-alikes. It is generally well-acted and very funny.

The Alien Boss is played by Kevin Hagen, LAND OF THE GIANT's Inspector Kobek.

Nexus is Liam Sullivan, who also guest-starred in third season STAR TREK.

EPISODE TWENTY-FIVE:
"The Space Croppers"
First telecast March 30, 1966
Writer: Peter Packer
Director: Sobey Martin
GUEST STARS: SYBILLA: Mercedes McCambridge, EFFRA: Sherry Jackson, KEEL: Dawson Palmer

When both moons orbiting the planet are full one night, the cowardly Dr. Smith imagines that a howl they hear must belong to a werewolf. Will and Dr. Penny, who are assembling a time capsule, think he's acting ridiculous. But on their way back to the Jupiter II, they're attacked by what looks like a werewolf, but the robot hits it with an electrical bolt and the beast retreats, reverting to human form as it does.

Smith is working on pipeline construction the next day, but Will wants Smith to help him track the werewolf. Smith reluctantly agrees and the robot takes over Smith's duties.

They track the man-beast but for their trouble find what appears to be a mute hillbilly. He leads them to a spaceship which for all the world looks like a log cabin with rocket engines on it. They meet the mute's sister, Effra, and the matriarch, Sybilla, who kicks Will and Dr. Smith out.

The visitors are there to plant and harvest a certain crop, which consists of mobile, ravenous plants.

Back at the Jupiter II, Effra and Keel (the mute) pay a visit to borrow some seasoning. Effra tries to come on to Major West, but he's unimpressed by her charms.

That night they hear the sounds of a ceremony coming from the direction of the visitors, and when John, Maureen and Major West investigate they discover a magical ceremony taking place aimed at making the plants grow faster. When Sybilla discovers the intruders, she chases them off.

When Will and Dr. Smith return to the scene the next day they find that the plants have expanded their territory, and for some reason the visitors aren't dressed like hillbillies any more. Smith sees the visitor's spacecraft as a means of returning to Earth and tries to befriend Sybilla.

Meanwhile, Effra is displeased by Major West's rejection of her and plans to use witchcraft. She tries to cajole Will into bringing her a lock of Major West's hair, but he doesn't trust her motives. The robot tells Will that the human appearance of these beings is a disguise.

When John examines a sample of the plants, he finds they contain a deadly virus. When Smith announces his plans to marry Sybilla, Will goes to warn Smith about what he;s learned about the beings and their plants.

Keel, the werewolf, attacks Will and knocks him into one of the plants, but he's rescued by Effra who thinks that the boy was bringing her a lock of Major West's hair. When she discovers that he wasn't, she's properly annoyed.

Smith soon learns that not only is Keel the werewolf, but that Effra is a witch. Deciding that things are getting too strange for him, Smith flees back to the Jupiter II, where they are just finishing the destruction of the alien plants which had attacked the ship in Smith's absence. The visitors take off in their spacecraft, leaving the planet and taking with them Smith's chance to return to Earth.

The only on-camera appearance by monster man Dawson Palmer, urually buried in alien make-ups. Palmer plays the Doltish Keel.

Actress Mercedes McCambridge (the voice of the demon in THE EXORCIST) brings a touch of class to the series as Sybilla.

The plants are reused from "Attack Of The Monster Plants."

EPISODE TWENTY-SIX:
"All That Glitters"
First telecast April 6, 1966
Writer: Barney Slater
Director: Harry Harris
GUEST STARS: BOLIX: Werner Klemperer, OHAN: Larry Ward

When John and Major West take the Chariot out to scout for additional water supplies, Dr. Smith is left behind with the rest of the Robinsons. Not far away, just over a hill, a being in a helmet is whipping two huge creatures while a man nearby hides from him.

The man who was hiding sees the Jupiter II and makes his way towards it. Dressed in rags, he suddenly is seen by Penny and Dr. Smith, and collapses in front of them. Smith is frightened and goes back to bring Judy and Maureen to help decide what to do.

Meanwhile, Penny helps the ragged man back to the Jupiter II and puts him in Smith's quarters.

When Smith returns to the scene with Judy and Maureen, they're surprised by two huge creatures which chase them back to the Jupiter II. Once on the ship they find that Penny is safe and see who it is that she brought back to the ship.

The fugitive is named Ohan, and is a professional thief. He leaves the next morning, having recovered enough to travel again.

Soon after he leaves, Bolix arrives with the two huge creatures at his beckoned call. He identifies himself as a law-enforcement agent from Tauron and he insists on searching the Jupiter II for his escaped prisoner. It seems that Ohan had stolen and hidden something of great value, and the police allowed his escape in the hope

52

that he might lead them to it. What no one else realizes is that Penny has the item in question, a small disc which Ohan left behind.

Ohan had described the disc as a key to the greatest treasure in the galaxy. When Smith learns what it is, he snatches it for himself after Bolix has left to continue his pursuit of Ohan.

Smith discovers that the disc can talk and it gives instructions that lead him to a small pile of rocks, which is actually a small casket which contains a metal ring, which Smith grabs and takes back to the Jupiter II.

That night Ohan returns and traces his missing disc to Smith, demanding that he return it with twenty-four hours, then Ohan leaves again to continue to avoid the pursuing authorities.

Smith puts the ring on a chain around his neck and soon discovers that anything he touches turns into platinum, a substance more valuable than gold. Having what he wants, he goes to Bolix and informs him that Ohan will be back at the Jupiter II at a specific time. Ohan is captured and Smith now feels that his treasure is securely his alone.

The next morning at breakfast, Smith cannot help showing off and demonstrates his power to the Robinsons. But he soon discovers that, like the Midas touch, he can't turn it off. His food and everything he touches turns to platinum. Smith finds that he cannot remove the ring, and so Maureen forbids Smith from entering the Jupiter II because if he should touch any of the ship's irreplaceable equipment, they'd never be able to repair it or have any chance of leaving the planet.

Feeling sorry for himself as usual, Dr. Smith wanders out into the barren wilderness to die, since it's impossible for him to eat anything.

Bolix returns to the Jupiter II, searching for the ring. He doesn't believe the Robinsons' story and arrests them, but Penny escapes and goes searching for Smith.

Penny tells Smith what has happened, but when she accidentally touches him, she turns to platinum as well.

Smith is beside himself, believing that Penny has been killed and that it is all his fault. He returns to the Jupiter II and by threatening to turn Bolix into platinum, forces the interplanetary policeman to flee the planet, taking his two monsters with him.

Smith is guilt-ridden over what has happened to Penny, and just then the disc starts speaking again, stating that Dr. Smith has learned his lesson. The disc deactivates the ring and restores Penny to normal again. But with the curse lifted, Smith quickly becomes his old self again.

Bolix is played by HOGAN'S HEROES "Col. Klink," Werner Klemperer.

EPISODE TWENTY-SEVEN: "The Lost Civilization"

First telecast April 13, 1966
Writer: William Welch
Director: Don Richardson
GUEST STARS: MAJOR DOMO: Royal Dano, PRINCESS: Kym Karath

Dr. Smith "borrows" a part from The Chariot right before John, Will Major West and the robot go off in it again to search for water. When its air-conditioning breaks down because of that missing part, they all seek shelter in a cave to avoid a treacherous heat wave.

They park the Chariot in the cave, and while John and Major West work on the air-conditioning unit, Will and the robot explore the mysterious cavern.

When a planet quake knocks them off their feet, Will and the robot tumble down a hole, but are unhurt. Since the hole is too deep to climb out of, they search for another way out. John and Major West realize what has happened and come looking for them.

Will is doing a good deal of exploring and comes upon and underground lake near an underground forest. Nearby, an armored warrior watches the approach of Will and the robot.

A falling rock almost smashes John and Major West, but it does momentarily pin Don's foot. When John frees him, Major West has an injured foot and needs help to walk.

Meanwhile, in the underground forest, Will and the robot come upon a young girl, apparently a princess, asleep on a cushion. The robot decides that this is Sleeping Beauty and makes Will kiss her.

The princess is awakened by the kiss and she takes Will and the robot to meet the rest of her people.

John and Major West have discovered the underground forest but are captured by warriors before they can catch up to Will and the robot. But after Will is introduced to Major Domo, he's taken to the prisoners, who are, of course, John and Major West.

Major Domo states that long ago his race planned to conquer the universe and they have an entire army placed in suspended animation, waiting for the right moment to attack. Since the princess has been awakened, they decide that now is the right time and they plan to begin with Earth.

Because Will awakened her, he is supposed to marry the princess, but he's not interested. Will would prefer to main unattached and have fun. The princess isn't familiar with the concept of fun, and when Will describes it to her, she decides to free John Robinson, since she can't have Will.

When another planet quake rocks the area, John is able to battle the warriors and free Will. During the conflict, Major Domo falls and is electrocuted by his own machinery.

Upon freeing Major West, they all escape the burning base. In the forest they find the princess returning to her cushion to once again enter a deep sleep to wait for another adventurer to awaken her with a kiss. Although the frozen army is still there in the caves somewhere, John says they should leave it behind for someone else to worry about. They return to the Chariot and exit the cave.

The interiors of the Seaview were used as the underground kingdom.

Kym Karath (Princess) co-starred with Angela Cartwright in Fox's THE SOUND OF MUSIC.

Story influence: 1930's Flash Gordon and Buck Rogers serials.

EPISODE TWENTY-EIGHT:
"A Change Of Space"
First telecast April 20, 1966
Writer: Peter Packer
Director: Sobey Martin
GUEST STAR: ALIEN: Frank Graham

Will sees a light off in the hills and he and Dr. Smith decide to go and check it out in case it might be a landing spacecraft. They climb up to a plateau to search for the source, but while up there Dr. Smith falls into a cosmic dust pit. Smith is certain he's going to die, but Will is able to help Smith climb out.

They continue their search for the source of the lights and encounter a spherical spacecraft rest by some strange looking machinery.

When John, Maureen, Major West and the robot arrive in the scene to examine the craft, the robot states that it appears to be an interplanetary space relay station, and that the craft before them is capable of traveling throughout the universe. It can do this by travelling at the speed of light squared and crossing the sixth dimension.

John decides that there's too much they don't know about the relay station and orders everyone to keep away from it until they can learn more. But as they're leaving, a ray shoots out and neutralizes the robot.

Although forbidden to go back there, Will returns alone to try and repair the robot, which he is able to do. The spherical ship has an aperture which the curious boy enters, whereupon it seals and takes off with Will aboard. The robot observed this incident and returns to the Jupiter II to report it. Everyone rushes back to the relay station and arrives in time to see the ship return, with Will still aboard.

Will exits the ship, but he has been altered by the experience. His brain capacity has been staggeringly increased, but he has become cold and arrogant. Although everyone is happy to see Will back, his attitude soon alienates everyone, except Smith. Smith wants to undergo the same experience and increase his own brain power. Although Will realizes that Smith is being friendly only to learn how to operate the spacecraft, the brain-boy gives Smith what he wants.

Dr. Smith takes off in the mystery craft, but when he returns, he doesn't emerge as a super-genius, but as an old man.

John and Major West try to think of a way to help Dr. Smith, but Will says the only way would be for Smith to make the journey again, but in the opposite direction.

Will decides to arbitrarily test test the theory himself, and takes the ship up again, against his family's wishes. But when the ship returns, instead of Will, an alien monster emerges. It has a laser finger and when Major West confronts the thing with his laser, it blasts the weapon from his hand.

The creature seems to be shouting at them angrily in an alien tongue. But the robot is able to translate it and reveals that it's looking for the sister ship which Will took off in.

They're finally able to convince the alien that his ship is returning, and indeed it does come back and Will emerges, a normal boy again. Will manages to convince the alien to take Dr. Smith in one of the ships to reverse the old age effect, and the alien agrees. Smith returns, young again, and his usual whining and complaining self.

After all this bother, the alien decides that this world is a bad place to leave a relay station and it packs up everything and leaves.

The alien ships are the Seaview's diving bells.
The alien suit was also used as a "Man-Fish" on VOYAGE.
Photography by Winton Hoch, Allen's favorite cameraman, also responsible for the pilot.

EPISODE TWENTY-NINE:
"Follow The Leader"

First telecast April 27, 1966
Writer: Barney Slater
Director: Don Richardson
GUEST STAR: KANTO: Gregory Morton

John Robinson and Dr. Smith are exploring a cave when Smith drops his precious laser pistol somewhere. While they're looking for it, a slight planet quake occurs and Smith panics and runs off. This leaves John stranded in the cave when the entrance collapses. While John is searching for a way out he encounters a wall which is obviously not of natural origin.

Suddenly he hears a voice that seems to be congratulating John Robinson on his strength when a huge statue topples towards him. John dodges it and then is faced with an attack by a giant lizard. . . which turns out to be an illusion.

The strange events continue when a doorway opens revealing a mummy in golden armor. These are the remains of the body of the great Kanto of the planet Quasti. But although the body is mummified, Kanto's spirit lives on and desires a new body. Kanto's spirit attempts to take over the body of John Robinson. John resists, but the alien stuns him and merges with John's form.

The Robinsons and Major West are attempting to dig John out from the collapsed cave entrance when the power of Kanto opens the cavern and John emerges unharmed.

But John is not himself and Dr. Smith suggests that John is having a nervous breakdown. Will disagrees, thinking it's just the strain of all that John Robinson has endured. Will tries to comfort his father, but John is strangely cold towards him.

Kanto, in John's body, comes up with plans to make an efficient fuel converter for the Jupiter II which will be able to manufacture all the deutronium they'll need to launch the spaceship again. In working on this, Kanto/John pushes everyone particularly hard and is oblivious to feelings and the strain he's putting everyone under.

When Smith goes to John and attempts to psychoanalyze him, Kanto/John blurts out the truth and threatens Smith to keep his mouth shut.

The robot has been keenly observing everything which has been happening and figures out what must be happening, stating its theory to the Robinsons, who find it difficult to accept, although they do admit that John hasn't been himself recently.

That night, when John returns to the cave where he'd been trapped, Will follows him. John discovers the boy and orders him back to the Jupiter II. But when John has still not returned the next morning, Maureen, Judy and Major West decide to go and see if John is still in the cavern. When they enter the cave, a wall lowers, trapping them in the cave.

John/Kanto returns to the Jupiter II, but now he's wearing a golden mask and speaking with the voice of the alien, Kanto, believing that no one will recognize him.

Kanto tells Will, Penny and Dr. Smith that Maureen, Judy and Major West have been taken prisoner by aliens from Quasti. Kanto states that he'll help them take the Jupiter II to Quasti to rescue the three.

Will challenges Kanto's story and the alien takes Will aside to talk to him and takes him to a bottomless pit where he plans to throw the boy in. Will reveals that he knows that Kanto has taken over his father's body, and when Kanto/John attempts to push Will into the pit, John Robinson resists. While Kanto is struggling to regain control of John's body, Will rips off the gold mask and hurls it into the bottomless pit, causing Kanto to leave John's body as the alien was linked to the gold mask. Trapped in the bottomless pit, the alien is too far out of reach to ever harm anyone again.

They return and rescue Maureen, Judy and Major West from the cave. The upside of all this is that the device Kanto had them build actually works, and they now have enough fuel to leave the planet.

This is the first episode showing Prof. Robinson turning against the family. It is also the final black and white episode.

GUY WILLIAMS: UPSTAGED BY A ROBOT

Although there was no question in the earliest episode of LOST IN SPACE that Guy Williams, in his role of Prof. John Robinson, was the main character in the ensemble of the Jupiter II clan, there is also no question that viewers could see Williams losing this position an inch at a time. Initially John Robinson was the driving force who made the command decisions and always took it upon himself to make the most dangerous forays when they were called for. Whether it was the space walk to repair the antenna, or flying down to the surface of the never named planet to investigate its suitability as a landing site, John Robinson was out in front.

But while he wasn't looking, treachery was at foot. Treachery in the form of a treacherous character, Dr. Smith, and a scene-stealing robot. The writers felt that it was more fun to write about the robot and Dr. Smith as though they were some sort of futuristic Laurel & Hardy, and soon John Robinson's role was reduced to often being no more than a spear carrier. While Guy Williams' character was frequently brought in for the climactic scenes ("The Challenge" and "The Lost Civilization") only in the final episode of the first season ("Follow The Leader") was Williams role allowed to be as active as it was in the earliest episodes of the series. The second season took the robot and Dr. Smith adventures (with Will along to kibitz) to new extremes until it became difficult to tell one episode from the other, with rare exceptions. Things changed in the third season for awhile as Williams was given more to do again, but soon the writers fell back into their self-generated formula, and the series continued to fall in the ratings.

Quite a letdown for an actor who thought he was the star of the show when he was hired. But then he was. It's highly unusual for a series to change its focus as completely as LOST IN SPACE did. Even though Williams received star billing throughout the three seasons of the show, the stories tended to ignore this little detail. Williams was still quite young (only 44) when LIS was cancelled in 1968, yet he never acted in front of a camera again. One could understand if it was because he felt embittered by how the producers and writers of LIS had treated him.

Born in New York City in 1924, his real name was Armando Catalano, and he was the son of Italian immigrants. He secured work as a photo model and acted in the Neighborhood Playhouse. It was during this period that he began using the name Guy Williams to keep from being typecast into ethnic parts.

Williams relocated to California and signed a contract with MGM for a time, and then moved on to Universal. His film roles were quite small at first, and his first picture at Universal was the now infamous BEDTIME FOR BONZO. He later appeared as the policeman who guns down Michael Landon in I WAS A TEENAGE WEREWOLF, but he wanted more. He'd married by then and had two children to raise and didn't see much of a future in bit parts in small films. So he started to consider work in television more and more seriously. At the time, TV was looked down on; many film actors felt threatened by the way it seemed to pull audiences away from theaters.

When Williams heard that Disney was planning a ZORRO TV series, he decided to try out for it, having more faith in Disney than in other companies. The role required someone who could perform a convincing Spanish accent as well as swordsmanship. Since Williams had been taught fencing by his father from the time he had been a child, it gave him that extra edge. That combined with his dashing good looks made him a natural for the role.

In ZORRO, Williams proved what he could do in a leading role. As the title character, the actor was in nearly every scene and had to carry the story himself. Although in the role of Don Diego de la Vega he had to play a character whom no one would suspect of being the masked adventurer, Williams chose not to play him as coward, but rather as a bookish intellectual who would nevertheless stand up to people when challenged. He gave Diego a sense of self and of character rather than overdoing the meek and mild-mannered angle.

ZORRO aired from October 1957 through September 1959. When it was dropped the ratings were actually quite good, but a behind-the-scenes clash between ABC, who was trying to force Disney to stay, and Walt, who wanted to go to NBC, caused Disney to cancel ZORRO just to spite ABC. Disney produced four additional one-hour episodes of ZORRO which aired on DISNEYLAND.

When Williams finally left the Zorro role in 1961, he went to Europe with his family for two years to make films, including CAPTAIN SINBAD in Italy and DAMON AND PYTHIAS in Germany.

When he returned, he appeared on BONANZA for several episodes in 1964 during the time when the series co-star Pernell Roberts was making demands the producers didn't want to meet. Williams was brought in to show Roberts he could easily be replaced. Guy Williams felt he was being used as a pawn and didn't care for the experience, just accepting that appearing on a continuing basis for one of the nation's top-rated shows could only boost his career.

In late 1964, the pilot script to LOST IN SPACE was offered to him and he accepted it. In STARLOG #114, Williams told writer Mike Clark, "I wasn't taken with the script. It was typical TV. If I had been asked to do 'Richard III', that would have been a surprise, but to go into LOST IN SPACE after having done ZORRO, it was just standard TV subject matter."

In describing what it was like doing the series, Williams went on to say, "The main idea of LOST IN SPACE was the special effects. Irwin is great at them, and our struggle was to stay away from all the flashing equipment when we were doing our scenes. They would stick us in front of equipment that was whizzing or whirring, and I knew that the audience would watch the machine. So, we moved to the left or the

right, and the camera would hopefully follow, and we would get *away* from the machine."

Although Williams discounted reports that he was angry that the scripts had made other performers the de facto stars, he was disappointed and felt that it was an overall malaise which went far beyond his character being relegated to the background. He said that LOST IN SPACE got a bad case of the "cutes."

"When a show gets the 'cutes,' it kills itself," Williams observed. "You can get campy and do stunts with style, and you can get away with amazing things and have people love it. In ZORRO, we did outrageous things but we did it in style, first class."

After LOST IN SPACE was cancelled, Williams was invited to appear in a charity show in Buenos Aires, Argentina by the wife of Argentine president Juan Peron. In gratitude she gave the actor carte blanche to make personal appearances in that country. Williams found much in that country to his liking and decided to settle there, making only occasional trips over the years to California.

One of his last trips was in 1983 when he was invited by Disney to consider appearing in a new version of ZORRO titled ZORRO AND SON. Unfortunately the scripts Williams read were terrible and he turned the series down, which did get produced but was quickly cancelled after only six episodes aired between April 6 and June 1, 1983.

In 1986 Williams made another foray stateside and appeared with June Lockhart and other former LIS cast members on the syndicated game show FAMILY FEUD. Williams had a great time seeing his old friends.

At the time, Bill Mumy had interested 20th Century Fox in a TV movie reunion/sequel for LOST IN SPACE, but Irwin Allen refused to even read Mumy's script and so the last opportunity for Williams to reprise his role of John Robinson was lost.

Guy Williams died in Buenos Aires on May 7, 1989, and news of his death made the wire services around the world, as his work remains very fondly remembered by his many fans, particularly by those of us who grew up watching him on ZORRO and LOST IN SPACE.

Guy Williams and June Lockhart enjoyed a close working relationship.

June Lockhart: Mother to the Stars?

Once LOST IN SPACE was approved for airing by CBS, they needed a cast to portray the characters. The first hired was June Lockhart.

June Lockhart gave us the human side of LOST IN SPACE. She portrayed the mother of three children, wife of Professor Robinson, friend to co-worker Major West—the all-around space-faring woman.

She was the only one sympathetic to Dr. Smith, even when the children were involved.

This was not an easy task.

Before she could learn what it was like to be LOST IN SPACE, June Lockhart had to take a VOYAGE TO THE BOTTOM OF THE SEA. "I did an episode called 'The Ghost of Moby Dick' and Irwin Allen asked me if I would like to be in his new pilot called LOST IN SPACE," says Lockhart, recalling how she landed her role of Maureen Robinson on the series.

Born into a theatrical family, her father, Gene Lockhart, and mother, Kathleen, were both performers in the theatre and in motion pictures. Even before she had completed her schooling at the prestigious Westlake School for Girls in Beverly Hills, she had appeared in supporting roles in such films as ALL THIS AND HEAVEN TOO and SERGEANT YORK, where she played Gary Cooper's sister. Following graduation, she went under contract to MGM and began her career with much larger roles in THE WHITE CLIFFS OF DOVER, MEET ME IN ST. LOUIS, THE YEARLING and SON OF LASSIE. The last proved prophetic for some years later, after leaving MGM for work in the live theatre and elsewhere, she landed the role in 1958 as the mother in the TV series LASSIE, which she held for six seasons. June Lockhart has two daughters: Ann, born in '53, and June Elizabeth, born in '55. Ann has appeared in a recent science

fiction series of her own, BATTLESTAR GALACTICA.

June Lockhart was the first actress cast for the LIS series, although when she read the pilot script it was called SPACE FAMILY ROBINSON.

"I'd finished my last episode of LASSIE in February '64 and did the VOYAGE in September. Then we made the pilot in December and went right into production on the series." But the pilot script she read and made in December was never aired in its original form. Besides lacking the characters of the robot and Dr. Smith, there were structural reasons why it was revised.

"The pilot had too many climaxes," she explains. "For instance, we were caught in a whirlpool and frozen, then we saw a one-eyed giant after we crash-landed and these sequences were finally edited and became the climaxes of the first five aired episodes. We had to shoot new scenes leading up to these climaxes, though. The pilot was never broadcast in its original form but all of the footage was eventually aired." All that is except for a scene of two aliens peering around a bush with apparent malicious intent.

Being lost in space was not all the gaiety it appears to be on the screen. For instance, the silver costumes the Robinsons wore during the first two seasons were actually fireproof aluminium race car drivers' suits, which under the stagelights were uncomfortably hot.

"We had to wear them because there wasn't any other fabric which had the same look to it, and they were so tight we couldn't sit down in them. In order to rest between shots, I had to be lowered onto a cot and then be helped to stand up. When we moved we were very stiff-legged. Underneath the suits we wore body stockings so that we could drop the suit tops down when we wanted to at least be comfortable from the waist up. By the time the third season came around mylar had been invented and then we wore silver jerseys made from that."

Every once in awhile Lockhart was called on to do other uncomfortable things, such as fly when she had to simulate the weightlessness of space.

"I had to wear a special suit with a harness around my pelvis," she recalls ruefully. "There were bolts which stuck out at the hip and were attached to wires outside the suit. When I was lifted up, the wires supported me by my crotch and I had to balance myself while lying out flat. It was very complicated. I could only stay up there for a short while and it was very difficult to do, but I got a kick out of it."

Guy Williams got more than a kick out of it. June and Guy were flying from their wires for a photo session with TV GUIDE when the worst happened.

"We were swinging together and then his wire broke. He fell twelve feet onto a hard cement floor. I was afraid he'd broken his neck but he was very athletic and so he rolled and landed on his shoulder. We didn't use the flying suits any more after that."

There were lighter moments on the show as well.

"Sometimes it was hard to keep a straight face," she admits. "My favorite time involved Stanley Adams when he played a giant talking carrot in 'The Great Vegetable Rebellion.'"

When the show was cancelled after the third season, she wasn't terribly upset. "I thought we had rung as many changes as we could on the boy, the doctor and the robot. However, had the series been renewed for a fourth season, I would have stayed with it. In the long run I was still the star of the show for three years. I had been in the business before LOST IN SPACE and I knew I would continue to work after the show ended.

"We had a lovely group of people on the show," Lockhart observes. "Guy was great fun to be around. He was a very bright man with a lovely sense of hu

mor. I've known Jonathan for years and he's a dear, funny man."

While a revival of LOST IN SPACE as a series remains uncertain, there was a partial reunion a few years ago on the game show FAMILY FEUD.

"It was so great to see everyone again. It's too bad Jonathan couldn't make it, too, as I really wanted all of us to do that show. We missed Billy, too, because he was on location filming something at the time. But it was great fun."

Mark Goddard — Lost in Space

Somehow I could really believe Major West knew all along how to get back to Earth, but he wanted the world to be spared the problems Dr. Smith would give us.

So he deliberately kept the Jupiter II lost in space all of those years.

Mark Goddard added a special honesty to his role. His portrayal of Major West seemed real. At times he held a story together because he would question what was going on around him.

Major West was just one of the elements that made LOST IN SPACE a dramatic series as well as a venture into fantasy storytelling.

Mark Goddard, as Major Don West, often served as the anchor for characters on LOST IN SPACE as he was not a part of the Robinson family and was there for his skills— unlike Dr. Smith who was there because he was trapped while sabotaging the mission. West was the only one who would really take Smith to task and who we believed would have been more than willing to drag Smith out of ear-shot of the base camp and give him a good working over. He never believed whatever Smith had to say and refused to be a part of the simpering Doctor's schemes.

Born July 24, 1936, Goddard's career began in Lowell, Massachusetts where he grew up.

"It was a small town," he recalls, "and I was brought up playing sports in a family of five, all older than I. I had a brother and three sisters and my dad had a Five & Ten with a clothing store in Lowell. I grew up like anyone in a small town. I played a lot of sports and in high school we went to the state finals in two sports and I was all state in basketball, and I played baseball, too. We played the state finals in Fenway Park in Boston for the baseball championship—it was really something I loved.

"When I applied to colleges like Dartmouth and Holy Cross, I discovered that Holy Cross had a really good basketball team. They were a Jesuit Catholic school and my older brother had gone there, so I went there. But I wasn't good enough to play on the team, so I turned to dramatics. I was in the dramatic society at Holy Cross and in my junior year I took a leave of absence for a year with the option that I could go back to Holy Cross if things didn't work out in New York."

Goddard went to the American Academy of Dramatic Arts in New York where he enjoyed studying acting so much that he decided not to return to Holy Cross.

"Instead I went to Florida and did Summer Stock and then came back to New England and did stock. When I came out to California I had an old, beat up Plymouth convertible and I ended up in Long Beach with about eight dollars in my pocket. I thought that Long Beach was Hollywood and I hung around there for about three days looking for stars, but I didn't see any. So finally I found Hollywood and I went to Paramount Studios. I wanted to go on the lot but they wouldn't let me in. Across the street was this place called O'Blatts and I was having a cup of coffee when I ran into this young man named Frank Dana who was doing a small part in a movie. He told me the director's name and I went up and spent my last couple of bucks on some paper, borrowed a pen and wrote a note to this Joe Anthony, just simply saying that my name is Mark Goddard, I just got out here, that I did stock in Florida, studied in New York and I needed some advice and left my phone number. I was staying with some relatives down in Long Beach. I gave the letter to the same guard at the Paramount gate who wouldn't let me in to see them shoot movies. He gave the note to Joe Anthony, who was really a Broadway director who was doing a movie called

CAREERS with Shirley MacClain. So Joe's secretary called me and we set up a meeting—Joe wanted to say hello and talk to me, and I said great! That following Monday I returned to Paramount, went on the set and they were shooting a scene—it was a courtroom scene. And then everybody left for lunch, but I kept sitting there since I had never met him and didn't know who he was. After lunch they returned and Joe walked up and said, 'Oh, you must be the young man who wrote the letter.' So we sat down and talked for ten minutes and set up appointments for me to see someone at William Morris and MCA.

"That's how it all started. The William Morris agency sent me out to Dick Powell and Aaron Spelling and the next week I tested and within three weeks I had my first series, called JOHNNY RINGO.

"Everyone asks me how to get started in show business and I tell them that it's different for each person. There is no formula or secret. If the timing's right and you're ready for it, something can happen. But there is no formula in our business, not like other jobs. You must know your craft and be ready for those chances. It's not just good looks, either. Most good actors seem to have something extra—a magnetism or something."

Goddard still has very fond memories of JOHNNY RINGO.

"It was only on for one year and it was something I really loved doing. Aaron Spelling was the producer and today he never mentions it so I don't think he has a very fond memory of it now. Aaron was great to work for and I imagine that he still is. He was a very special person and we became good friends because I was out there in Hollywood alone and he was married to Carolyn Jones then—they were like sister and brother to me. They really took me under their wing and took care of me. When the holidays came around and I was without family, they took me with them to all the people they visited, like Alan Ladd, Danny Thomas and people like that. I was in awe, as you can imagine.

"Aaron and I travelled to New York one time and since he doesn't fly, we took a train across country. We went through Dallas and met his parents and he showed me where he went to school and it was really nice. He was later best man at my wedding."

When JOHNNY RINGO ended, Goddard went on to other series work and films.

"I did a few movies and then went into THE DE-TECTIVES with Robert Taylor for three years at Four Star for Dick Powell, who was very good to me. He gave me the choice of a couple of series to do and I chose to work with Robert Taylor because of his professionalism. He was a wonderful man and I learned a lot."

When that ended around 1963, Goddard did guest shots on such well known series as PERRY MASON and THE BEVERLY HILLBILLIES. Then LOST IN SPACE soon followed.

"That came about because I was with the same agency that Irwin Allen was with at the time and they sort

of packaged it. I thought it was just a pilot that wouldn't sell because no one at the time had a space show on the air, even though in reality space was beginning for our country. I didn't think a show like this would work because of the cost to do it each week."

As we all know, LOST IN SPACE was launched on what would become a three year voyage. Goddard was very pleased to work with his co-stars, although by the time the third year came around, not everyone was really happy with the way things were going.

"There was a lot of tension on the set during the third year because of the way the show had evolved. We all thought that the show was going to be different, more of a STAR TREK type of show, and I thought I would have become a bigger star and the show was going to be a bigger hit. This was something I had no right to think or feel because it affects the others around you. That's what contributed to the tension on the set, which no one had the right to make. In other words, when Jonathan's part grew on the show, that was due to the writer and creator of the show. It was their right to turn it that way and we were paid to follow their plan.

"Guy and I got along real well because Guy is easy to get along with. Everything was fine between us except for maybe one time when the script called for scenes that were mine and Guy was doing them instead. I guess that because Jonathan was taking his scenes, he was protecting himself because he had lost so much to Jonathan. But I did enjoy working on LOST IN SPACE because we had a lot of nice people, like little Billy Mumy and Angela, and all of them were really great."

Even though by the third year things were difficult for them, it was during that season that LOST IN SPACE produced Mark Goddard's favorite episode.

"I liked 'The Anti-Matter Man' because Don West had two sides to him in that one and I had a little scar on my face. It was a chance to do a little something different and it was fun."

Mark Goddard during the second season

67

SEASON TWO

Introduction by Paul Monroe

The second season of LOST IN SPACE saw color come to the show, allowing us to see alien landscapes, monsters and spaceships as we never had before. Airing in color meant that props and sets could be modified to look more impressive on the country's TV screens. The futuristic gadgets and alien flora and fauna of LOST IN SPACE were the perfect environment in which to capitalize on the new medium of color.

Inside the Jupiter II, changes included the addition of a control panel below the main viewport windows, a scale around the interior of the astrogator, and the redesign of the atomic clock assembly and the communication area. Outside the ship, the alien planet set was transformed from a desolate, desert area into a kaleidoscope of brightly colored trees, rocks and exotic plants. Changes to the equipment began with the robot, who was overhauled from bubble to treads. His elliptical sensors were colored, his claws made a deep red, and his legs re-molded to give them a smoother look.

The laser pistol used in the pilot, as well as the first season laser rifle, were all discarded in favor of new designs, although they would frequently turn up in the hands of aliens and visitors during the second and third seasons. Other modifications were made to the Chariot and the force field hardware.

The most significant change in the series, however, was the shift in its story lines away from survival adventures into outrageous, and at times absurd, fantasy. Over on the ABC network, a show called BATMAN was quickly racking up ratings with its high camp style of adventure, and LOST IN SPACE began adopting at least some of this style. A younger, larger audience was beginning to tune in, but unfortunately, what the program gained in viewer numbers, it lost in credibility. The character of Dr. Smith was reaching the apex of a transformation from a cold enemy into a comedic troublemaker, which seemed the perfect fuel for the program's "camp" fires.

While this move to more humorous stories seemed to begin with the second season, a review of the first year clearly reveals the roots of this alteration. In the beginning, Smith was cold, merciless and deadly. He kills an Alpha Control security guard when he is caught sabotaging the robot's programming ("The Reluctant Stowaway"), possesses no reservations about killing the Jupiter crew, and makes several additional attempts to kill them after the launch ("Island In The Sky"). Despite this seemingly cold, unflinching front, we do glimpse the cowardly, comedic side of Smith which would soon define his character completely.

In both "The Reluctant Stowaway" and "Island In The Sky," Smith lies to cover his cowardice of spacewalking. By the end of "Island In The Sky," he shows the first, genuine signs of concern for any of the Robinsons, worrying that the robot, which Smith programmed to eliminate each family member in "The Derelict," might harm Will. From this point on, Smith's selfishness, cowardice, untrustworthiness, incompetence and, fortunately, affection for the Robinsons, rises more and more to the surface.

Throughout "There Were Giants In The Earth," much of the Doctor's time is spent dodging work on the force field hardware and the hydroponic garden. Later, when a pea that he plants in the planet's soil without permission grows into a giant mutation, Smith runs for protection behind the ladies, a reaction that would soon become second nature when facing any danger.

In "The Hungry Sea," the episode which brings the first storyline to a close, the Robinsons had set off in the Chariot to find a warmer climate, leaving Smith and the robot behind in the Jupiter II. In these scenes, Smith seems almost pleased that the planet's hostile climate will destroy the family until he learns of the planet's elliptical orbit and, in a fit of compassion, warns them of the coming heat wave by sending the robot with a message. From "Welcome Stranger" on, Smith continues to betray the Robinsons, often placing one or all of them in danger to save himself ("Invaders From The Fifth Dimension," for example), but his character is much less harsh.

Another member of LOST IN SPACE's cast who played a significant part in the program's shift to more humorous scripts was the robot. During the first season, the robot had developed from Dr. Smith's evil tool into a helpful resource and trusted guardian of the Robinson's. By year two, TV GUIDE was listing him in the credits and more episodes featured him.

Early into the first season, Jonathan Harris started thinking of the robot in human terms and began treating him as if he were a real person. Suddenly, this new twist to the program's format was recognized by the writers, who began creating more situations for them. The verbal abuses endured by the robot gave us some of LOST IN SPACE's best moments and became one of its trademarks, but much of the first year drama was now gone. Add the robot developing human characteristics such as laughing and crying, include Will for Smith to get into trouble, and the formula which would dominate the remainder of the series was born.

Highlights in year two included the premiere "Blast Off Into Space" featuring a spectacular lift-off sequence as the Jupiter finally leaves the first year planet which, for a short time, we get to see in color. In the next episode, "Wild Adventure," the Jupiter is nearly destroyed in Earth's sun, due to Smith's tampering with the astrogator, and actually talks to Earth over the radio, although they cannot make a course change to land. Not knowing what lies ahead for them, they exit Earth's galaxy for uncharted space, becoming lost for the second time.

The robot was showcased in several second season stories including "Trip Through The Robot." As a result of his failing power, the robot strays from the ship and collapses in a valley where alien gasses cause it to grow to the size of a house. Upon finding him, Will and Smith go inside the machine to revive his mechanical heart, restore his power levels and return it to normal size. In "Wreck Of The Robot," aliens called the Saticons steal the robot and dismantle it. By doing so they learn the basic principles of Earth machines and build a device to conquer the Earth.

Season two featured some excellent guest star appearances. Wally Cox played Tiabo, the sole inhabitant of "The Forbidden World," when the Jupiter crashes on the planet where they would stay for the remainder of year two. Gerald Mohr appears as Morbius, the political prisoner when Smith makes "A Visit To Hades." Malachi Throne portrays "The Thief From Outer Space" searching for his princess. The relationship struck by Will and the thief is similar to the warm friendship shared by the boy and Captain Tucker in year one's "The Sky Pirate" and year two's "Treasure Of The Lost Planet" in which the talented Albert Salmi reprises his role as the intergalactic pirate. John Abbott appears in "The Dream Monster" as the scientist Sesmar, who tries to impress human feelings on his robot Radion by depriving the Robinson family of theirs. In the season's finale, "The Galaxy Gift," John Carradine portrays Mr. Archon, an alien who employs Penny's help to defeat the evil Saticons, first seen in "Wreck Of The Robot."

In "The Cave Of The Wizards," Smith is controlled by an alien computer and, wearing blue, Spock-like makeup, becomes the leader of the Draconian civilization. This episode is one of Jonathan Harris' favorites. Another interesting story was "The Questing Beast" for the uncharacteristic way in which Smith behaves. Will loses faith in people because of his disappointment with an old knight named Sir Sagramonte who is searching for the beast that he has pursued his whole life. Smith, also feeling responsible for Will after being caught in yet another lie, acts out of total unselfishness to help Sagramonte restore the boy's innocence.

CAST AND CREDITS

CREATED AND PRODUCED BY IRWIN ALLEN
STORY EDITOR: Anthony Wilson
ASSOCIATE PRODUCER: William Faralla
MUSIC SUPERVISION: Lionel Newman
PRODUCTION SUPERVISOR: Jack Sonntag
PRODUCTION ASSOCIATE: Hal Herman
UNIT PRODUCTION MANAGER: Ted Butcher
DIRECTOR OF PHOTOGRAPHY: Frank Carson
ART DIRECTORS: Jack Martin Smith, Robert Kinoshita
SET DECORATORS: Walter M. Scott, James Hassigner
COSTUME DESIGNER: Parl Zastupnevich
SPECIAL PHOTOGRAPHIC EFFECTS: L.B. Abbott, A.S.C.
MAKE-UP SUPERVISION: Ben Nye
SUPERVISING SOUND EFFECTS EDITOR: Don Hall, Jr.
SOUND EFFECTS EDITOR: Frank White
THEME: Johnny Williams
EXECUTIVE IN CHARGE OF PRODUCTION FOR VAN BERNARD: Guy Della Cioppa

AN IRWIN ALLEN PRODUCTION IN ASSOCIATION WITH:
Jodi Productions, Inc.
Van Bernard Productions, Inc.
Twentieth Century Fox Television, Inc.
CBS Television Neywork

CAST
PROFESSOR JOHN ROBINSON: Guy Williams
MAUREEN ROBINSON: June Lockhart
MAJOR DON WEST: Mark Goddard
JUDY ROBINSON: Angela Cartwright
WILL ROBINSON: Billy Mumy
DR. ZACHARY SMITH: Jonathan Harris
THE ROBOT: Bob May
THE ROBOT'S VOICE: Dick Tufeld

Commentaries by Mike Clark

EPISODE THIRTY:
"Blast Off Into Space"

First telecast September 14th, 1966
WRITER: Peter Packer
DIRECTOR: Nathan Juran
INCIDENTAL MUSIC: Leith Stevens
GUEST STAR: NERIM: Strother Martin

The planet quakes which have plagued that world ever since they landed there are now reaching a critical peak, and the entire planet is in danger of breaking up. Calculations indicate that the planet will explode within twenty-four hours.

The Robinsons are packing up, and Will and Dr. Smith are out at the drill sight when there is an explosion and an old miner, Nerim (read it backwards, gang) appears. It seems that the planet quakes were actually the result of Nerim's blasting. The miner is searching for the rarest and most valuable substance in the universe, which he calls cosmonium. Cosmonium is supposedly the actual essence of pure life force.

Nerim takes Will and Dr. Smith down to show off his mine, and insists that he knows what he's doing with all his blasting. Dr. Smith is particularly fascinated by all this, and the mention of cosmonium appeals to the larceny in him, but then what doesn't?

At the Jupiter II, another quake rocks the planet. When their calculations reveal that the ship would be too heavy to lift off with their present fuel supply, they start throwing out all non-essential items.

Although the quakes are being caused by Nerim's explosions, those explosions have been damaging the world's core until it has become dangerously unstable.

When Smith wants to bargain with Nerim for some Cosmonium, the miner offers some in exchange for a thruster pack. It seems that the miner's mule, Rover, has chewed up his thruster control, effectively stranding Nerim on the now unstable planet.

Smith swipes a thruster from the Jupiter II, since he doesn't believe that the planet is going to blow up, and uses it as his part of the bet in a card game with the miner. When Nerim wins the thruster pack, he quickly makes his exit, admitting that he knows perfectly well that the planet is getting ready to blow up. But when Nerim flees, he leaves behind two vials of the precious cosmonium.

While Will and Dr. Smith are returning to the Jupiter II, Smith accidentally breaks one of the vials of cosmonium and the substance gets on a statue he'd made. Much to their surprise, the statue comes to life. Needing more of the substance to sustain its life, the statue pursues Smith to get the other vial.

While John Robinson is searching for Will and Dr. Smith, Smith is cornered by the statue and forced to surrender the other vial. John arrives in time to drive the stature off and they all return to the ship to get ready for blast off.

The Jupiter II lifts off as the world starts to break up. When the ship has trouble reaching escape velocity due to thruster problems, Smith admits his theft and Major West is able to make a hasty but successful repair.

Free from the disintegrating planet, they start taking readings of the constellations to chart their position.

This is the first color episode of LIS.
There is new footage of the Jupiter II liftoff. The lights surrounding the lower

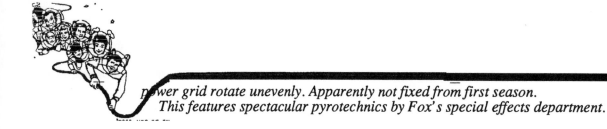

wer grid rotate unevenly. Apparently not fixed from first season.
This features spectacular pyrotechnics by Fox's special effects department.

EPISODE THIRTY-ONE:
"Wild Adventure"
First telecast September 21, 1966
Writers: William Read Woodfield and Allan Balter
Director: Don Richardson
Incidental Music: Alexander Courage
GUEST STAR: LORELEI: Vitina Marcus

They are trying to plot a course back to Earth when the robot states that because the sun is between them and the Earth at this time, that it would be unsafe to go on that direction. And so John and Major West reset the ship's controls for Alpha Centauri.

Dr. Smith tries to reset the astrogator for Earth by using a magnetic ring, but all he manages to accomplish is to jettison all of the Jupiter 2's reserve fuel. They only have twenty hours of fuel left, but upon contacting Alpha Control they learn that a fuel barge had been launched into space and occupies a position approximately twenty hours distant.

They arrive safely at the fuel barge, but while Major West is refueling he notices that much of the fuel in the barge has already been siphoned off. Major West sees something out of the corner of his eye, or at least thinks he does, but nothing is detected there.

When the Jupiter II departs on course for Alpha Centauri again, Dr. Smith manages to trick Penny into resetting the controls for Earth.

While below decks, Smith sees a green girl wearing a gold-colored costume outside his window, but when he reports it, no one will believe him. They think it's another one of his devious tricks. Will gives Smith the benefit of the doubt and stays up with him to watch for the green girl to reappear, but she never does. But when Smith is alone with the robot, she reappears, singing in a language which the robot is able to translate. She claims to be of the People of the Green Mist, and states that she's in love with Smith.

The collision warning sounds in the Jupiter II as it's in danger of being pulled into a star. They plot a new course around the star and have just enough fuel to make a course correction. Their new course will enable them to return to Earth.

When the green girl reappears, her voice hypnotizes Smith, who is able to don a space suit and sneak to the airlock where he exits the ship to meet with the strange space girl.

When Smith is discovered, the robot reveals that the green girl wants the Jupiter 2's atomic fuel because she feeds on it. Complicating the situation is that if they stop to rescue Dr. Smith, they'll miss their course correction point and be unable to return to Earth. Still, Major West goes outside and manages to drag Smith back aboard.

As they begin passing out of range of Alpha Control, they're informed that the Jupiter II is leaving the galaxy for parts unknown. Once again, the Jupiter II is lost in space.

The Jupiter II actually contacts Alpha Control as they rocket out of the solar system and become lost in space once again.

EPISODE THIRTY-TWO:
"The Ghost Planet"

First telecast September 28, 1966
Writer: Peter Packer
Director: Nathan Juran
GUEST STARS: THE SUMMIT: Michael Fox, OFFICER 03: Sue England

Dr. Smith hears a voice over the speaker in his room which claims to be "Space Control" giving directions for landing. Smith is certain that they are near Earth and he changes the course of the Jupiter II, which takes it directly into a radiation storm which buffets the ship.

No one else has heard the voice and thinks Smith has flipped as no planet is detected anywhere nearby, but Smith sticks to his story. Suddenly the Jupiter II emerges from the radiation belt, a planet comes in sight and the voice of Space Control is heard over the communications system. But when John tries to contact Space Control to find out who they are, he gets no reply.

The Jupiter II is pulled into the planet by a directional beam and set down outside gate 115. Dr. Smith is eager to go outside, convinced that he's on Earth, but when John points out that if he's wrong Smith could be putting his life in danger, he relents and goes along with John's idea to send the robot out to reconnoiter.

The planet is dark and misty, and looks barren. As the robot approaches gate 115, it opens and the robot is zapped by another robot before it can give it's report on what it has detected.

Smith is still convinced that he's on Earth and sneaks out of the shop. He encounters several cloaked beings led by a robot, Officer 03. The woman offers Smith rewards in return for his cooperation. When Smith is shown previous beings who were turned to stone when they didn't cooperate, Smith decides to help them.

The Robinson's robot is repaired and brought back to the ship along with Smith, but when Smith tries to get the Robinsons to come out, John won't allow it. When they try to take off from the planet, a mysterious force holds them in place.

That night Smith gathers up the lasers and sneaks out with them, but he's seen by Will. Will follows Smith with the robot, but is captured. While Smith meets with Officer 03, Will and the robot are taken before The Summit, which is a machine in the shape of a gigantic human brain. The Summit proclaims that the robot is guilty of disloyalty to cybernetic life-forms for helping the humans. The robot agrees to mend its ways and joins the force of The Summit.

The robot takes Will away and forces him to work on an assembly line while Dr. Smith's reward turns out to be putting together cybernetic circuits.

Although Smith took the larger laser pistols, he accidentally left behind two small lasers, which John and Major West arm themselves with to go searching for Will, the robot and Dr. Smith. When they encounter the robot, it promises to free Will and Dr. Smith, explaining that it has been pretending to join the forces of The Summit. It tells John and Major West to return to the Jupiter II where they'll be safer.

The robot encounters Officer 03 and short-circuits her, as well as destroying the machine which holds the Jupiter II imprisoned on the planet's surface. The robot rescues Will and Dr. Smith and they return to the Jupiter II, which flees the ghost planet. But a hyperatomic missile is shot after them, and to avoid it, they must dive into the atmosphere of another nearby world. But while the missile misses them, it impacts on the planet ahead of them and explodes, resulting in damage to the Jupiter II.

This is the first episode in which the robot falls in love with an evil female robot. Her voice was provided by Sue England, who does the voice of other characters later in the series.

There's some exciting footage of the Jupiter II evading the missile launched from the Ghost planet. It's used again in several later episodes.

EPISODE THIRTY-THREE:
"Forbidden World"
First telecast October 5, 1966
Writer: Barney Slater
Director: Don Richardson
Incidental Music: Robert Drasnin
GUEST STARS: TIABO: Wally Cox, PARROT THING: Janos Prohaska

When the Jupiter II is damaged by an exploding missile fired at it from the Ghost Planet which they had just escaped from, it is forced to crash-land on another world. The fog-shrouded planet doesn't look very inviting and the damage to the ship's navigation system is so extensive that the projected time for repairs is weeks at best.

Because the atmosphere could possibly be corrosive, John Robinson doesn't want to risk sending the robot out to reconnoiter, and forbids anyone else to leave the ship either. But Dr. Smith gets antsy and sends the robot out behind John's back. The robot reports that the atmosphere contains cosmic dust, thus necessitating breathing apparatus for anyone who should exit the ship. The robot also detects something approaching in the in the fog, but before it can identify it, communication with the robot is abruptly cut off.

When John discovers what Smith has done, he's furious and sends Dr. Smith out to find the robot and bring it back to the ship. Once outside, Smith soon finds his way through the fog and emerges into an area where the air is fresh. But just then something large and hairy grabs Smith and the Jupiter II loses radio contact with him.

Feeling responsible for anything that might have happened to Smith (and still wanting to find the robot), John and Major West go out and search for him, but without success.

Despite everything that's happened, Will decides to search on his own that night and encounters an alien being which looks like a crossbreed of a monkey and a parrot. It is approaching Will menacingly until a strange looking man in rags calls it off. Will tries to explain who he is and what he's doing there, but Tiabo isn't interested and takes Will prisoner.

Dr. Smith and the robot and chained up inside a cave used by Tiabo as his encampment. The raggedly dressed man explains that he is Captain Tiabo of special intelligence for the forces on that planet. Tiabo plans to take his prisoners before his commander, General Andos, and leaves them all guarded by the parrot-thing.

On a viewscreen they seen a soldier report in, and then the face of General Andros, and Will can't help but notice that they all look like Tiabo. General Andros orders the intruder (the Jupiter II) to leave immediately or they'll unleash their secret weapon on it. When Will tries to explain their predicament, General Andros cuts him off.

When Tiabo and his monster pet leave the prisoners alone, Will, Dr. Smith and the robot take the opportunity to escape. But unbeknownst to them, Tabo is watching from nearby, having planned to allow them to escape.

Dr. Smith had been thirsty and taken a drink from a cask of liquid. As they're leaving the cave, Smith throws the cask away, and it explodes! The robot analyzes the contents and reveals that it is a liquid explosive and Smith may now be a walking time bomb, and must stay securely away from the ship.

Will reports in at the Jupiter II about the warning of General Andros, but as time passes it seems that no attack is forthcoming.

Finally, upon the robot's suggestion, Will decides to go to Tiabo to see if he has a remedy for what Dr. Smith drank. Will catches Tiabo disguising himself as different people and recording messages to play back on his viewer. Tiabo admits that he's alone on that world, and that he's actually a hermit who came to that planet to live alone and just wanted to make the Jupiter II leave so that he'd have his peaceful solitude back again. Will finally convinces Tiabo that they don't intend to stay long and so the alien decides to move to another part of the planet until the Robinsons leave.

Meanwhile, the robot has hooked up a detonator to Dr. Smith to end the situation once and for all so that Smith cannot endanger the Robinsons or the Jupiter II. Smith is beside himself until Will shows up with the antidote, which the robot confirms is indeed effective.

The alien bird is a recycled costume from THE OUTER LIMITS episode "Amusement Park," and the original STAR TREK pilot, "The Cage." Operated by Janos Prohaska, who portrayed the Horta on the STAR TREK episode "The Devil In The Dark."

EPISODE THIRTY-FOUR:
"Space Circus"
First telecast October 12, 1966
Writers: Bob and Wanda Duncan
Director: Harry Harris
Incidental Music: Herman Stein
GUEST STARS: DOCTOR MARVELLO: James Westerfield, MADAME FENESTRA: Melinda Fee, NUBU: Michael Greene, BISHO: Harry Vartresian, COSMIC MONSTER: Dawson Palmer

Dr. Smith is taking one of his many naps when he's awakened by a huge, white hairy monster. Smith screams in horror and the monster runs off. His screams are heard and soon Will, Penny and the robot arrive to see what the ruckus is this time. But they aren't the only ones attracted to the scene.

Also arriving is one Doctor Marvello, who apologizes for the incident and explains that the creature was simply a cosmic monster from Supernova 12, but it's safely back in its cage now. He invites them to accompany them to his circus, which he dubs, "the greatest show in space." In reality it's rather rundown and has clearly seen better days.

Doctor Marvello shows them what his carnival contains, which includes a variety of beings and entertainment. There's Nubu, who has machinery which which he can create and juggle cosmic forces. The cosmic beast which Smith had scene is there to wrestle with Bisho, the strongman. There's even a clairvoyant named Madame Fenestra. Marvello rather hoped there'd be a larger population on this world to attend his circus than the seven stranded wayfarers of the Jupiter II. Marvello is pretty down on his luck and agrees to have his circus perform for the Robinsons in exchange for a hot meal.

Dr. Smith sees this as an opportunity to get off this world and tries to convince Marvello to let him join his circus and travel to Earth. Smith maintains that he's an accomplished song and dance man.

But because their purifier has broken down and they have a food shortage, thanks to a blight on the planet, John Robinson maintains that they don't have any food to spare for Doctor Marvello. But Maureen somehow convinces him that it would be worthwhile to have this show as they would then be able to escape from the stress of their situation for a little while.

The circus performance begins and leads off with Bisho wrestling the cosmic monster, but the monster wins. The cosmic monster is safely returned to its pen by Doctor Marvello's hypnotic powers.

After Nubu performs his act, then Madame Fenestra is on stage. She had Will assist her and plans to make a golden goblet appear, but somehow, through Madame Fenestra, Will actually is able to make things appear for real. After Will makes things like a purple frog appear, Marvello is amazed and insists that Will Robinson join his circus.

Marvello spins tales of the fantastic life Will would leave travelling to exotic alien worlds, but Will is equally insistent that he won't leave his family.

Dr. Smith tries to audition for the circus, but he's pretty hopeless. Marvello gets an idea and says that Smith could come along to act as Will's manager if only the boy would agree to join the circus. Smith thinks this is a wonderful idea and launches a devious scheme to convince Will to join the circus.

Smith makes the food shortage seem worse than it is and explains that were Will to join the circus then there'd be more food for his family. Will reluctantly agrees and he and Smith make plans to leave.

Meanwhile,, John and Major West have figured out that Smith has been deliberately creating a food shortage and when confronted by them, Smith reveals that Will is leaving to join Doctor Marvello.

When John Robinson tries to stop Marvello from taking Will, the circus owner unleashes the cosmic monster which attacks John. Will agrees to go along quietly with Marvello if he'll call off the creature. But then Marvello has a change of heart. He states that if Will isn't coming along voluntarily, that he'd only be a liability to the circus, no matter how talented he is. And so the circus leaves, leaving Smith behind as well.

Because of the temporary food shortage Smith created, he's punished by being forced to listen to the robot's atonal singing.

EPISODE THIRTY-FIVE:
"The Prisoners Of Space"
First telecast October 19, 1966
Writer: Barney Slater
Director: Nathan Juran
GUEST STARS: JUDGE IKO: Dawson Palmer

Dr. Smith is busy preparing to make wine, while Will and the robot look on, when a a cyclops creature comes into view, carrying an odd machine. It follows Will, Dr. Smith and the robot back to the Jupiter II where it leaves the machine outside the ship and then leaves.

The machine announces that it has been brought there from the Galaxy Tribunal of Justice and is putting the Robinsons on trial for a crime they allegedly committed in space. Oddly enough, Dr. Smith is not being charged with anything. A force field is placed around them to prevent the Robinsons from escaping.

That night, Dr. Smith sneaks up to the device and offers to provide any evidence the Galaxy Tribunal needs so long as they'll return Smith to Earth. Smith is turned down.

The following morning, John Robinson is summoned by the device, which transmits him to the world of the Galaxy Tribunal for a hearing. Alien beings coldly observe as John's brain is picked and a screen shows the launch of the Jupiter II as recalled by John Robinson.

After John is returned to the Jupiter II, Major West is summoned. He's given a wrench which is the same one that John lost when he was on a space walk to repair the inertial guidance system. The wrench is described as dangerous litter.

Don is returned and Will is the next summoned to testify. Will is shown that when they entered the derelict ship and awakened a bubble creature, thus causing its life-space to be shortened. Will is charged with criminal negligence for this action.

The device returns Will, stating that Dr. Smith will be summoned to testify the next morning. Smith is certain that under questioning by the alien machines that he'll incriminate himself. With the help of Will and the robot, Dr. Smith tunnels under the force field and escapes.

When Will confesses what he's done to the device, it states that helping a prisoner to escape carries a five-year sentence. The device allows Will and the robot to leave the area confined by the force field so that they can track down Smith and bring him back.

Dr. Smith is tracked to the area where he was making wine, but he refuses to come back, even though Will faces a prison sentence if he doesn't. But the robot insists that Smith return voluntarily or the robot will drag him back. Smith relents.

Smith is taken before the Galaxy Tribunal of Justice and the memory machine reveals Smith's sabotage of the Jupiter II and that Smith attacked the bubble creature. One of the judges on the tribunal, Judge Iko, is himself a bubble creature and looks down on Smith's dislike of monsters.

When the Tribunal reaches their verdict, sure enough the Robinsons are found innocent while Smith is judged to be the true felon behind all of the crimes involved. Smith is returned to the Jupiter II to await sentencing.

John Robinsons draws up a petition which they all sign, asking for clemency on Smith's behalf by reason of insanity. Dr. Smith is outraged by the suggestion, but sees no other recourse. The Tribunal takes this under consideration and agrees, releasing Smith into the custody of the robot.

As the Robinsons are surrounded by walls of shimmering plastic, look for foot prints of the crew appearing in the dirt every time one appears.

The outer space jury consists of various Irwin Allen monsters. The Judge is the alien from "The Derelict."

Black and white footage from the series pilot is viewed as evidence during the trial.

EPISODE THIRTY-SIX:
"The Android Machine"
First telecast December 26, 1966
Writer: Bob and Wanda Duncan
Director: Don Richardson, GUEST STAR: VERDA: Dee Hartford, ZUMDISH: Fritz Feld, SECURITY GUARD: Tiger Joe Marsh

When Dr. Smith comes upon an alien machine, he decides that it's some sort of artwork machine because when he pulls a lever, pictures of a beautiful woman appear. But the machine instead creates a life size beautiful silver female android. The robot explains that it's an android, but that it has something in it that does not compute.

The android announces that her name is Verda. Since Smith used the machine to apparently order her from the "Celestial Department Store," she has been delivered for Smith's personal use. She states that she will be Smith's forever, an idea he's not entirely thrilled by.

John and Major West are working out at the drill site and discover mysterious tracks. Concerned about what might be wandering around, they decide that the drill site should be declared off limits for fear of what might be lurking inside a nearby cave, although John believes whatever is in there is probably nocturnal.

At the Jupiter II, Verda the android takes over as the children's teacher, supplanting the robot, which is not happy to be replaced.

Dr. Smith is annoyed with Verda already because even though the android proclaimed herself to be Smith's property, she won't side with Smith when he's in the wrong. Since the robot also has a grudge against the android, Smith finds it easy to conspire with the robot against the silver android.

Smith plants flowers which he thinks will lead Verda to the cave which John and Don had declared off limits. But before Smith's plan can bear fruit he is attacked by the thing in the cavern, although the robot succeeds in driving it off before Smith can be harmed.

While Verda is conversing with the Robinson children, she explains that she was manufactured by UNIT 12, RDS REMOTE UNIT and doesn't possess emotion. She doesn't understand what happiness is and Will and Penny try to teach her about it.

Since the machine which brought him Verda is an interplanetary mail order catalog, Smith uses it to bring him a suit of clothes which make him look like a dashing cavalier, but he looks ridiculous and wants his old clothes back. When Will, Penny and Verda see Smith in his new wardrobe, they cannot help but laugh.

Will and Penny see the flowers Smith had planted, and they begin to follow them. They are soon attacked by the beast in the cave, but Verda distracts it until John Robinson is able to arrive at the scene and shoot the creature with his laser. John is grateful to Verda for her unselfish act, but the android doesn't understand why she was willing to endanger herself for the children.

Dr. Smith continues to fool with the machine and manages to contact the complaint department of the Celestial Department Store. A Mr. Zumdish arrives in a spacecraft which looks like an elevator. Accompanying Zumdish is a security guard who looks like an elevator operator.

Zumdish takes back the cavalier garb and then gives him a bill for Verda. Smith claims that the android is defective and refuses to pay the bill. When Zumdish inspects Verda for himself, he has to agree that she isn't functioning like a normal android and isn't responding to orders the way she normally should. Zumdish agrees to accept the return of the android, which will be scrapped.

The Robinsons like Verda and don't want her taken away. They tell Zumdish he can't take Verda until they discuss it. Zumdish is annoyed and threatens to destroy the Jupiter II in five minutes if Verda isn't returned. The Robinsons put it to a vote and Smith is the only one who votes against her. Even the robot votes in her favor. Verda cries tears of happiness, revealing that she is more than just a machine. They try to negotiate a trade with Zumdish of some of their fuel in exchange for the android. But Penny fears the worst and she runs off with Verda to find a place of refuge.

The security guard tracks Verda for Zumdish, and when he threatens Penny, Verda moves to attack the guard. Zumdish is impressed by this as the android has exceeded her programming and displayed free will and other human characteristics, which actually make her more valuable than a normal android. Thus Zumdish recants his order to have Verda scrapped, and she agrees to return with him to the Celestial Department Store.

Dr. Smith has the robot drag the mail order machine off as he plans to order more androids and retrain them to sell at a profit.

Zumdish wants his machine back and with a snap of his fingers it appears, with Smith programmed inside it. He leaves and Smith is summoned from the machine. Smith claims he just dreamed he was merchandise in a galactic department store. "Yeah," says Major West, "in the bargain basement."

The first guest-star role for Dee Hartford and Fritz Feld. Both will return in later episodes.

EPISODE THIRTY SEVEN:
"The Deadly Games Of Gamma 6"
First telecast November 2, 1966
Writer: Barney Slater
Director: Nathan Juran
GUEST STARS: MYKO: Mike Kellin, ALIEN LEADER: Peter Brocco, GEOO: Harry Monty, GROMACK: Ronald Weber, ALIEN GIANT: Chuck Robertson

Will, Smith and the robot are setting up a weather relay station to connect with the Jupiter II. Smith refuses to listen to the robot's claim that he forgot to attach two wires, so when Smith starts up the machine it shorts out.

Just then a tall man approaches and stands unspeaking nearby. John Robinson can't get it to speak and when he goes up to it and offers his hand in friendship, it attacks him. John is thrown around but then manages to defeat the man. But no sooner does he accomplish this than another large man steps out from behind the rocks and grabs John, lifting him over his head.

The man holding John is named Gromack and he's called off by Myko, a bearded man who explains that he arranges fights. He's impressed by John's expertise and invites him to participate in the Gamma Games, which are help on this planet once a year. John isn't interested, even though he would be paid for his efforts.

After John leaves, Smith tells Myko perhaps they can come to some arrangement for payment to him if Smith could induce John Robinson to participate in the Gamma Games.

After the others return to the Jupiter II, Myko finds that the fighter John defeated has a broken arm from the conflict, so Myko destroys him. Myko contacts his superiors and explains that humans are on that world now. The aliens have always wanted to have Earthmen participate in their contest. The aliens decide that they'll stage a bout with humans, and the outcome will decide whether or not the aliens will invade Earth.

Smith is not successful at talking John into fighting in the Gamma Games. Will is also disappointed because he thinks that his father would win, but John explains to Will that he never fights for fun, only when he has no other choice.

Will and Dr. Smith visit Myko's training camp and observe his fighters at work. Gromack, the one who had been grappling with John earlier when Myko arrived on the scene, demonstrates his training by crushing stones and lifting forty times his own weight.

Myko shows off something called The Wheel of Life. It contains six identical lasers, but all are duds except for one. Two contestants pick up lasers and fire at each other until one of them is killed. Myko states that he needs a human fighter and decides that Smith is his only remaining option.

Smith agrees, so long as he can choose his own opponent from those assembled. When he sees a dwarf nearby being thrown around, Smith chooses him. But he doesn't realize that this was all staged as the dwarf's name is Geoo, and he's capable of turning invisible.

Back at the Jupiter II, Smith embarks on a campaign of personal training, which everyone else regards as harmless amusement. When Myko stops by, they question him about the Gamma Games but he deliberately avoids answering certain questions, which arouses the suspicions of John and Major West.

John and Don follow Myko back to his training camp and overhear him communicating with the alien leader, and learn that Earth will be invaded if Smith loses his contest.

They decide not to let Smith fight and they lock him up. But Smith tricks the robot and escapes. Smith arrives just in time to discover that he's on first, and the robot and Will show up to act as Smith's seconds.

When the bout begins, in an Earth-style boxing ring, Geoo turns invisible and quickly knocks Smith down. Geoo is declared the winner and Myko announces that Earth is the loser.

John Robinson discovers that Smith has escaped and arrives just as Myko is making his announcement. John demands a rematch and Myko agrees. John enters the ring with Geoo, but when the dwarf turns invisible, John uses his belt to swing around and discover just where Geoo is. Because of this, he's able to defeat Geoo.

Myko states that the invasion of Earth will proceed as planned, so John challenges Myko to play him on The Wheel of Life. They pick up lasers and point them at each other, but Myko finally loses his nerve and quits, declaring John the winner. Upon checking, they discover that had Myko not chickened out, he would have won.

The aliens call off the invasion of Earth, deciding that Earthmen are too brave to challenge in combat. Although Dr. Smith lost he does have one prize from his combat—a black eye! John is amused and says that maybe Maureen can find him a beefsteak for his eye while Smith blames the robot for all his problems.

Story influence:"The Challenge."

EPISODE THIRTY-EIGHT:
"The Thief From Outer Space"
First telecast November 9, 1966
Writer: Jackson Gillis
Director: Sobey Martin
Incidental Music: Robert Drasnin
GUEST STARS: ALI BEN BAD: Malachi Throne, PRINCESS: Maxine Gates, SLAVE: Ted Cassidy

Following a ravaging meteor shower, Penny finds a strange alien bottle on the ground.

The next day, Will and Dr. Smith are checking the deutronium drill sites, or actually Will does while Smith lies down to take a nap. They see a thief stealing some of their equipment, and the thief is outfitted like something out of the Arabian Nights. At first the thief pulls out a huge sword and attacks them. Smith defends himself with a shovel until Will pulls out a laser and orders the thief to halt.

But when they're able to calm him down and talk to the thief, he explains that he's Ali Ben Bad, the thief from outer space. Seeing potential here, Ali summons up a slave who grabs Will and Smith so that Ali can interrogate them. Ali wants to know where the rich people are with their treasure. When Will explains that they're poor and stranded on the planet, and since he doesn't want Ali to find out about the Jupiter II he claims that they're alone on the planet. Ali is both disappointed and annoyed, and disappears with his slave. Even though Will and Dr. Smith both tell the Robinsons what they saw, there's no evidence and so John believes they imagined it all. Even the stolen tools are all lying back at the site of the mineral drill.

Will later comes across what looks like an abandoned sedan chair such as sheiks on Earth used to be carried around in. It's resting on a platform which pulses and glows, and which has a pulsating mushroom shaped light on the top. When Will steps inside, the door swings shut and the "sedan chair" takes off and transports Will to an asteroid which is in orbit around the planet. Will gets out and the device takes off without him.

Exploring the caves on the asteroid, Will discovers that this is where Ali Ben Bad lives, and as if to confirm it he's soon captured by the thief's slave. The slave is there to keep the furnace working, which sustains the life support systems on the asteroid. The slave takes advantage of Will's opportune arrival and has the boy do his work for him while the slave takes a nap.

When the thief returns, he finds Will asleep in his vast treasure room. Even though the thief has vast amounts of treasure, he considers it all worthless. He explains that two hundred years before, the beautiful princess of his caliph was kidnapped by the evil Vizier. The thief has been trying to track the Vizier down ever since in order to secure the safe return of the princess. Ali has a golden arrow with him which helps him find clues to where the princess is. Since the golden arrow device indicates that there are clues to the whereabouts of the princess on this world, he asks Will to help him locate those clues.

Penny and Dr. Smith soon turn up on the asteroid in the sedan chair and they, too, are captured by the thief's slave. Penny is put to work in the furnace room where Will had been, but Dr. Smith is tied up beneath a huge, swinging pendulum blade because the thief doesn't like him.

When Will and Penny make up a story about a map they'd found, the thief believes them. The thief returns to the planet with Will and Penny, but Smith is left behind. The thief is getting weary of his quest, though, and says that Smith isn't really in danger as the blade isn't really very sharp.

The reason the thief dislikes Smith so much is because of his resemblance to the evil Vizier. But the Vizier was the slave's former master and because Smith's resemblance, the slave frees him.

When Will, Penny and the thief arrive at the Jupiter II, John Robinson engages the thief in a sword fight and Don then jumps out and captures Ali.

Just then Smith appears with the slave, only Smith is now decked out like the evil Grand Vizier, and he proceeds to order the slave to kill Ali. The slave prepares to do so, but Will throws a vanishing ring at the slave, thus saving the thief.

The golden arrow device the thief uses to find clues now points to the bottle which Penny found after the meteor shower. Upon examination they find that the Princess had been reduced in size and placed inside the bottle.

She's freed by the thief, but after two hundred years of doing nothing but eating marzipan, she's grown fat, bored and is a ceaseless talker. The thief reduces the Princess back into the bottle and leaves her behind, where the robot agrees to talk to her to keep her company.

EPISODE THIRTY-NINE:
"Curse Of Cousin Smith"
First telecast November 16, 1966
Writer: Barney Slater
Director: Justus Addiss
Incidental Music: Robert Drasnin
GUEST STAR: JEREMIAH SMITH: Henry Jones

Will, Penny and the robot are bird-watching. They get into an argument over who should use the binoculars. They see a bird but it has already been catalogued and has Dr. Smith's name in it as Smith names all birds he discovers on that world after himself. When a strange spacecraft flies over and proceeds to disgorge pieces of luggage, one of which appears headed directly for Will until the robot pushes the boy to safety. Upon opening the trunk, they find that it's filled with games and devices used for gambling. Nearby a man lies, dazed, and Will runs to get the others.

The man introduces himself as Colonel Jeremiah Smith, a traveller. But Dr. Smith doesn't like him and stays in his quarters with a gun kept within reach. When there's a fire in Smith's cabin that night he's sure that someone is trying to kill him and he flees the Jupiter II.

Jeremiah explains that he's Dr. Smith's cousin, and that they had a falling out years before. But although likeable, at least at first, Jeremiah demonstrates that he just as lazy as his cousin.

Dr. Smith is afraid of his cousin and has gone into hiding, and only the robot knows where. While the robot is packing supplies for Dr. Smith, Jeremiah slips a cream pie into the in with the clothes and food—a pie with a time bomb inside.

Jeremiah amuses the Robinsons with card tricks while waiting for the explosion, but then he turns around and finds that the robot has brought back the pie, which explodes in Jeremiah's face. Jeremiah claims that Smith put the bomb in the pie, but for some reason the Robinsons find this difficult to believe. Violence? Dr. Smith?

The robot explains that the two cousins are the last surviving relatives of Maude Smith, their great aunt. Her will left her million dollar estate to her last living relative, which explains why the two cousins would want to do each other harm.

Jeremiah tracks Will and the robot to lead him to Dr. Smith so that he can shoot him, but Smith has dug a pit which Jeremiah falls into.

Since Jeremiah isn't hurt by the fall, John Robinson tries to settle the feud and have the two cousins bury the hatchet, but he has no luck.

Jeremiah is determined to eliminate Dr. Smith and contacts Little Joe, a gambling boss, and makes a deal to have Little Joe eliminate Dr. Smith for non-payment of gambling debts, whereupon Jeremiah will then pay Little Joe.

Little Joe sends a gambling machine down to the planet to set up Smith, who won't be able to resist it. Smith finds the machine and the first time he plays it he wins. But eventually Smith loses big and the machine is prepared to rub him out.

For some reason John Robinson offers to wager the Jupiter II against Smith's outstanding debts. But he won't play the machine's game, suggesting a different game—the shell game of three cups and one ball. The machine loses and promptly disappears. When Jeremiah tries to guess which cup the orange ball is under, he's wrong. But before Dr. Smith can pick up the third cup, John clears the table, leading Smith to believe that John didn't put the ball under any of the cups. He acts offended at the thought that he might have cheated, but he won't even tell Maureen for certain if he did. "There are some things men have to keep to themselves, and this is one of them," he states.

Defeated, Jeremiah Smith leaves the planet.

EPISODE FORTY:
"West Of Mars"
First telecast November 30, 1966
Writer: Michael Fessier
Director: Nathan Juran
Incidental Music: Robert Drasnin
GUEST STARS: ENFORCER CLAUDIUS: Allan Melvin, DEE: Mickey Manners, PLEIADES PETE: Ken Mayer, BARTENDER: Eddie Quillan, SMITH'S DOUBLE: Charles Arthur

The lonely planet, which seems to be in the middle of some sort of interplanetary traffic lanes due to all the visitors it attracts, is due for visitors once again. Space Enforcer Claudius is journeying to the planet on the trail of a notorious gunfighter named Zeno. A probe from Claudius appears on the planet and announces his coming and demands that the "superswift" Zeno prepare to surrender.

Meanwhile, Will and Dr. Smith are working in the mine and are being secretly observed by a mysterious figure garbed in black. Smith is afraid that Zeno will kill them all before the Enforcer can arrive and explains that a "superswift" is a gunfighter who kills for the thrill of it and for no other reason. But when the ship of the Enforcer begins landing, Smith feels that not only are they saved, but that they should try to get some of the reward for Zeno's capture. As Will and Smith are going to greet the Enforcer, Zeno grabs Smith as the Enforcer's rocket is landing on the planet. The reason he grabs Smith is because he looks enough like Smith to be his twin. Under threats, Zeno forces Smith to change clothes with him. Zeno is under a death sentence and is a desperate man. At gunpoint, Zeno forces Smith to masquerade as him and surrender to the Enforcer. Smith does an excellent job, even to confessing to twenty-six murders. The Enforcer takes the false Zeno prisoner and makes Will accompany him as the witness to his prisoner's confession.

Meanwhile, Zeno is now masquerading as Smith and when the robot encounters him he claims to have been attacked by Zeno, which resulted in a concussion. Thus

bizarre behavior could be rationalized. But as pat as the explanation is, it still arouses some suspicion among the Robinsons.

Aboard the Enforcer's spaceship, which is taking the prisoner to his execution, Smith attempts to convince the Enforcer that he's not really Zeno, but Claudius won't believe anything Smith says. Even Will is confused and uncertain by the turn of events.

When Smith says that he can prove it at the trial, Claudius reveals that there won't be any trial, just the hanging, since "Zeno" has already confessed.

At this revelation, Smith panics and hurls himself at the controls, causing the spaceship to crash-land. The Enforcer is knocked out and Smith takes Will and they head for the nearest settlement. On the way there they encounter Dee, an old associate of Zeno's, who becomes frightened upon seeing him. Smith likes the feeling of power he gets from this and decides to continue the masquerade and have a good time.

Nearby, another super-gunfighter, Pleiades Pete, arrives, looking for trouble. Seeing "Zeno," he decides to add to his reputation and takes him on. Through dumb luck, Smith knocks Pete out but now everyone else is after him, including Claudius who has recovered and has been searching for his prisoner.

Smith and Will escape on robot horses and find their way back to the Enforcer's ship. They take off in it and Will is able to operate the controls and guide the ship back to the world where the Jupiter II is.

The Enforcer pursues them in Pete's spaceship. When the Enforcer arrives, he's confronted by Zeno and Smith, who both claim to be Smith. There's no way to tell them apart until the real Zeno gets tired of all this and escapes, but with Claudius in pursuit once again.

Another Smith look-alike episode.

EPISODE FORTY-ONE:
"A Visit To Hades"
First telecast December 7, 1966
Writer: Carey Wilber
Director: Don Richardson
GUEST STAR: MORBIUS: Gerald Mohr

Dr. Smith, Will and the robot are out bird-watching when Smith comes upon a gateway shaped like a keyhole. In it is a golden lyre, and since it looks like it might be valuable, he immediately picks it up. The robot tells Smith that it is a piece of alien technology and could be dangerous, but as usual, Smith doesn't pay any attention to what thew robot tells him.

Smith tries to play the lyre, and upon plucking three chords, Smith vanishes and reappears in a cave where fires burn all around him. A being known as Morbius, realizes that Smith thinks he's in Hell, and so he laughs and tells Smith that he's long been looking forward to having him there. Dr. Smith is terrified and insists that this is all some book-keeper's mistake, but Morbius just laughs.

Morbius shows images of Smith's past misdeeds on a screen, which show Smith as a child snitching on a classmate and stealing the answers to a test. Morbius then shows Smith his future, which consists of nothing but flames, and tells him that he'll be his guest in the fires of Hades for a long time to come. A hell of a long time, you might say.

Dr. Smith pleads with Morbius, offering to do anything. Morbius suggests that if Smith would destroy the golden harp, then he'd relent and let Smith go free. Smith returns to the surface of the planet.

The robot tries to explain that Smith was in an alien dimension, but Dr. Smith won't listen to any of it as he's certain he has just glimpsed the gates of hell. They return to the Jupiter II, but that night Smith sneaks out of the ship and returns to the alien gateway. Smith tries to destroy the harp, but without success. All his efforts accomplish is to create a lot of weird sounds from trying to destroy the harp, and these noises seem to torture Morbius.

The next day, Morbius observes Judy wandering around in a fine snit. He appears to her and charms the young woman. Judy decides to take Morbius back to the Jupiter II with her to introduce him to everyone else. But as soon as Dr. Smith sees the man, he panics. Smith is certain that Morbius is spying on Smith and the doctor proceeds to go off in search of good deeds to do.

When the robot attempts to warn the Robinsons that Morbius is an alien, the robot's power pack mysteriously malfunctions.

Judy goes off for a walk with Morbius, who explains that he's from a world called Lyre (liar?) and was exiled for being rebellious.

When Smith accidentally discovers that the lyre can be used to inflict pain on Morbius, the doctor thinks he has a way to control the Devil. But Morbius manages to trick Smith into playing the chords on the lyre which return him to the dimension he was in, but because Judy was standing close by, she vanishes with Morbius as well.

Will manages to repair the robot's power pack and it completes the warning it had started to give about Morbius. When they discover that Smith knows what's really going on, they confront him and force the doctor to play the notes on the lyre which transported Morbius. Smith vanishes with the lyre. The robot reconstructs the sounds so that John and Major West can follow in pursuit to that fiery dimension.

In the other dimension, Morbius admits that he's a prisoner who can only be freed if the lyre is destroyed. Morbius had been banished to that place for leading a failed revolution.

Judy is angry and wants to return home. Smith is confronted by a monster which turns out to be harmless to humanoids as it's just there for pest control.

When Major West encounters Morbius, they get into an argument when the alien states that they're all trapped there just as surely as he is. When Major West and Morbius get into a fight, Judy tries to help Don and uses the lyre as a club, but she accidentally hits Don with it, causing the lyre to break. Since the lyre could only be destroyed by someone pure of heart (ergo, Smith's failures in trying to destroy it), the prison disappears. Morbius plans to return to his planet to start another revolution while the others return to the surface of the planet they'd been on before as the former prison of Morbius starts breaking up.

Back on the planet, they all reappear but Dr. Smith is stuck in a tree and it takes the rest of them to try to figure out how to pull him down.

EPISODE FORTY-TWO:
"Wreck Of The Robot"

First telecast December 14, 1966
Writer: Barney Slater
Director: Nathan Juran
Incidental Music: Bernard Hermann (DAY THE EARTH STOOD STILL music)

GUEST STAR: ALIEN LEADER: Jim Mills

When Will and Dr. Smith are playing ten-pins with the robot. Dr. Smith has lost five games in a row and so he switches bowling balls with Will. But when Smith goes to roll the ball, his finger gets stuck in it and he falls flat on his face. They struggle to free Smith and then the ball falls off and rolls down the "alley" and knocks some pins over. But then the ball starts rolling back by itself, only instead of a pink bowling ball, it's a black one with a fuse which explodes!

When the smoke clears and the dust settles, a golden ball is in sight, which rolls off and leads them to a cavern. The cave is filled with alien machinery guarded by three beings garbed in black bowler hats and long black cloaks. The aliens express interest in their robot, but Will says they don't want to part with it, even though the aliens offer to trade gold, which Dr. Smith wants to go for. But Will refuses and the aliens become threatening. They leave the cave and return to the Jupiter II, much to Dr. Smith's relief.

Will tells his parents what happened, and John says they should just take more precautions since the aliens probably won't attack during the day. Dr. Smith is terrified and the robot indicates the aliens are dangerous. The robot offers to go to the cave by himself, but Maureen says that the robot is a part of the family and will stay with them. Later, when John is playing chess, the aliens use a chess piece to communicate with John their interest in meeting with him.

John and Major West go to the cave which Will had described and there the three aliens indicate their wish to purchase the robot from the Robinsons. When John turns down their offer, the aliens become angry and threatening.

The robot is upset over what is happening and goes off to be alone. That night the aliens enter the Jupiter II and confront the robot. They threaten to harm the Robinsons, who are all sleeping, if the robot won't come with them quietly. Not wanting to see the Robinsons harmed, the robot agrees to leave with the aliens.

The next morning the Robinsons realize that the robot is gone and decide that the logical place to search would be the aliens' cave. Upon arriving at the cave they find that the aliens do indeed have the robot, and that they've taken it apart. The aliens promise to return the robot when they're finished with it. The three aliens keep their promise, only they don't bother to reassemble the robot before they give it back.

John and Major West work on putting the robot back together, and with Will's help they seem to get it working normally again. But now the other machinery in the Jupiter II is acting abnormally. When Judy is attacked by a compressor hose, the robot reveals that the aliens disassembled it to learn about Earth machinery and how to control it so that they can invade Earth.

The Jupiter II has lost power so John and Major West decide to attack the aliens in a frontal assault on their cave. But upon reaching the cave they discover that their lasers won't function.

The Alien Leader is cocky and arrogant, stating that his machine cannot be destroyed by either men or machines. But since the robot is not a man and is more than just a machine, it is able to destroy the alien device. The three aliens vanish, leaving just their hats and cloaks behind.

The series' cheapest aliens appear. They are actors covered in black velvet wearing bowler hats.

There's a good comic scene when Major West tortures Smith by using the robot's disassembled bubble, and claiming to be his ghost.

EPISODE FORTY-THREE:
"The Dream Monster"
First telecast February 21, 1966
Writer: Peter Packer
Director: Don Richardson
GUEST STARS: SESMAR: John Abbott, RADION: Dawson Palmer, First Dwarf: Harry Monty, Second Dwarf: Frank Delfino

Dr. Smith is having the robot fan him in his quarters during a heatwave. The air conditioning unit isn't working because someone overloaded it. While John and Major West are working on the unit, they almost get in a fight because of the stress caused by the heat.

Penny and Debbie the Bloop are watering some flowers to try to keep them alive during the heatwave. Suddenly a tall, gold clad android appears and acts in a threatening manner, lurching towards Penny without speaking.

But the appearance of an alien scientist, Sesmar, halts it. Sesmar is the creator of the android. The android's name is Radion and Sesmar is still working to perfect it. When Penny mentions the emotions she feels when looking at the flower she was watering, Sesmar says that he's interested in getting some of those for Radion. Penny decides this conversation is getting too weird and she takes Debbie and returns to the Jupiter II.

Sesmar has two small assistants, golden dwarfs, who babble incoherently. Radion also wears an orange box on its chest which contains an old style reel-to-reel tape recorder. Sesmar plucks the flower and hands it to Radion to see the effect, but the android just tears the flower apart.

Meanwhile, Dr. Smith gets in trouble again and gets kicked out of the ship for overloading the air-conditioning system. But Smith doesn't have long to wait to find out where to go because the two golden dwarfs immediately kidnap Smith and take him to their master, Sesmar.

Sesmar considers using Smith's emotions in Radion, but he considers Smith's emotions to be useless for his purpose. When Sesmar decides to just break Dr. Smith down into his component molecules and restructure him, Smith panics and desperately offers to get Sesmar the emotions he needs from the others. Sesmar accepts Smith's offer and gives him a portable transporator to record the appropriate emotions to bring back to him.

Smith returns to the Jupiter II and records the positive emotions generated by the Robinsons. He returns successfully to Sesmar, but the scientist discovers that the plates produced by the transporator are not perfect enough to transfer the emotions to his android. To complete the emotion transfer, Radion must come into physical contact with the Robinsons.

Sesmar decides to send Radion to visit the Robinsons in person. Radion makes a good impression by repairing the broken air-conditioning which Smith had overloaded. Radion helps out in other ways, but Major West remains suspicious of the android's real intentions as he's sure there must be an ulterior motive for it being so helpful.

When Radion invites the Robinsons to the laboratory, they agree to the visit. Upon arriving, Radion shakes hands with them all, excluding Major West, and thereby completes the successful transfer of their positive human emotions. But soon after, Don discovers the Robinsons sitting around, seemingly listless and completely lacking in will power.

Even though Radion has absorbed the human qualities of the Robinsons, Sesmar doesn't feel that his android is complete as it still may be unable to cope with liars and reprobates like Dr. Smith. To complete this, Sesmar has his golden dwarfs kidnap Major West and takes a transporator picture of Don's emotions, and Dr. Smith's, to give Radion a more aggressive side to his personality, as well as deviousness.

But this final transfer is unsuccessful because the transporator only works on people when they are unaware of what is being done to them. Don and Smith escape by tricking Radion into releasing them and in the conflict the android short-circuits and begins to wreck the laboratory.

Radion pursues Don and Smith back to the Jupiter II where a battle results. The android is resistant to laser fire but when it tries to force the robot to become its servant, the robot is able to blow the androids circuits by hitting it with an electric arc. Don then rips out and destroys the transporator plates, thus restoring the human emotions to the Robinsons.

When Sesmar arrives on the scene he sees that his android is destroyed, his whole life's work shorted out. He admits his mistake in stealing the emotions, and by trying to make Radion all powerful he corrupted him and himself. He recovers his android and decides to start over with it again.

When Smith says he's decided to stay with the Robinsons because of the sadness he'd cause by leaving, the robot laughs.

Guest star John Abbott appeared in several other Irwin Allen shows.

EPISODE FORTY-FOUR:
"The Golden Man"
First telecast December 28, 1966
Writer: Barney Slater
Director: Don Richardson
GUEST STARS: KEEMA: Dennis Patrick, FROG ALIEN: Ronald Gans,
HANDSOME ALIEN: Bill Troy

Dr. Smith and Penny are out collecting wild flowers when they encounter an alien craft. It's a globular shaped craft but the creature in it cannot be clearly seen in the dome of the craft and demands to be left alone, pointing a laser cannon at Smith and Penny to emphasize its point. It fires a warning shot and insists that they leave it alone. When Penny protests, it orders them to leave the area and then fires another warning shot.

Back at camp, Dr. Smith urges Maureen and Judy to set up the perimeter defenses, particularly since Will, John and Major West have gone off on a survey expedition.

Another alien craft arrives and when Dr. Smith sees it landing he goes into another panic. But the following morning a gift box turns up at the Jupiter II filled with special items like caviar, perfume and even a ham. Then Keema, a golden man, arrives in a puff of smoke, offering his friendship to the Robinsons. Keema states that he's the enemy of the other alien that arrived first, but that both are envoys from their respective planets. The two envoys will engage in battle and the winner will resolve the dispute between their worlds. The other being, a frog-alien, represents the Zedams, whom Keema claims has made unreasonable demands on his world.

For some reason Penny is suspicious of the handsome gold man bearing gifts, while Maureen states that she'd rather reserve judgment until she hears what the alien has to say for itself.

Penny visits the first spaceship which landed, which bears the representative of the Zedam, and explains what Keema related to them. When Penny asks to see what this other alien looks like, he reveals himself to be a giant frog, which is certainly not as pleasing to the eye as the soft spoken golden man.

The frog alien claims that Keema is a deceiver and uses his appearance to trick people.

Meanwhile, Keema is starting to reveal his true side when he meets clandestinely with Dr. Smith and explains that he needs weapons to fight his battle with the other alien. Keema states that if Smith steals some weapons for him from the Jupiter II, that Keema will see to it that they all return to Earth.

Smith takes this offer to Maureen, who turns it down, stating that she still doesn't know enough about the golden man, the other alien or the actual reasons behind the conflict.

The robot offers to check out the encampment of the golden man to secure additional information. When the robot rolls up to the scene, he overhears Keema reporting to his superiors. Keema states that he expects to secure weapons from the humans, and that after he's destroyed the Zedam that he'll destroy the humans as well. Just then Keema realizes that the robot has overheard him and he knocks the robot out of commission so that it cannot report what it heard to the Robinsons.

The next day, Judy Robinson stumbles into a mine field whose explosives are detonated by sound waves. Keema rescues her and claims that the Zedam planted the mine field there heedless of whether any innocent people would walk into it.

This pretty much convinces Maureen, but Penny is still suspicious of appearances. Penny visits the Zedam, who insists that he planted no mines anywhere. But the Zedam realizes that because he looks so repulsive by human standards, that he'll be disbelieved. Penny convinces the Zedam to meet with her mother. Maureen is meeting with the Zedam when the golden man shows up, and Maureen is barely able to prevent a battle right then and there.

When Smith delivers the weapons to Keema, the golden man explains that since both sides were evenly matched to start with, the contest was to be one of skill. But not that Keema has the lasers, it puts him at a distinct advantage. Keema alters his appearance to reveal that he's actually a hideous alien and Dr. Smith realizes that he's been duped by the evil creature.

Dr. Smith runs screaming back to the Jupiter II, admitting what he's done. Penny forces Smith to go with her to warn the Zedam, but Keema attacks the frog alien before they can get there.

Penny and Dr. Smith and pinned down near the Zedam ship where the frog alien lies injured. Keema comes with a grenade to finish the job, but Penny grabs it off the ground and throws it to Dr. Smith, who shrieks and tosses it back to Keema, where it explodes, destroying him.

The frog alien is thus triumphant, and before leaving it alters its form to that of a handsome human man before leaving, so that Penny will remember him fondly instead of as that ugly little alien. But Penny says that she'd like him no matter how he looked.

When John, Will and Major West return in the chariot, Maureen and Judy.

According to director Don Richardson, Allen turned thumbs down on spending $10,000 for an alien ship. The craft that appears in this episode is actually a large, plastic champagne glass used in a 50's Marilyn Monroe feature. Richardson turned it upside down and had the art department dress it with a frame.

EPISODE FORTY-FIVE:
"The Girl From The Green Dimension"

First telecast January 4, 1967
Writer: Peter Packer
Director: Nathan Juran
Incidental Music: Alexander Courage
GUEST STARS: ATHENA (LORELEI): Vitina Marcus, URSO: Harry Ray-bould

Will and the robot are using the electronic telescope to study the Omega Nebula. But Dr. Smith wants to get back to camp because he feels a chill coming on. The robot warns that a high velocity solar gale is sweeping in, and keeps shouting, "Danger! Danger!" The telescope acts as a focal point for the gale, drawing energy into it and exploding. This results in the telescope being charged with positron particles.

When Will looks into the telescope he sees the green girl that they once encountered in space. When Dr. Smith sees who it is he becomes frightened. The robot indicates that the green girl can also see Smith. Smith wants to go back to camp, stating that just thinking of the green girl is a menace. Using the telescope as a transitional device, the lorelei is able to pass from the green dimension to the planet. Upon seeing her, Smith is terrified and runs shrieking back to the Jupiter II.

Smith is afraid of her because of the way she bewitched him before. But soon he comes around when he finds that she can communicate with him in English and is able to use the positron charged telescope to peer into the future. Dr. Smith quickly sees the advantages of this.

Smith is out at the telescope, trying to find some useful future event when a green man appears. He's big and strong and very angry. Athena, the green girl, is able to get the green man settled down. She explains to Smith that this is Urso, an old lover. Because Athena wants Smith now, Urso is angry and jealous.

Athena wants some deutronium and so Smith steals some for her from the Jupiter II because he wants to be able to see into the future with the green girl's help.

Urso is still around and when he sees Will with Smith, Urso changes Will into a green boy as a joke. Will tries scrubbing the green but it won't come off his skin. When Smith asks Athena for her help, she explains that since Urso made Will green, only Urso can undo it.

Athena says that if she fights Urso for her that he'll change Will back. Smith wants no part of a fight, but John Robinson insists that Smith go through with it in order to help Will.

The fight between Smith and Urso mostly consists of Urso chasing Smith. When Urso makes Smith look into the telescope, Smith thinks he sees his own immediate future—a funeral in which the Robinsons are all present, but not Smith.

Dr. Smith is carving his tombstone when the robot convinces him to go out with glory. Will goes to Athena and tries to explain to her that Dr. Smith isn't brave but is really just a scaredy cat.

Dr. Smith and Urso choose weapons, stand back to back and start pacing, but Smith panics, drops his gun and flees. Smith comes upon the Robinsons burying a piece of radioactive equipment in what looked to Smith like a funeral when he viewed the scene through the telescope.

Smith is relieved, but still begs Urso not to kill him. Smith keeps running with Urso in pursuit. Urso catches up with Smith, who goes down on his knees begging for his life. Athena is disappointed by the pathetic sight of Smith pleading with Urso and decides that Smith isn't worth having. She takes Urso back and the green man undoes his spell which turned Will green. Ursa and Athena return to the green dimension and the telescope returns to normal.

Vitina Marcus returns as the Green Girl.

EPISODE FORTY-SIX:
"The Questing Beast"
First telecast January 11, 1967
Writer: Carey Wilbur
Director: Don Richardson
Incidental Music: Cyril Mockridge
GUEST STARS: SIR SAGRAMONTE: Hans Conried, THE QUESTING BEAST: Jeff County, GUNDEMAR'S VOICE: Sue England

The atomic regulator threatens to overload, but the robot manages to bring it under control. Smith sits idly by while all this is going on, unconcerned whether the robot will be destroyed in the process.

The robot is attacked by a knight, who is on foot, when it is checking the atomic regulator. But the knight isn't very powerful and his attack is rather inept, mostly just making a nuisance of himself by driving his lance into the ground until the robot yields just to end the nonsense.

The knight, Sir Sagramonte, then summons his basset hound, Bayer (a dog which wears square eyeglasses). The knight explains that he's on the trail of Gundemar, the Questing Beast. The knight wants someone he can ransom and so takes Dr. Smith and Will as hostage, since the robot (which the knight thinks is another knight) states that it cannot pay ransom for itself. Sir Sagramonte forces Smith to be a vassal and work for him while Will is made to act as the knight's squire.

Maureen is concerned about Will being gone at knight, but John reassures her that he's all right with Smith and the robot to protect him.

Following the Questing Beast is the knight's reason to be, although he admits to Will that he's been following it for forty years and hasn't even caught a glimpse of it yet. Sir Sagramonte teleports from world to world in pursuit of the beast, although he really doesn't understand how he does it.

Smith flees his forced servitude at the first opportunity but is pursued by the fire-breathing Gundemar, a creatures which is something like a dragon. The knight goes off in pursuit of Gundemar.

The robot returns to the Jupiter II and reveals what has happened to Will and Dr. Smith, so John and Major West set out in search of them.

Penny encounters Bayer, the eye-glass wearing basset hound and follows it, only to run into Gundemar. Gundemar is a lady creature and explains to Penny what is happening and how Sir Sagramonte is pursuing her on a quest to slay the dragon-like beast. Penny feels sorry for Gundemar and agrees to help her hide from the knight.

Will catches up with Sir Sagramonte, who starts telling Will about things which the boy clearly knows are exaggerations. Will realizes that the knight is not all that he had led him to believe and the boy becomes very disenchanted about knighthood and chivalry, deciding that it is not all that the knight claimed it to be.

When Will returns to the Jupiter II, he overhears Dr. Smith exaggerating about what happened to him even more that Sir Sagramonte was. Embittered, Will goes off by himself to think things over.

Meanwhile, Penny has found a cave which Gundemar can use for a place of refuge from the knight.

Will has come to believe that anything an adult says is a lie, and when Dr. Smith tries to talk to him the boy says that he's finally outgrowing his childhood.

Smith realizes that this is partially his fault and he actually feels guilty about it. Going to Sir Sagramonte, Smith explains what Will is going through and the knight feels ashamed at what he's caused. Sir Sagramonte explains that on his world, Antare, things have become so complex and complicated that people elect to return to a simpler time, in this case the time of knighthood and the days of chivalry.

Dr. Smith suggests a way that he might inspire the boy again and reveals that he's discovered the hiding place of the Questing Beast. At dawn of the following day, Sagramonte will fight the beast and Smith will make sure that the boy is there to see the great contest.

Smith returns to the Jupiter II and reveals what is going to happen. At first Will doesn't believe him, but Smith convinces Will that he's seen the beast and begs Will to believe him now as Smith regrets all of the other lies he's told in the past.

Penny overhears and runs to warn her friend that the knight is coming for her. Gundemar appreciates Penny's warning, but she's grown weary of the long chase and has decided to put on a good show but to ultimately allow the knight to slay her. Penny won't hear of it and tries to talk Gundemar out of this course of action.

The next morning the contest takes place just as Smith promised Will that it would. Will is very excited by this duel, but also concerned that the knight will really be hurt. Finally Penny stops the fight, refusing to let the knight finish Gundemar off. And as soon as Sir Sagramonte hears the Questing Beast speak and hears that it is female, he cannot bring himself to finish the duel. Penny suggests that each of the antagonists return to their own planets.

Gundemar reveals that she was the one who had been teleporting the knight hither and yon around the galaxy in order to keep him interested by the thrill of the chase, and Sir Sagramonte admits that they've been the greatest years of his life. Will offers to stay with the knight, but he's depressed, stating that the quest is ended.

Gundemar deliberately gets the knight worked up and angry and the quest begins all over again as Gundemar and the knight vanish in a burst of energy on their continuing chase across the galaxy.

MAKE ROOM FOR DADDY's Hans Conried guest stars as the alien knight. Sue England ("Ghost Planet") voice-overs the poor quality dragon lady.

EPISODE FORTY-SEVEN:
"The Toymaker"

First telecast January 25, 1967
Writer: Bob and Wanda Duncan
Director: Robert Douglas
GUEST STARS: MR. O.M. : Walter Burke, ZUMDISH: Fritz Feld, WOOD
SOLDIER: Larry Dean, SECURITY GUARD: Tiger Joe Marsh, MONSTER:
Dawson Palmer

Dr. Smith is preparing a flower arrangement for Penny's birthday when Will
and Smith come upon the old inter-galactic mail order machine which caused so
much trouble earlier when Smith accidentally ordered Verda the android from it.
Smith talks Will into fussing with it and there is an explosion. But when the smoke
clears, they're unhurt so Smith decides to give it another try. This time there's no
explosion but Dr. Smith vanishes and is entered into the catalogue of merchandise
available from the machine. Will sees a picture of Smith on the screen now instead
of the toys which had appeared on the order screen before.

Will runs back to the Jupiter II looking for John and Don, but they've gone to
search for a fissure. Will explains what's happened to Dr. Smith. Maureen agrees
to look for John.

Elsewhere, John and Major West are examining an open crack in the rocks
which needs to be sealed. They fear that the fissure could deepen and cause serious
planet quakes. They are unaware, though, that the crack was caused by using the
inter-galactic mail order machine.

Will returns to the machine and tries to get Dr. Smith's picture on the machine.
When Will tries to operate the machine to retrieve Dr. Smith from it, the boy is
also absorbed into it. After taking Will, the machine explodes, causing serious
damage to it.

Meanwhile, Will has appeared in what appears to be a gigantic toy store. He is
surrounded by huge alien puppets, wood soldiers, stuffed toys and wind-up things.
When Mr. O.M., the toymaker appears, he just assumes that Will is another lifelike
toy creation. Smith has already been placed with the other toys, and is hanging by
strings with all the puppets.

John and Major West take readings at the fissure and discover that the crack
must be sealed within twenty-four hours or it will cause permanent damage to the
crust of the planet.

Will and Smith try to escape from the toy store, but the toymaker activates a
wind-up minotaur to stalk them.

Back on the planet, John and Major West have determined that Will and Dr.
Smith have been taken by the mail order machine. They're making plans to go after them when a spaceship lands nearby bearing Zumdish, whom they hadn't seen
since he left with Verda the android. Zumdish has been transferred to the demolition department of the Celestial Department Store and he's come for the old mail
order machine. John and Major West force Zumdish to abandon his plan for now,
but the wily man is not to be outdone by these mere Earth people.

Will and Dr. Smith come upon a strange boarded up door. Through it they can
see Earth, where Christmas is being celebrated. But before they can go through,
the minotaur catches up to them and takes them back to Mr. O.M. in the huge toy
room. Will is forced to do some cleaning up while Mr. O.M. thinks that Smith
needs some repainting, still believing that they are both recalcitrant toys.

Will sees that there is a key sticking out of the wind-up minotaur and the boy
pulls it out, disabling the thing. He and Dr. Smith make another break for it, this
time running straight for the room where they saw the doorway to Earth.

John and the robot manage to enter the mail order machine in search of Will and Dr. Smith, but as soon as they depart, Zumdish returns with one of his super-powerful security guards. They overpower Major West and place a vacuum activator on the old mail order machine. When the vacuum activator warms up it will destroy the old machine and anything inside it.

Meanwhile, Mr. O.M. has reactivated the minotaur with a spare key and it catches up to Will and Smith just as they're opening the doorway to Earth. When they are brought back, Mr. O.M. finally figures out that these two are not really toys at all. Just then John and the robot are ensnared by the toymaker, but Will convinces Mr. O.M. to set them all free.

The structure starts to shake as the vacuum activator begins warming up. Mr. O.M. realizes what is happening and leads them all to a device which he operates and through which they return to the planet just before the machine explodes.

On the planet, John and Zumdish have a confrontation, but things are settled when John convinces Zumdish to rehire the old toymaker. Mr. O.M. had been forced to retire years before by the Celestial Department Store. By rehiring the toymaker the store won't lose any more toy business.

Zumdish is grateful for this turn of events and, upon discovering their problem with the fissure, gives the Robinsons the device they need to plug it and end its menace. The device is lowered into the fissure which will conform itself and become a perfect seal.

Penny's birthday party is a success and she receives many gifts.

Fritz Feld returns as Mr. Zomdish of the Celestial Department Store.

EPISODE FORTY-EIGHT:
"Mutiny In Space"
First telecast February 1, 1967
Writer: Peter Packer
Director: Don Richardson
GUEST STAR: ADMIRAL ZAHRK: Ronald Long

Dr. Smith has put together a rain-making experiment which involves launching a small rocket into the clouds. The robot warns Smith to recheck his calculations, but Smith refuses. He launches the small rocket, but unfortunately his calculations are a bit off and the rocket veers wildly off course and heads right for the Jupiter II. But instead of hitting the spaceship it destroys the weather station the Robinsons had built right next to it.

Smith has done it again and is once more exiled from the Jupiter II since he won't return to the ship to face John Robinson's wrath. He finds a wrecked alien spaceship and hatches a plot. He'll act as though he's repairing it, and when the Robinsons see how dangerous this craft is they'll feel sorry for Smith and ask him to rejoin them rather than ignore him and refuse to talk to him, such as the Robinsons are doing now.

But this is no ordinary derelict alien spacecraft. It is the lifeboat from the flagship of the Imperial Casseopean Navy and belongs to one Admiral Zahrk, who observes Dr. Smith by the lifeboat craft. The Admiral's vessel was the victim of a mutiny led by Mr. Kidnoe, who cast Zahrk adrift in the lifeboat ship. Zahrk is nearby observing Smith's movements.

While Smith carries out his charade, the lifeboat is actually being repaired by the robot, as well as by Admiral Zahrk himself.

When Will arrives with some food for Dr. Smith, Zahrk steps out and attempts for kidnap the boy and blast off with him in the lifeboat. But the repairs are far from complete as the drive unit is still burned out. Thus Will is able to make good his escape.

Major West has figured out Smith's game and attempts to show him up by leaving a working propulsion unit near the lifeboat ship. When Zahrk discovers it, he forces Smith do actually do the work of installing it in the spacecraft.

Will comes back and Zahrk kidnaps him again. This time the vessel is on full working order, and with the robot at the helm, the Admiral forces Will and Smith to be his crew when the vessel lifts off.

Zahrk decides that all Smith is good for is swabbing the decks, and so that becomes his task. Dr. Smith tries to make the best of a bad situation by slyly bringing up the subject of Earth and what a good idea it would be to visit there, but the Admiral isn't interested.

Admiral Zahrk is bent on tracking down his mutinous crew, and Mr. Kidnoe in particular. But the Admiral's navigation just succeeds in directing his spacecraft through a solar fire, which knocks them all about inside the vessel.

Back on the planet, the Robinsons are concerned about Will's absence and the disappearance of the robot, considering that the ship Smith had supposedly been working on is missing as well.

Since the propulsion unit that Don had left for Smith works via a magnetic drive, John Robinson believes he can draw the ship back to the planet by building a negative magnetic power beam generator, which turns out to work just as John planned.

On the lifeboat ship, the Admiral thinks he's about to catch up to Mr. Kidnoe, and Dr. Smith is too frightened to carry out his mutiny. Zahrk fires his cannons three times, but seemingly at random with no target in sight. Will gives Zahrk a piece of his mind and states that the reason his crew mutinied is because he's too strict and harsh, but the Admiral refuses to listen to him.

Smith finds a gun and gives it to Will as they launch their own mutiny against the Admiral. But when the negative magnetic power beam generator begins drawing the lifeboat back to the planet, the Admiral is convinced that he's being attacked by Mr. Kidnoe.

When the spacecraft lands again, Admiral Zahrk finally realizes that Mr. Kidnoe isn't there, and after releasing Will and Dr. Smith, Zahrk lifts off again in his lifeboat ship, on the trail of Mr. Kidnoe and the mutineers. After leaving, the robot starts going an imitation of Admiral Zahrk.

EPISODE FORTY-NINE:
"The Space Vikings"
First telecast February 8, 1967
Writer: Margaret Brookman Hill
Director: Ezra Stone
GUEST STARS: BRYNHILDE: Sheila Mathews, THOR: Bern Hoffman

As fate and this story would have it, Will, Penny and Dr. Smith are rehearsing a play about Norse mythology which Dr. Smith is directing. Penny and Will want to play Odin, but Smith states that the part is perfect for him. When a storm begins to roll in, pair of gloves fall down out of the sky and Smith is terrified that giant hands are coming for him until the gloves suddenly appear on Smith's hands. The gloves are covered with Nordic runes and when Smith removes the gloves, the storm dissipates. But when Smith puts the gloves back on again, fascinated by the wers they seem to give him, a huge hammer appears, which Smith casts aside. The hammer falls near the Jupiter II, and when it hits the ground an explosion results, and then the hammer flies back to Smith's hands, just like the legendary hammer of Thor.

Smith is impressed by what these gloves can do and he's certain that whoever they belong to will be returning to reclaim them. Not wanting to give them up, he has the robot manufacture a duplicate pair of gloves to cover just such a circumstance.

Smith's bravery quotient hasn't increased any, for when some horned monster appears out of nowhere and attacks him, Smith just panics and throws the hammer at it. The monster is destroyed and the hammer zips back into Smith's hands. But if that isn't enough, Brynhilde, a singing Valkyrie, appears on a flying horse and lands in front of Smith, whereupon he faints.

Brynhilde, not being the observant type, decides that Smith is dead and prepares to carry him off to Valhalla. But when Smith comes around, she decides to take him and the robot back to her anyway.

They arrive and they find themselves in the company of others where they feast and drink. But lurking outside are the Frost Giants who are waiting to attack Asgard, the home of the gods, should they learn that Thor has lost his power. Since Dr. Smith now possesses the power of Thor through the gauntlets and hammer, he'll have to fight Thor in order to keep them. Smith has decided that he doesn't want them as badly as he thought he did, and upon being informed that Thor is arriving, Smith tries to find a good place to hide.

Thor finds where Smith is cowering and reclaims his enchanted hammer, but Smith only has one of the gloves. As punishment, Thor takes Smith down to the realm of the elves and trolls, Nifleheim, where two elves give Smith a hard time by subjecting him to their silly antics.

Back on the planet, Will finds the imitation gloves which the robot had made, as well as one of the real gloves of Thor which Smith had thoughtlessly dropped when Brynhilde carried him off.

When Thor appears looking for his missing gauntlet, he agrees to take the boy to where Dr. Smith is in exchange for the magic glove. Will is transported to Nifleheim where he chases off the two silly elves who had been teasing Dr. Smith. Thor decides to take Dr. Smith back to Valhalla so that they can have the duel over the gloves and hammer which Thor believes Smith attempted to steal.

In Valhalla, the robot attempts to prepare Smith for the duel by teaching him fencing, but with no luck at all. Smith is expert at screaming and cowering, but not at fighting. But one other thing that Smith is very good at is cheating, which the robot suggests Smith try when all else fails.

Brynhilde confides to Will that this duel with Thor was her idea from the beginning. Thor is very insecure and needs constant challenges for him to face in order to keep his spirits up.

Smith has taken the robot's advice and has to manufacture two sponges which look just like rocks. Smith takes them with him to the hall and tricks Thor by having the man hand Smith a real rock, which Smith substitutes the sponge for. Dr. Smith then proceeds to squeeze the water out of the "rock," much to Thor's amazement. Baffled by this display, Thor attempts to duplicate the feat with a real rock, but fails.

Smith then tells Thor that all his problems come from an unhappy childhood, but then Thor can't even remember ever being a child. Completely depressed and downhearted by the experience, Thor is in no condition to defend Asgard and so the Frost Giants choose this moment to attack.

Brynhilde leaps to Asgard's defence, but is quickly knocked aside. Infuriated by the sight of this, Thor leaps to the attack and defeats the Frost Giants, which restores the warrior's self-respect. Quickly recovered from the battle, Brynhilde returns Will, Dr. Smith and the robot to the planet.

Irwin Allen regular Shiela Mathews (the future Mrs. Allen) guest stars as Brun Hilde.

EPISODE FIFTY:
"Rocket To Earth"
First telecast February 15, 1967
Writer: Barney Slater
Director: Don Richardson
GUEST STAR: ZALTO: Al Lewis

Will, Penny and Dr. Smith are playing baseball when a strangely garbed wizard appears and catches a ball which was headed for Smith. But only Smith can see the wizard. The wizard, Zalto, proceeds to harass Smith before disappearing. Since Smith is the only one who saw it and Will and Penny claims that nothing was there, Dr. Smith starts to doubt his reason.

Later the wizard reappears, accompanied by a ventriloquist dummy which proceeds to berate and bedevil Smith. Dr. Smith really thinks he's flipped now and flees to the privacy of his quarters aboard the Jupiter II. But just as Smith has convinced himself that everything is going to be all right, the wizard appears in Smith's room and continues his calculated campaign of cruelty.

But the robot is able to detect the energy of the wizard's appearances, and along with Dr. Smith and Will, they trace the wizard to a cave. Upon arriving at the cave, a red carpet unrolls before them. They follow it into the cave and encounter the dummy urging them to continue on to the wizard's laboratory. When they arrive at the lab they find that it contains devices which are scientific as well as some which clearly have magical purposes and origins.

Zalto introduces himself as the universe's great magician. His only shortfall is that he has real problems getting his spells function correctly. He keeps causing things to appear which are not what he had wanted to summon up, and since his dummy has a mind of its own, it is constantly berating him.

When Smith discovers that Zalto has a spaceship there in the cave, the wizard admits that it could take them to Earth if he chose to travel there. Smith immediately offers to become the wizard's assistant. which Zalto deliberates on and then agrees to. It just so happens that he needs some assistance in preparing a publicity stunt that he's hatched. Zalto teaches Smith some tricks, but none of them come off well, except for a rabbit that Smith pulls out of a hat.

The wizard is planning to make a comeback and he wants Smith to fly his spaceship to a barren asteroid and blast it with two missiles which will set the asteroid on fire in the shape of Zalto's name. Smith agrees to this idea, but secretly plans to steal the spaceship in order to return to Earth.

But when the Robinsons learn Smith's plan, they don't approve of stealing the spacecraft.

Smith plans to proceed with his scheme, and while he's waiting to launch, Will goes to take Smith a book to read and after he boards the spacecraft, Zalto launches it prematurely, eager to get his publicity stunt underway. What Smith didn't realize until Will points it out is that the missiles will blow up the spacecraft when they detonate the asteroid.

When the robot determines this and reveals it to the Robinsons. John, Maureen and Major West rush to Zalto's cave to confront him. When confronted by them, Zalto gets upset and vanishes into thin air. John Robinson attempts to contact the spaceship by radio.

The spaceship is approaching Earth and is contacted by the United Defense Council which demands that the spacecraft identify itself, but Will can't get the radio to transmit a reply.

When Smith launches the signal rockets, they explode in the Pacific Ocean and seem like a hostile act. When Earth fires on the spacecraft, Will reverse course and flees back into space and return to the planet where Zalto and the Robinsons are. The magician is already hatching another plan for his great comeback and leaves in his spacecraft.

Grandpa Munster, Al Lewis, guest stars as Zalto.

Bob May (the robot) did double duty in this episode, working as Zalto's ventriloquist dummy and the robot during several scenes.

Zalto's ship, carrying Will and Dr. Smith, almost reach Earth but are repelled by a missile barrage.

EPISODE FIFTY-ONE:
"The Cave of the Wizards"
First telecast February 22, 1967
Writer: Peter Packer
Director: Don Richardson
Incidental Music: Alexander Courage

The Jupiter II finally has enough fuel for liftoff and they are planning to blast off the next day at 8 A.M. Will and Dr. Smith are out prospecting when Smith's prospecting causes a spark and ignites so gas, causing an explosion.

Smith bangs his head in a fall, resulting in amnesia. Smith is lured into a cave by an alien force by a mummy. Will and the robot attempt to follow him but rock-like monsters force them back. But since these rocky guardians are chained to the cave wall, Will and the robot are able to slip by just out of the robot's reach.

They find Dr. Smith in a cavern containing a computer system which is controlling Smith's mind. The robot recognizes that Smith has amnesia and decides to use the cliche remedy of another hit on the head with a rock. While Smith's memory returns, the chances of periodic relapses are very likely.

Will and Dr. Smith return to the Jupiter II but something strange is going on. Parts of the Jupiter II keep disappearing and there's no sign of Major West and the rest of the Robinsons. They soon realize that this isn't the Jupiter II at all, but just an incredible simulation created by the same mysterious force which lured Smith into the cave. The robot is able to lead Will and Dr. Smith to the real Jupiter II.

Smith decides to return to the alien cave with the robot, having decided that he could use the power of the machines to create duplicates of the Jupiter II for his personal gain. When Smith and the robot arrive at the cave, the rock creatures are not menacing at all.

Inside the control room in the cave, the computer is activated and Dr. Smith finds a skullcap and a pendant which he decides to put on. The computer informs Smith that he's out on the crown of the Draconians, but Smith then finds that he can't get them off again. The computer has chosen Smith to absorb all the knowl edge once possessed by the Draconians and thereby restore the lost civilization to its former glory once possessed of that knowledge.

But Smith is mollified when the computer has Smith given a huge diamond as a show of gratitude.

The Jupiter II is being loaded for its planned lift-off when the robot arrives at the ship. It has been painted gold and dispatched by Smith, who is glorying in his new role as the savior of a dead civilization. The robot is even singing.

Will accompanies it back to the alien cave where he finds that Smith is changing. The man's skin is silvery, he has pointed ears and his eyebrows are slanted upwards. Smith informs Will that he wants to remain on the planet when the Jupiter II leaves.

When the rock creatures enter, Smith's face goes blank as he's prepared to receive the implanted memories of the Draconians.

Will returns to the Jupiter II and tells his father what's going on. John and Major West go to the cave to see what's going on, but when they arrive Smith is already completely controlled by the alien computer. Smith repeats his claim that he doesn't want to return to Earth with the Robinsons. The computer forces John and Major West to leave the cave.

Back at the Jupiter II they explain to Will that Smith refuses to leave and there's nothing they can do for him. But Will won't accept this and believes that something can be done.

At the alien cave, Smith has been completely dominated and is now called by the Draconian name Oniac. Will attempts without success to appeal to the human side of Smith. Since the robot is also being held there by the alien force which is dominating Smith, a dejected Will Robinson leaves the cave alone.

But suddenly Will's pleading starts having an effect on Smith and he starts to fight against the alien domination. The battle of wills is so great that the computer short-circuits in a shower of sparks, allowing Smith and the robot to flee the cave and race back to the Jupiter II.

The launch time comes and goes, but Smith and the robot were detected approaching and so John Robinson delayed takeoff. But since the launch window has passed, they'll have to wait for another.

The four foot Jupiter 2 miniature is used as a prop in the cave.
Dr. Smith's pointy ears were actually borrowed from STAR TREK.

EPISODE FIFTY-TWO:
"Treasure of the Lost Planet"
First telecast March 1, 1967
Writer: Carey Wilber
Director: Harry Harris
GUEST STARS: CAPTAIN TUCKER: Albert Salmi, SMEKE: Jim Boles, DEKE: Craig Duncan

When Penny stumbles on a gold coin, Smith gets gold fever and convinces the others to help him search for treasure. Will, Penny and the robot are helping to look when Smith uncovers a large ring. When he pulls on it, a trap door opens and Smith falls into a pit. He's unhurt and discovers a treasure chest. Nearby is a box which has the skull and crossbones on it. The box has a metal head in it which the robot can hear speaking, but no one else can.

Upon rescuing Smith from the pit and returning to camp, the robot announces that there are four and one-eight aliens present. The one-eighth is the metal mead in the box.

That night, while Smith is asleep, the box enters Smith's quarters and communicates with him.

Meanwhile, Will encounters Nick, a familiar metal parrot. It leads Will to where Captain Alonzo Tucker, an acquaintance met on the other planet they'd been marooned on (see "The Sky Pirate"). Tucker is tied up, and upon being freed by Will, the Captain explains that his from Bootes turned renegade and expected him to join them in their pirating ways. When Tucker refused, they tied him up, or so he says. In reality, Tucker is the leader of a gang of pirates but his crew no longer trust him.

Tucker's crew consists of Deke, a lizard creature; Isralim, a bull-like being, and Smeke, a furry man. They'd been out searching for Beely Bones' treasure.

Will wants to help his friend Captain Tucker and so he leads him back to where the Jupiter II is. Tucker is put in Smith's room, where he sees the box with the metal head and immediately recognizes it as having belonged to Beely Bones. The head is still attuned to Belly Bones and has mistaken Dr. Smith for its old master because of how alike they are.

Tucker realizes that he can find the treasure of Beely Bones. The robot explains that the metal head can lead them to a treasure, and while Smith uses it to do so, accompanied by the robot, they are followed by Tucker as well as by Tucker's former compatriots.

Tucker and his comrades make a truce and is able to keep the pirates from killing the Robinsons.

Deke captures Smith and Will, and the pair then learn that Tucker is really their leader, although they don't really have much respect for him, nor trust.

Soon John and Major West decide to search for Will and Smith because they should have returned by now.

Smith leads the pirates to the pit where he found the box and the metal head continues to guide them towards the treasure. No one is certain exactly what the treasure is and Will suggests that what Belly Bones valued may have been very different from what the pirates value.

The route to the treasure is booby trapped, and at one point when they arrive at a stone wall, Deke, the lizard-man, strikes it, causing a pit to open beneath his feet and the creature plummets to his doom. Later, Isralim is blown up when crossing a mine field.

They finally arrive at the spot where the metal head indicates the treasure is buried. Fearing more traps, Smeke forces Will to dig, but Tucker helps him. When they find a box, Smeke takes it and opens it himself. The box is filled with pig iron. Thinking this was all a trick, he attacks Tucker, Will and Smith. John arrives just then, having followed them, but his laser blasts leave Smeke unharmed because he feeds on energy. Only cold steel can affect Smeke.

Tucker eventually overcomes Smeke and saves the others. Tucker explains that Will had guessed right. Because on the world where Beely Bones came from iron was rare, he valued it highly. Tucker leaves, once more free to resume his old ways.

Albert Salmi returned as Alonzo P. Tucker.

EPISODE FIFTY-THREE:
"Revolt of the Androids"
First telecast March 8, 1967
Writer: Bob and Wanda Duncan
Director: Don Richardson
GUEST STARS: VERDA: Dee Hartford, IDAK ALPHA 12: Don Matheson,
IDAK OMEGA 17, AND THE MONSTER: Dawson Palmer

Smith has been out hunting rubies and having some luck until he's attacked by a hairy monster which eats the rubies Smith had been unearthing.

Dr. Smith is pouring out his tale of woe to Will and the robot when something materializes near them. The robot explains that it is not just an ordinary android, but a super-android. The android is frozen in position because it's controls need to be tightened.

When Will repairs the controls, the android comes to life an attacks them. The reason is has no gratitude is because it is an Instant Destroyer and Killer (IDAK) android. But this is a clumsy robot which stumbles over a rock and falls. The robot observes this and states that it doesn't think that this android is going to leap tall buildings in a single bound.

The IDAK explains that it was dispatched to this world to destroy another android which is there, but it is having trouble making its super-powers function.

Dr. Smith wants the robot to repair the IDAK's problems (despite the fact that it just tried to attack them), but the robot resists the suggestion, referring to the IDAK as a foreign import. But the robot does go ahead with the repairs to IDAK.

Meanwhile, Judy and Penny find a female android which they soon recognize as Verda (see "The Android Machine"). Verda looks more human than she did before and reveals that the Cosmic Department Store was taken over by someone else and all the other androids like her were turned into scrap metal, but she just managed to escape. Verda explains that an IDAK has been sent to hunt down and destroy her.

The IDAK soon detects Verda's presence and proceeds to the Jupiter II to complete its mission. John and Major West fire on the IDAK with their lasers, but to no effect.

Penny spirits Verda out the rear exit of the Jupiter II, but the IDAK keeps tracking them. When the IDAK tracks down and confronts Verda, because she looks so human now she is able to convince the IDAK that its tracking unit must be malfunctioning because she's obviously not an android. They actually succeed in winning the IDAK over and befriending him.

They all return to the Jupiter II and IDAK begins to fit right in, even learning to play baseball. It can't quite get the hang of hitting the ball with the bat, though, as every time it connects it hits the ball into solid rock. Just when things are proceeding well, Smith lets slip that Verda is an android, too.

The IDAK confronts Verda once again, but this time it realizes that it likes her and can't bring itself to follow its programming. The IDAK short-circuits and becomes immobilized.

Verda is returning to the Jupiter II for help when the Factory Machine arrives and inspects the IDAK. It decides that it is defective and replaces it with a more powerful model, an Omega 17. This other IDAK will even harm humans if they attempt to contravene its programmed mission.

The Omega 17 follows Will and Dr. Smith back to the Jupiter II. Meanwhile, the robot comes to help the other IDAK and repairs its damage. But the other IDAK, an Alpha 12, while working again, no longer has super-powers.

The Alpha 12 thinks it's pointless to battle the Omega 17, but when it sees the robot attack it anyway, it is shamed into joining in. The Alpha 12 manages to destroy the Omega 17's belt, which deactivates it. When the Factory Machine returns to retrieve and destroy both IDAKs, Prof. Robinson is able to destroy it with a disintegrator capsule.

The IDAK Alpha 12 is becoming more human, just as Verda did. Verda and the Alpha 12 bid the Robinson's goodbye, planning to journey to another world where they can safely go into hiding without endangering their human friends.

Dee Hartford returns as Verda, the android. Her pursuer is Don Matheson.

EPISODE FIFTY-FOUR:
"The Colonists"
First telecast March 15, 1967
Writer: Peter Packer
Director: Ezra Stone
GUEST STAR: NIOLANI: Francine York

When the Robinsons are building three additional remote radio stations, the first thing their receivers pick up is a powerful alien sound wave designed to destroy their equipment. Not only are the receivers knocked out, but Penny and Judy vanish as well.

A voice over the radio informs them that they are all prisoners. Major West's laser is destroyed by remote control to show that they mean business. Then Smith and Major West are ordered to return to the Jupiter II.

Upon reaching the Jupiter II they find that Will and the robot are missing, but this is because they'd detected the source of the alien broadcast and have gone to investigate.

Will and the robot reach a cave where the alien signal was transmitted from, but before they can discover anything further they are taken prisoner by gray, unspeaking guards who drag them before their master, the Amazon warrior Niolani. She makes it clear that she despises all men.

Niolani goes to the Jupiter II and insists that all weapons be turned over to her, and she points out that she has taken the children as hostage. The Robinsons feel they have no choice but to do as Niolani demands.

The Robinsons are then taken to Niolani's encampment and imprisoned behind a force field wall. Niolani reveals that her world of warrior women are going to colonize this planet and she is their advance scout.

Niolani puts the male prisoners to work building an arch and clearing the ground for a colony rocket to land. The arch will enable the women to be altered so that they can breathe the air of this world.

Maureen is taken to join Judy and Penny, who are undergoing an indoctrination to brainwash them into despising men. Penny has taken to this and shows her contempt for her brother, Will. John and Major West attempt to resist captivity and try to escape, but they are quickly recaptured.

Niolani likes Dr. Smith's craven ways and makes him her consort since he's clearly afraid of her.

Maureen shuts down the force field so that John and Major West can escape, and although they are once again recaptured, Will and the robot manage to get away.

Will and the robot go to their drill site and retrieve some explosives and they return to Niolani's encampment. They plant their plastic explosives on the archway, planning to detonate it when the colonists arrive in order to disgrace Niolani before her people while making the planet unsuitable for her people to colonize. Their plan succeeds. Not only is Niolani recalled from the world in disgrace, but instead of being a warrior she'll be reduced to such menial tasks as house cleaning, laundry and looking after children.

EPISODE FIFTY-FIVE:
"Trip Through The Robot"
First telecast March 22, 1967
Writer: Barney Slater
Director: Don Richardson

John and Major West are testing the Jupiter 2's electrical systems when Smith bungles and causes an overload which results in a power failure which will take weeks to repair.

The robot is also having power problems and needs to be recharged, but they can't spare the extra power right now because of the state the Jupiter II is in. The symptoms of the robots power problems cause it to state that it feels faint and ill. But without the recharge, the robot will run down and, as the robot puts it, it will "die."

Will is very angry that no one wants to help the robot, and because of the conflict this is causing the robot choose to trundle off into the wilderness to "die" alone.

When Will realizes what the robot has done, he convinces Dr. Smith into accompanying him to track down the robot and try to help it. They follow the robot to a place called the Valley of the Shadows where strange gasses causes weird effects on those who enter the valley. In the robot's case the gasses have caused it to grow to a gigantic height. This has happened because the robot's ionic processes have reversed, and the only chance the robot has of reverting to its normal size is for Will to cause those ionic processes to be restored to their normal state. But the only way to accomplish this would be to enter the robot and repair it from the inside. Finding a hatch on the robot's lower section near the tread, Will and Dr. Smith enter.

The robot has a laser unit which is designed to track and destroy any alien contamination. But in the robot's current enlarged state, Will and Dr. Smith are determined to be just such a type of contamination. When it comes after them, they flee through the power cables and circuitry and in the process get separated in the maze of machinery.

Dr. Smith gets trapped in the robot's temperature control unit and the robot has to expend some of its precious remaining power in order to free him.

Meanwhile, back at the Jupiter II, John and Major West have become aware that Will and Smith are missing and decide that they should try to find them, at least for the boy's sake. John and Major West track them to the Valley of the Shadows and encounter the gargantuan robot. Finding the open hatch they determine what has happened and enter it to search for Will and Dr. Smith.

The laser antibody defense locks onto John and Major West, but John knocks it out of action with his own laser pistol.

Elsewhere in the robot, the equivalent of its heart (the robot's diode timer) fails. Will is certain now that the robot has died, but then he remembers the robot's emergency power system. Will manages to get the backup power system activated and it restarts the robot's diode timer. The boy then re-routes most of the power to the robot's tread section so that it will be able to move and return to the Jupiter II when it is restored to normal. When Will manages to reverse the ionic process so that it resumes its normal state, the robot immediately starts to return to its normal size.

Will and Dr. Smith are racing for the hatch when they get separated again, but Smith encounters John and Major West, warns them of what's happening, and they all make it to the hatch in time.

The robot is returned to the Jupiter II where they decide that they can recharge it using the batteries in the Chariot.

A plethora of Irwin Allen gadgetry is used to provide a setting for the robot's interior.

EPISODE FIFTY-SIX:
"The Phantom Family"
First telecast March 29, 1967
Writer: Peter Packer
Director: Ezra Stone
GUEST STAR: LEMNOC: Alan Hewitt

The Jupiter II has been under attack by an unidentified alien force for several nights. The Robinsons guess that it is trying to weaken their defenses with the nightly assaults. Following the latest offensive, Major West forces Dr. Smith to accompany him while they go outside to check their force field generator defenses.

A nearby rock wall mysteriously opens and an alien with a red crest on its head fires a gun at Smith which seems to stupefy him. The alien then begins to use a wrist device to begin controlling Smith's actions.

The next day the family is cleaning up after the latest attack when another offensive is launched. This time the alien zaps Judy, Penny and Major West with the strange gun. They are stunned by the gun and apparently turned into zombies with a device on each of their wrists which controls their actions.

The robot has determined that these are actually duplicates and Will accompanies the robot to search for the real Smith, Judy, Penny and Major West. They discover the base of an alien named Lemnoc. In the control room are body molds for creating human duplicates. The real people are held in stasis in nearby tubes.

When confronted, Lemnoc explains that he has created duplicates of the Robinsons in order to instill the will to survive in his own race and teach his people the meaning of survival. Lemnoc says that if Will can teach the duplicates to have human qualities, then he'll free his prisoners. The twenty-four hour deadline is crucial because the humans will die if they are kept in the tubes longer than that.

Will has no choice but to agree, but after he leaves, Lemnoc reveals that he has other plans. Awakening Major West, Lemnoc instructs him to teach his duplicates to fly the Jupiter II. When Major West flatly refuses, Don is put into the stasis tube again.

Back at the Jupiter II, the robot is helping Will to teach Penny and Judy to sing and to adopt other human qualities. When a storm strikes, the Dr. Smith and Don West duplicates are incapacitated, but the robot explains that thumping them on the chest will reactivate them, which it does.

When Lemnoc arrives at the Jupiter II to view Will's progress, the duplicates of Don and Smith grab Lemnoc for being a hostile alien because they have now become more human than alien themselves.

Will tells Lemnoc that he's got to release the real humans now and the alien agrees. When Will goes to Lemnoc's cave, he finds Judy, Penny and Major West there and frees them.

At the Jupiter II, the duplicates free Lemnoc, as they had been obeying his orders all along.

When Will, Judy, Penny and Don return to the Jupiter II, the duplicate Dr. Smith is still there. Lemnoc wants the robot Smith to learn how to fly the Jupiter II.

John and Maureen Robinson finally return to the ship, having been gone on a trip performing some experiments. When they learn what has been happening, John and Major West go to track down Lemnoc once and for all and end this trouble.

When confronted, Lemnoc states that he'll release Dr. Smith only in change for the Jupiter II, which he feels would be the perfect symbol of survival to take back to his planet and show to his people. John refuses, which means that when the twenty-four hours elapse that Smith will die in his stasis tube.

Back at the Jupiter II, the duplicate Dr. Smith explains how much he is enjoying becoming like a human in actions, but Will doesn't want to talk to him. He wants the real Dr. Smith back. The robot double understands the boy's feelings and goes to Lemnoc where he subdues the alien and ties him up so that he can set the real Dr. Smith free. When the robot meets the original, the robot disintegrates, which frightens Smith and sends him screaming back to the Jupiter II.

Another look-alike episode. This time it's the entire family, save for Will.
The real Robinsons are stored in what looks like the Jupiter II freezing tubes.
Story influence:"Dream Monster."

EPISODE FIFTY-SEVEN:
"The Mechanical Men"
First telecast April 5, 1967
Writer: Barney Slater
Director: Seymour Robbie
Incidental Music: Alexander Courage

Dr. Smith is trying to come up with a fuel substitute to enable the Jupiter II to return to Earth, but his experiment fails, causing an explosion. Because of Smith's carelessness in the experiment, he could have endangered everyone's lives, and after John Robinson gives Smith a good tongue-lashing, Dr. Smith becomes offended and goes off to take a nap among the rocks.

But when Dr. Smith awakens from his snooze, he finds himself fastened to a platform, chained there by tiny mechanical men which all look like duplicates of the Robinson's robot, but six inches in height. The leader of the tiny robots is purple and moves on a platform which glows when it speaks.

John and Major West have decided to search for Smith, but aren't successful.

Suddenly the Jupiter II and the Robinsons come under attack when their force field generator and their weather station explodes. When they ask the robot if it knows what it happening, it refuses to reply out of loyalty to what it deems its "own kind."

The tiny mechanical men are from the planet Industro and have been waiting ten thousand years for a leader, and have chosen the Robinson's robot for that honor. They move in on the encampment, demanding that the robot be turned over to them. In the face of hundreds of little robots, the Robinsons have no choice but to comply.

Will accompanies the robot to the camp of the mechanical men, where he finds the bound and typically terrified Dr. Smith. When they next see their robot, it is wearing a crown and robe and carrying a royal scepter as it has accepted the mantle as leader of the tiny mechanical men.

It soon becomes apparent, though, that the robot is not all that the mechanical men want. Being ruthless and power hungry by nature, the mechanical men want a more aggressive leader. They see these qualities in Smith and want to transfer his personality into the robot.

Will runs back to the Jupiter II to explain what is happening, but before anyone can plan to try to do anything about it, Smith returns to camp. He now talks like the robot did and is eager to work.

The robot then rolls into camp, talking like Smith used to and displaying all of Smith's negative personality traits. The robot is now enjoying being the ruler of the mechanical men and has decided that it needs the Jupiter II so that it can return to the planet of the mechanical men, Industro, since the space ships of the mechanical men are too small to accommodate it.

Once again, in the face of overwhelming odds, the Robinson's are forced to surrender.

Dr. Smith is now as brave as the robot was and he goes with Will to spy on the camp of the mechanical men. They overhear the robots planning to attack and destroy the Robinsons as practice for their planned conquest of the galaxy. Will and Dr. Smith run back to the Jupiter II to warn everyone of the impending sneak attack.

When the robot and the mechanical men attack, they manage to hit their former robot with a laser blast, causing it to collapse. Dr. Smith does as well, since there is still some linkage between the two. The tiny mechanical men flee in hopeless defeat.

Dr. Smith awakens with his personality restored while John and Major West restore the robot, although Smith questions the wisdom of making it work again. Things have returned to normal.

Scores of Remco toy robots are sprayed silver and used as the tiny robot army.

EPISODE FIFTY-EIGHT:
"The Astral Traveler"
First telecast April 12, 1967
Writer: Carey Wilber
Director: Don Richardson
GUEST STARS: HAMISH: Sean McClory, ANGUS: Dawson Palmer

When Will, the robot and Dr. Smith get caught outside during an electrical storm, they seek refuge in a nearby cave. As Will and Dr. Smith enter the cave, whose entrance is too small to accommodate the robot, lightning strikes outside, causing a rockslide which seals them in the cavern.

Dr. Smith starts to panic in the dark, but then two torches mysteriously appear to light their way. Since they can't get out the way they came in, Will says they'll have to look for another exit and their search leads them to a revolving mirrored door. Will decides to try the door, but when he enters it he disappears.

Meanwhile the robot has returned to the Jupiter II to get help, and the Robinsons return to the cave entrance to try to dig Will and Dr. Smith free.

After passing through the door, Will finds himself in a dark area near a huge castle. When a monster crawls out of the moat and tries to chase Will, the boy runs into the castle to escape.

Inside the castle Will finds a plaque embedded in stone which proclaims that in 1497, Hamish Rue Glamis, the ninth Laird of Glamis, was executed for treason. To all appearances Will has returned to Earth in Scotland. Outside, Will sees a vast body of water and pulls a leaf off a nearby plant and puts it in his pocket.

Back on the planet, the Robinsons are successful in digging away the rockfall and Smith is rescued, expressing his undying gratitude. But they cannot find Will, and when Dr. Smith explains what happened, Major West suggests that the electrical storm created a warp in the planet's magnetic field which they must duplicate in order to retrieve Will.

In the castle's torture chamber, Will observes such things as ghosts escorting a man to the headsman's block. When a tall Scotsman appears he introduces himself as the ghost of Hamish. At first Will thinks this is just another alien, but finally the ghost convinces him of his identity.

Hamish explains that the thing that Will saw in the moat is Angus Glamis, who is living under a curse.

Will finds his way back through the warp to the cave and relates his experiences to his family. He even has the leaf with him as proof of where he's been. Dr. Smith identifies it as Scottish ivy.

Hearing bagpipe music, Will returns to the cave and finds that Hamish has come through the warp and is no longer intangible. In fact he's suffering from gout, which Maureen treats for him.

Major West states that with a field generator they could reconstruct the gateway, but only two people would be able to pass through it successfully. Dr. Smith quickly volunteers to go and take star charts with him so that a rescue ship can be dispatched from Earth.

Hamish mistrusts Smith, and rightly so. Smith doesn't want to see the Robinsons rescued because they would reveal how Smith stowed away on the Jupiter II, which would send him to prison for a very long time.

The gateway is reopened and Smith and Hamish go through it, but as they are doing so, Smith drops the star charts. Will dives after them, causing an overload in the gateway, closing it before Will can return.

In Scotland, Angus appears, frightening Smith, and Hamish has decided to keep Smith in the castle's torture chamber, as a ghost. Smith tries to appease Hamish by revealing that he's descended from the Ruthven clan, which infuriates Hamish all the more because it was a Ruthven who betrayed Hamish to his executioners. Hamish decides that by executing Smith, he'll be able to go to his eternal rest with his vengeance satisfied.

An executioner is dragging Smith to the block when Will runs up and pleads for his life. Hamish is moved by Will's pleas and frees Smith, who returns with Will through the gateway. Hamish is prepared to continue his exile in the castle with Angus, but because he demonstrated the quality of mercy, he's forgiven by the higher powers and allowed to go to his eternal rest.

Back on the planet, Will and Dr. Smith return, but the field generator has burned out and the gateway cannot be re-established to return them to Earth.

EPISODE FIFTY-NINE:
"The Galaxy Gift"
First telecast April 26, 1967
Writer: Barney Slater
Director: Ezra Stone
GUEST STARS: ARCON: John Carradine, SATICON #1: Jim Mills

Dr. Smith, Penny and the robot are rehearsing a play which Smith wants to put on to demonstrate his thespian talents. Suddenly a hideous alien appears in their midst. It's dying from the air and somehow its death throes cause flames to appear around Penny. It forces Dr. Smith and the robot to leave and then communicates with Penny.

The alien reveals that its name is Arcon and begins altering its appearance to find one which will accommodate survival in an oxygen atmosphere. First it changes into something which is frog-like, and then human.

Arcon reveals that he's being pursued by Saticons, who are cruel creatures from a dead world. When a missile bombardment hits the planet, Arcon disappears.

Arcon is later found sleeping in Smith's quarters aboard the Jupiter II. But suddenly three of the deadly Saticons appear outside the Jupiter II, demanding that Arcon be turned over to them. Maureen Robinson refuses to cooperate with the creatures so they retaliate by causing the temperature to drop to levels dangerously low for human survival.

Inside the Jupiter II, Arcon reveals to Penny that he's unaffected by this because of the amulet which he wears that protects him from the Saticons. Arcon needs to entrust it to someone and he decides that Penny is the logical choice. He explains that it must be kept from the Saticons at all cost or his planet could suffer annihilation. Arcon then disappears again, explaining that he always gets away.

Smith accompanies the robot to attempt to come to some kind of understanding with the Saticons. The aliens can read minds and they can see that Dr. Smith plans to betray the Robinsons, so they offer him transportation to Earth if he can bring them the amulet.

Dr. Smith agrees, but plans to betray the aliens in his own way by having the robot manufacture a duplicate of the amulet. The Saticons are also planning to cheat Smith by creating an imitation Chinatown street plucked from Smith's memories. When Smith thinks he's safely on Earth and hands over the amulet, the Saticons will kill him.

The Saticons discover Smith's ruse and destroy the fake amulet, demanding that the real one be turned over to them. Penny won't do it but Smith says that she will if and when they are returned to Earth.

A transporter has been provided by the Saticons which they claim will take the humans to Earth, but which actually transports one to the fake Chinatown street. Smith has Debbie the Bloop test it and she appears on the fake street where the Saticons giver her a hot dog and a Dodgers pennant as evidence of her trip. When Debbie returns through the transporter with these things, Smith is certain she was on Earth and is tremendously excited.

Smith goes through the transporter with Penny, but the robot examines the hot dog and discovers that it is a phony. The robot is concerned and uses the transporter to follow Smith and Penny.

Penny and Smith have arrived in what Dr. Smith believes is Chinatown, but the robot soon appears and warns them that this could be a trap. The robot points out that there is no one there except them.

Meanwhile, Arcon appears to Maureen, Judy and Will and reveals that Penny, Smith and the robot are on an asteroid, lured into a trap by the Saticons. Arcon has been searching for hundreds of years for someone to give a galaxy gift to and has yet to find someone who has not betrayed him. Penny is his latest test subject. Penny will remain safe if she keeps the amulet, but if she surrenders it to the Saticons, she will be destroyed.

The robot tries to tell Dr. Smith that this is a trap, but he refuses to listen to it and insists that Penny turn over the amulet, which she does. The Saticons then prepare to kill Smith and Penny until another Saticon appears and grabs the amulet, hurling it to the ground which causes an energy discharge which kills the Saticons.

The new Saticon was just Arcon in yet another form. He listened to Maureen's explanation that Penny was not being selfish in handing over the amulet, but rather was just trying to help her family.

Arcon returns Penny, Smith and the robot to the planet and then leaves again on his continuing mission.

Guest star John Carradine also performed on LAND OF THE GIANTS and is one of the most prestigious actors to appear in guest-starring roles on Sixties television. He even turns up in an episode of THE GREEN HORNET.

MARTA KRISTEN: THE ELDEST DAUGHTER

"Get me the girl with the big earrings," commanded Irwin Allen, and that girl was Marta Kristen.

"I had been doing a lot of television," she recalls. "I was in the first two-parter on television for DR. KILDARE. I was doing Emmy Award-winning material and shows. In fact, I wasn't auditioning for anything back then. They were simply calling me in, asking me to do the shows and giving me the script. I feel that I had gotten to a point in my career, even though I was just eighteen years old, where I had a good reputation. So when I went in to interview for LOST IN SPACE, they didn't have me read for it at all. But I remember that I was wearing an off-white winter suit and great big gold dangling earrings and Irwin Allen said afterwards, 'Get me the girl with the big earrings!'"

Kristen was born in Norway in 1946 and raised in Detroit. She appeared in the movies SAVAGE SAM (1963), BEACH BLANKET BINGO (1965) and BATTLE BEYOND THE STARS (1980). Her other television appearances included ALFRED HITCHCOCK PRESENTS ("The Gloating Place), THE MAN FROM U.N.C.L.E. ("The Neptune Affair"), MR. NOVAK, WAGON TRAIN, MY THREE SONS, THE GREATEST SHOW ON EARTH and others.

And yet, Judy Robinson, as a character, never had a great deal to do on the show. "I'll tell you the truth," Kristen states. "Even now, Judy Robinson is never clear to me because I wasn't given much to do. I went to Irwin often and said, 'please, give me something,' or 'I've got an idea here we could develop more, about my relationship with Don.' But I don't want to complain, because I think that, all in all, it was a good experience. But every actor wants to be able to fulfill their creative potential because that's what we're here for. Not to have that opportunity is very frustrating. I love acting. Acting is

actually my therapy—my way of being able to get outside myself and use myself at the same time, use all the emotions that I have without making my family crazy so that I can do it in my work rather than in my personal life."

Kristen agrees that working with her co-stars on LOST IN SPACE for three years did engender feelings much like one would experience with a genuine family.

"We cared about each other to some degree, especially in the beginning. It was a whole new concept for television with its family in space approach to science fiction. We did a lot of laughing—that was certainly the truth—partly because of the silliness of some of the scripts. We all have to admit today that they were fun but some of them were very silly."

Working on the show was something she really loved doing. "You see, I love getting up early in the morning, being out on the freeways before everybody else and going into the studio and having my breakfast and coffee, talking with the make-up group, the hairdressers and going to my trailer. I love that. It's something that makes you feel like this is really show business, folks! I was working and being happy, so I was always happy to go to work. There's no doubt about that. No matter what you do in television or anything, actually, you're going to be typecast and it's just impossible to get away from that unless you're like Sally Field and you have the opportunity and a very strong personality."

At the time, Kristen never thought about what it would be like with the show still playing in re-runs around the country twenty years later.

"It's amazing to me that people still come up to me or stare at me for a long time because this is twenty years later but they still ask, 'Were you Judy on LOST IN SPACE?' and it never ceases to amaze me because I don't think I look the same. It's always a pleasant surprise."

Kristen explains that the cast member she became the best of friends with was the youngest castaway—Billy Mumy.

"Billy and I really had a good time. I remember listening to music with him," she states, "and I made him aware of Bob Dylan and Donovan. He was a very bright and precocious child and was very good with the guitar. He was the only one to have a stereo in his dressing room. I never finished my dressing room (sort of keep your bags packed) and Mark's room had graffiti all over it. Everyone had to sign his. We had the oldest dressing room that anyone would possibly find on the lot. They were sort of fun and looked like little eggs which were green on the outside and brown on the inside."

Being right on the 20th Century Fox lot offered many opportunities to explore other things around the studio.

"THE TIME TUNNEL was right next to us and so was THE LAND OF THE GIANTS set. All of Irwin Allen's shows were done there. I'd go over to VOYAGE TO THE BOTTOM OF THE SEA, which was right near us. I didn't go to visit any other shows, though. I never felt really comfortable walking around in my space suit."

Since the actors were together so much of the time, strong friendships developed on the show, such as the one Billy Mumy had with Angela Cartright. Kristen was also good friends with another one of her fellow performers.

"I must say that I had a crush on Mark, although we were both married. We cared for each other. We'd go to lunch at Chez-J's in Santa Monica and we'd bring bagfuls of peanuts for the crew. It was nice but of course it never culminated in anything other than just a friendship."

Kristen was also good friends with a crew member who worked as Irwin Allen's assistant and who helped the actress deal with some personal problems she was having at the time.

"Rick Husky was a very sweet man and I just adored him," she explains. "He helped me through some very difficult times. Rick had the short end of the stick when it came to our relationship because I was having trouble with my first marriage. He helped me through that and I wished in many ways that I had not stayed in my marriage and had pursued Rick in a long term

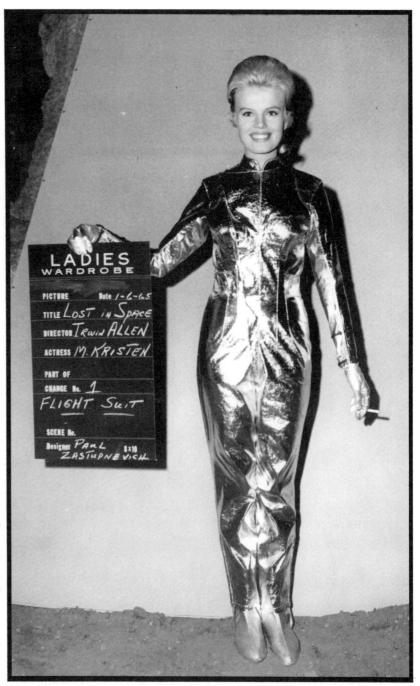

relationship. He was very kind and a very sweet person and I would tell anyone that. Rick was there when I needed him and he was a very bright and witty man. He always made me laugh."

While no reunion movie has been made with the LOST IN SPACE cast, some of them reunited a few years ago on the game show FAMILY FEUD.

"I loved it!" Kristen states enthusiastically. "I'm a game freak. I love any game you put in front of me and I'll try to work it out. I guess it must be because I'm competitive, although I say that I'm not. We made it right to the finals for the week. We were all concerned about Guy because he'd recently had a ma-

113

jor stroke. It wasn't because we were concerned whether he would or wouldn't do well on the show but because we care about each other. Even though, like a family, we had our differences, we all cared about each other. It was so good to see everybody, although Billy and Jonathan were not there. Still, it was so nice to be together."

Kristen also thinks it would be fun if they could all get together again for a new LOST IN SPACE story. "I've thought about that and I think it would be fun to have it return, but I would be the mother and June and Guy would have gone back to Earth somehow or remained on the planet. Don and I would become the parents of other children. That would be fun and I would enjoy doing that."

Mark Goddard and Marta Kristen take a break on the set

ANGELA CARTWRIGHT—BRIGHT AS A PENNY

For Angela Cartwright, LOST IN SPACE "was great fun"

"The show contained many things that children dream of—adventure, excitement and monsters."

She also recalls working on Irwin Allen's feature film, BEYOND THE POSEIDON ADVENTURE. She costarred in that one.

Long before that came to pass, she was called to journey where no family had ever journeyed before, as the youngest daughter—Penny.

Angela Cartwright has been acting most of her life. Born Sept. 9, 1952, she is the daughter of art designer John Crawford. Her career started shortly after arriving in California when a neighbor encouraged Angela's mother to put her and her sister, Veronica, into children's fashion modeling. When she was three and a half years old, Cartwright was chosen to appear in SOMEBODY UP THERE LIKES ME because her long, dark hair and huge hazel eyes made her an idea choice as the daughter for Pier Cartwright and Paul Newman. Another small part followed in SOMETHING OF VALUE, also for MGM. She also appears in the film LAD: A DOG.

By the time she was four, Cartwright was well known by the top photographers and appeared on a McCALL's magazine cover and in many advertisements. It was this exposure that led to her selection for the part of Linda on THE DANNY THOMAS SHOW. She grew up before millions of viewers during the seven years she was with that series. She also appears as one of the Von Trapp children in THE SOUND OF MUSIC, which helped bring her to the attention of Irwin Allen.

"He had seen my work on DANNY THOMAS and THE SOUND OF MUSIC," Cartwright recalls, "and he knew what he wanted. He called me in to see if I would be interested in doing his pilot. It seemed like a very exciting thing to do, having rocks falling on you, and being sprayed with water when we went through the whirlpool. So as a child it was a lot of fun. The crew would rock the Chariot back and forth and it was great fun."

Like any actress, her favorite episodes are the ones in which she had more than just an average amount of screen time, since Dr. Smith, the robot and Billy soon became the de facto stars when the story emphasis shifted almost exclusively to them.

"I liked the plot, and generally the ones I had things to do in, such as 'My Friend, Mr. Nobody.'"

There were also shows she didn't like. "I didn't like the one where I had to dance to Rock music. ('The Promised Planet.') And in the third season they wanted me to cut my hair for some dumb reason. I told them that I didn't want to and they ended up making me wear a wig for the third season and I never understood why."

Cartwright also doesn't give very high marks to the directors on the show.

"I didn't think that any of the directors were that great. My favorite director is Robert Wise—he was wonderful when we did THE SOUND OF MUSIC.

"Irwin Allen directed the LOST IN SPACE pilot and—let me think, how can I explain him? Well, he was interesting. Yes, I guess that 'interesting' is the word. He had a lot of faith that things would somehow magically come together while filming a scene. I guess that's why he always tries to get big name stars for his projects. I think he feels that something special will just happen when all these stars come together. But sometimes it doesn't work, like in BEYOND THE POSEIDON ADVENTURE which I did for him."

As Billy Mumy also notes, they became more than just friends after the

show was cancelled. This is a subject she apparently finds too private to discuss.

"Billy and I were very good friends," Cartwright explains.

"After the series ended we started dating," she adds with a good-natured laugh.

Prophetically, when asked about the future of LOST IN SPACE, Cartwright replies, "I think it would have happened already if there was a chance. So many people are involved and I guess they can't agree. I know that Billy tried to get something going with a script, but nothing has happened."

What many fans don't remember is that while Cartwright was playing the daughter, Penny, on LOST IN SPACE in 1965, she was also still playing the daughter, Linda, on THE DANNY THOMAS SHOW. THE DANNY THOMAS SHOW was cancelled in 1965 but returned for a full year in September 1970, with Cartwright appearing as the now very much grown up Linda Williams.

Cartwright also appeared in several made for television productions such as MR. & MRS. AND THE MAGIC STUDIO MYSTERY (1969), UMC (1969), SCOUT'S HONOR (1980) and HIGH SCHOOL USA (1983).

BILL MUMY — A BOY AND HIS ROBOT

Not only was Bill Mumy the central focus of one of television's most popular science fiction series, but, as if that wasn't enough, he is also a comic book writer—COMET MAN for Marvel Comics—and a talented musician, playing with Barnes and Barnes. He has even written songs for the group America, and produced the first album of actor/performer Crispin Glover.

All this aside, to LOST IN SPACE fans he will always be known as little Will Robinson.

LOST IN SPACE was launched into TV orbit on September 15, 1965, one year before STAR TREK as well as the year before all network shows went to color. When the black and white first season episodes appear on the screen they serve as a signal to fans twenty-five years later to stay tuned for adventure!

When he began in the show as one of the supporting players, young Billy Mumy was already a veteran of episodic TV. He would later be elevated in importance in stories. Mumy's acting credits include bit roles on such series as PLAYHOUSE 90, DR. KILDARE and PERRY MASON. He had a small role in the TWILIGHT ZONE episode "Walking Distance" and was featured in roles in two others, "In Praise of Pip," and It's a Good Life." When the story for the latter was rewritten and filmed for TWILIGHT ZONE: THE MOVIE, Mumy was included in a cameo appearance. Aside from appearing in such feature films as THE WIZARD OF BAGHDAD and TAMMY TELL ME TRUE, he returned to series television in 1974 for a brief run on the series, SUNSHINE.

Even though twenty-two years have passed since he did his last LOST IN SPACE episode, those days have never entirely been left behind as his fans still recognize him for that widely seen role, just as they do his friend Mark Hamill from STAR WARS.

Mumy's memories from those days are, of course, the recollections of a youngster to whom working on the show was a great adventure. Working at Twentieth Century Fox proved an adventure for him in many ways, and he'd involve his friends and co-stars in these escapades as much as possible.

"For instance," Mumy recalls, "underneath Twentieth Century Fox there are tunnels which go under the whole studio. I discovered these tunnels one day with Angela (Cartwright.) Whenever we had some time off, she, Mark, Marta and I would go exploring, and these are serious tunnels! We're talking way underground with pipes which would go for miles. I don't know what they were built for. They have all of the air conditioning and heating equipment down there. We're talking labyrinths of huge underground systems. I used to love exploring those. It was adventurous, exciting and scary!"

Mumy goes on to describe his days at Fox by talking about his dressing room, which he really loved. "I was the only one who had a stereo in his dressing room. Everybody'd come over; Mark would bring his records, which were by Richie Havens. Marta turned me on to Bob Dylan and The Byrds, which I really thank her for.

"I still have the same friends I had when I was ten years old. I used to bring some of them down to the set, but none of them appeared to really be impressed with what I was doing. Acting and being around weird sets and famous people is something that I've been doing since I was five years old, so my friends were used to it. If you've ever been on a set of any type of show, in reality it's pretty boring. Everybody just sits around while they get the lights right and then you walk through it a bunch of times and everybody has to be quiet. When the bell rings you shoot it and then you're done. It's not like some scored piece of action that you see on television. And sometimes

Showbiz is rough. Sitting through make-up was no picnic. It took many hours. And sometimes explosions were bigger than expected. But all in all it was a fun shoot."

As the first year of LOST IN SPACE progressed and the series started tinkering with the format, certain elements were emphasized while others were de-emphasized. One character who was pushed into the background was Guy Williams, and Mumy admits that Williams couldn't have helped but have been disappointed by that.

"I think that Guy is a really good actor—not in the sense of Dustin Hoffman, but a great leading man adventurer, and I really like what he did in the first season of the show. I really mean that. But he watched his role go from the star of the show to *not* the star of the show. I'm sure it was disappointing for him but he never really made a stick out of it. I'm sure he didn't like the way the show turned. I don't think anybody liked the way the show turned, outside of Jonathan. I didn't like the way the show turned. I much preferred working as part of an ensemble group with everybody else than working mostly with Jonathan and Bob. I thought the show was a thousand times better the first season than any other. I enjoyed the original creation that we did. I thought that when Jonathan came on the show, his character added a lot to it because he was really despicable and a really formidable foe."

Supposedly Jonathan Harris has stated that Billy Mumy himself could be a formidable foe on the set.

"I'm not sure what he meant by that," Mumy wonders, "although by then I was probably secure enough with my place on the show to let my opinions be known that I would have preferred the show to be a little more serious. Let me put it this way: When we did something like 'The Anti-Matter Man,' then I would have said that I thought it was a good show—let's do more like this as opposed to the really silly ones. I don't remember ever giving Jonathan a hard time. Certainly never when we were acting together. I didn't hang out with Jonathan as much as I chose to hang out with Mark, and Marta and Angela, but that seems obvious to me. Here I was, thirteen, and Angela was fourteen and Marta was into Rock 'n Roll.

"I think that Jonathan's a wonderful actor," Mumy continues, "and we're very good friends. He came to

my home just a couple months ago and he's doing a segment in the Barnes & Barnes package we're putting together right now. Obviously the characterization of Smith that he created, and I give him sole credit for that, was a big success and was probably the main reason the show ran as long as it did. The pilot was shot several months before we started working with Jonathan and Bob (May) and I always wanted the show to be like a superhero comic. But it became more of a farce, a spoof and a campy, fantasy thing. My job was to show up, hit my mark and read my lines and do whatever they tell me to do. But as a personal note I enjoyed it more as an adventure show. I

like the first season best. I hate 'The Great Vegetable Rebellion.'"

Still, Mumy does have some favorite directors that he worked with on the show.

"Harry Harris was a wonderfully nice man and I enjoyed working with him very much," the actor recalls. "Maybe he's my favorite. Sobey Martin was a nice guy although I didn't think that he was the world's greatest director. But he was real sweet. So I guess that Harry was my favorite of the regulars."

Since Billy Mumy and Angela Cartwright were the two youngest cast members and so close in age, it was inevitable that they would become good friends. Later, they became more than just good friends.

"It started out as most young relationships start out," Mumy recalls fondly. "I had a crush on Angela from the day I met her, but I forced myself to wait until I was sixteen and had my own car before I did anything about it.

"First of all, there's a big difference between a twelve year old and a fourteen year old and I just had to wait until I was in the kind of position to be taken seriously, and when I did I made my move and I kissed her in a park. We'd been best friends for a long time. We used to go out a lot and I guess there was a certain energy between us, but we never did anything physical about it until five years later. It was a wonderful time in our young lives. I was sixteen and she was seventeen and we were a couple for a few years."

It was the first relationship for either of them and eventually they drifted apart. Today they don't really have very much communication with one another.

"We've just grown apart over the years, but we had a nice relationship together. We were engaged and then we broke up. We spent about six years together, being with each other every day and after we broke up it just wasn't that comfortable any more."

Although LOST IN SPACE was cancelled after its third year, when the season finished shooting, everyone on the show believed that it would be back.

"What I have been told, and which I assume to be the truth, is that we were picked up for a fourth season. But CBS wanted to cut the budget because it was an expensive show. Irwin (Allen) said that he couldn't do it, so CBS said good-bye and Irwin took it to another network, but he couldn't get them to pick it up. We had all been told that we would be back."

When Mumy was notified of the cancellation, it came as quite a shock.

"I was at home with my mom and dad and my agent called and told me. He said, 'that's it, the show's cancelled.' I cried and cried. I'd spent about four years doing the show. It was like a family. It was different from when you make a feature film or a guest shot on a TV show because you always know it's going to

end soon. And if we had known at the end of the third season that that was that, it wouldn't have been so hard because we would have had time to prepare for it. But I was just a little kid and it was a sad time for me."

His love for LOST IN SPACE manifested itself creatively a couple years ago when Bill Mumy and a friend co-wrote a script which would have reunited the cast and presented a final episode. But even though it looked for a while as though it had every chance of being made, it finally hit an immovable obstacle from a surprising direction.

"I had the cast ready to go," Mumy states. "I had CBS ready to go. I had 20th Century Fox ready to go. I co-wrote the script and sent copies of it to everyone in the cast, with the exception of Guy who I didn't know how to find. I got everyone's feedback as to what they would like to see done differently with their characters. I revamped it towards making everyone real happy about their characters and I took the script to Andy Siegel, who at the time was head of movies and television at CBS and he thought it was a great idea. He'd worked on LIS as a production assistant. Andy gave me some suggestions about what I could do to make the script stronger, which we implemented, and got it back to him. He was very happy with it and thought it would make a lot of money and wanted to see it happen.

"I then took it to 20th Century Fox, to the lady who was head of the movies and TV there and she thought it was a natural. There were all these reunion shows being done and they were all making money. LOST IN SPACE was a castaways story which had never been resolved, but we resolved it! The studio was very interested in being a part of it."

Then Mumy called Irwin Allen.

"I had been doing some science fiction conventions solely to see what the fan energy was like out there for the project, and within less than a year they had received 300,000 signatures which were all sent to Irwin Allen. I respect Irwin a lot and I always treated him with respect. I told him that I had this project which I felt was really, really good and that everyone I spoke to was really positive about doing. He told me that if I sent it to him, he wouldn't read it, and that if I tried to discuss it with him, he wouldn't listen. He said that LOST IN SPACE was a castaway story and there were only a handful of plotlines which could be followed. If he ever did one, he said that it would be his own script, his own plot, at a time that he wanted to do it and he didn't want me suing him for using my ideas. I tried to make him understand that I wasn't interested in suing him and that this was not done as a way to get rich. It was done as a total labor of love. I felt that I was close to the project and regardless of what the legal realities were that he was worried about, I assured him that I wasn't interested in infringing on the characters that he created and that no matter what happens, he would need a good script or plot and I felt like I had a great one. He very, very firmly made it clear that he was not the slightest bit interested in anything I had to say. He shut me down so fast and so firmly that I just washed my hands of the whole idea," Mumy explains regretfully.

"I don't want to get hung up on the past and I don't want to have any bitter taste in my mouth about LOST IN SPACE because I had a wonderful time on that show and I care very much for those people that I worked with. So I really don't want to dwell on what could be, but I cannot understand for the life of me why the project has not been done. To me it's a natural. Everybody who's in this business is in it to make money and I don't understand why Mr. Allen chose not to make his project because I know he would have made money. Everybody in the cast looked great and was alive, healthy and ready to get involved in the project. But I just don't want to dwell on that any more. The energy that I put into that epilogue script was really a labor of love because I wanted to be true to the characters. I knew how the cast members felt. It was certainly a nice-ensemble-serious-adventure script—a damn good script.

"I'm not trying to say that I'm the world's greatest script writer," Mumy continues, "but I really think I had a good thing going there. It's a shame that Irwin would not even read it because I assured him that I wasn't interested in infringing on his copyright. I have a great amount of respect for Irwin—he created the show!

"You've got to remember that when it comes to business dealings and stuff like that on the old show that I was still a kid and wasn't really aware of most of the things that were going on. I got there early in the morning and went to school three hours a day. I went to lunch for an hour and I worked all the time. I had quite a heavy workload on LOST IN SPACE. So whatever down time I had was usually spent listening to music or playing with Angela. They had a birthday party for me and Angela every year. I remember that we had a cake. It was very nice of them. I never heard from Irwin after the show was cancelled. I saw him maybe once when I was at 20th Century Fox with Angela. In fact I remember going up to his office when I was seventeen."

Something not remembered by many fans today is that the second season of LOST IN SPACE was on opposite the briefly popular BATMAN series.

"We were on the air before BATMAN and went off after BATMAN, so we were on the air seventeen shows before him and went off about fifteen after he was cancelled," Mumy observes. "BATMAN was the big success but we were around longer."

LOST IN SPACE also had more episodes in its three seasons than STAR TREK did in theirs.

"I won't compare LOST IN SPACE to STAR TREK," Mumy states firmly. "I don't want to get into that. STAR TREK's obviously a much better show in terms of being a serious adventure, but I look at STAR TREK as a military show while I view LOST IN SPACE as mostly a fantasy show. Nonetheless, they have their Tribbles and we have our 'Reluctant Stowaway' episode, so it gets balanced out a little bit. I'm a Trekkie myself and I love that stuff. People think 'C'mon, man, you're not really into that?', but I love STAR TREK and I always did."

Mumy still loves music, which is why he's involved in making melodies with Barnes & Barnes. "My band Barnes & Barnes recently released ZABAGABEE: THE BEST OF BARNES & BARNES on a 45 minute video cassette, CD, audio cassette and LP on Rhino Records. We've co-written and produced the debut album by actor/artist Crispin Glover on Enigma Records, and I wrote for Marvel Comics the graphic novel DREAMWALKER, as well as THE COMET MAN, SPIDER-MAN, HULK, IRON MAN, etc."

He sees his old co-stars on occasion.

Bill Mumy with the robot and Mike Clark, who wrote the episode guide for the LOST IN SPACE 25th ANNIVERSARY TRIBUTE.

JONATHAN HARRIS—TWIRLING MOUSTACHE

"Special Guest Star" is a term that Jonathan Harris invented. It is used today on television shows and features to give special credit. The Dr. Smith character became a key role for the series, and owes much to Harris's hard work.

Before he was lost in space, Harris co-starred with Michael Rennie in THE THIRD MAN, a popular TV series in the Fifties. Around that same time he was featured in the motion pictures THE BIG FISHERMAN and BOTANY BAY. Just prior to LOST IN SPACE he played the long-suffering hotel manager for THE BILL DANA SHOW. Then came LOST IN SPACE.

"As nearly as I can remember," Harris recalls, "my agent rang up and said that Irwin Allen wanted to see me and was doing a series. I went to see him and we chatted for a moment. The person who was in charge of casting for the show was there at the time. As I remember, Irwin said, 'Make a deal with him.' That was it. It later turned out that they had already made a pilot in which my part didn't exist. After the pilot CBS decided they needed an actor who could play a villain, so to speak. They sent for me and the rest is history!"

All these years later, Harris still has fond memories of the series.

"I think it was a very good show of its kind," he observes. "It was very creatively written. We did 83 episodes and I think that of the 83 we surely had 30 wonderful scripts—that's a damn good average. Then maybe 20 very good ones and a small number of duds. But we had a good record of creative ones, of imaginative ones, and I think that's marvelous. I very much enjoyed doing the really creative ones. They took us far afield and we were able to introduce new points of view. We did adventure and fantasy. As soon as I hit on the happy idea of comedic villainy, I think that helped us tremendously. I think that deep, dark villainy in a television series is not very palatable—not week-to-week. People would get bored. Comedic villainy has great longevity. A comedic villain, on one hand, you want to kill. So many times in all parts of the world I had it said to me that, 'Oh, I wanted to hit you,' but the next minute they always add, 'Then I thought I'd give you a kiss,' which is perfect. That is exactly what the reaction is.

"Dr. Smith was into everything," Harris continues. "He was devious, a coward, a sneak and yet I considered him adorable. The audience felt the same way. He was a wicked man but he had comedic overtones so you could hate him one minute and kiss him on the nose the next. That's what I designed. That was his charm. Smith adjusted to whatever was going on at any given time. He was not so much interested in whether he was telling the truth, he was interested in adjusting to any particular situation. If the situation arose where he and Major West were entombed (it happened in 'Space Primevals'), and the end was near, he would make his peace with anyone. But the moment the situation changed, he would go back to doing what he always did. His meetings with aliens were the same way. He would make a quick adjustment to the situation which had nothing to do with the truth or anything else. He was a survivor. He would do anything, but he would survive."

When asked to reflect on what his best acting work has been, Harris replies, "Such a difficult question for the actor to answer. Of course I admired Zachary Smith. I thought he was one of my best creations and a very full character of many facets. There have been other things I did which I liked. It seems to me that as far as series are concerned, the one I'm doing at any given time is the one I liked the best.

"I think that the man I created in my first series, THE THIRD MAN with Michael Rennie, was a most interesting character. He was called Bradford

Webster and I deduced he was a true eccentric. He always wore the same suit and kept his watch only at New York time. It was not unusual for him to have breakfast in Afghanistan at five P.M. because his watch said 7 A.M. I found him tremendously interesting and exciting. That was in 1958.

"There were also isolated guest shots I really enjoyed," the actor adds. "I remember once doing a BONANZA in which I played Charles Dickens on a mythical visit to Virginia City and it was a great pleasure doing him. He was really a full blown, well rounded character and was well written. I make it a point to take joy in what I play or I won't play it at all. I think it shows up on the screen and I don't like apologies on the screen: 'Well, I took this part for the money.' Of course we all work for the money, but I really do try, for the most part, to succeed in having a good time whenever I'm acting. I like playing strange, eccentric characters—they are so interesting! I love doing villains, heavies. It is true, that in these parts you don't get the girl because you already killed the girl in the preceding scene, and what a scene it was!"

Dr. Smith is not the only science fiction character that Jonathan Harris has played. He also starred as Commander Gampu on SPACE ACADEMY.

"That was a departure. A kind, decent man, 300 years old! I did have a chance to explore the comedic aspect of my theatrical nature. One was called 'My Favorite Marsha'. I did that with Dena Detrich, who is a marvelous actress. Dena played Marsha and, in the script, we apparently had a romantic fling years ago and she turned up again on this particular planet. Great fun for both of us. Then, years later, there was a very serious story in which I threatened to resign my commission because I was 300 years old. That was beautiful."

In describing what those halcyon days on LOST IN SPACE were like, Harris recalls that, "A typical day was arriving at the studio at seven o'clock, having gotten up at five. Then in the make-up chair at seven fifteen, having the eyes propped up with toothpicks so that the dear make-up man could do something about them.

"The first shot was at eight o'clock. I was usually in it. I would generally work until twelve thirty or a quarter to one. Then lunch—one hour. If you're a professional actor, you come back in a shorter time so you can go to makeup to get done up again. Then you resume with a little less energy because I find that lunch is always a mistake. I'd rather go right through without having lunch because my energy seems to sag after lunch, a common complaint among actors. Then you work until six, seven, eight or nine. We generally did about twelve pages a day, which is an awful lot, and one must keep one's energy up and one's wits about them.

"There were always problems which arose during filming," Harris continues. "Some of the things we did were very involved. We frequently had wars be

tween aliens which involved explosions and that takes a great deal of time and care to set up.

"We had a genius named Stu Moody—I will never forget him. He was originally a college professor who went into special effects. These were carefully designed to protect the actors so they wouldn't get hurt or killed. It would take hours, and you can imagine what that costs! We had a running bit, Stu and I, when he announced that the scene was ready to be shot. I would always say, 'Moody, is this going to hurt me?' and he would always say, 'You bet!' Then I knew I was safe. There was a degree of tension, you see, because if it mis-exploded it would have to be re-rigged. Moody was awfully good.

"I love actors and I love what I do, but I think the true genius of movies is the effects, the make-up men, the technicians—the Stu Moody's. That's the genius. In LOST IN SPACE I remember they had to make a death mask of me so that everyone in the show could wear it. Billy Mumy wore one and so did many other people in the show. (Note: it happened in 'Space Destructors.') Of course they had to make the mold for the mask on my face. An extraordinary makeup man named John Chambers, who did PLANET OF THE APES, made the plaster mask. I am very claustrophobic and I hate to be enclosed, so it was agonizing for me to lie still in the makeup chair while they poured the plaster. I hated it, but John was so kind and constantly reassuring that I was perfectly safe. From that one mold he made all the masks. They gave me one to keep in a plastic case, but I'll be damned if I know where it is now. I think it crumbled with time. I kept it on a stand in the plastic case and visitors used to shriek because it really looked like me."

Harris says that he doesn't really have very many souvenirs of his work in film (both TV and movies.) "No, I had a pair of boots. I don't know how I got those. I used them for gardening. I have every script from my work on Broadway, but nothing from television. It would be impossible to store all of them as I just finished my 610th film. I have no real interest in saving them—when I finish a job I am done with it. I've done eight series, BATTLESTAR GALACTICA being my eighth. I have fond memories of all of them, but to save scripts holds no interest for me."

Jonathan Harris also has fond memories of people he worked with on the series, such as the script continuity person, Helen Parker. "One of the old timers," Harris recalls. "I don't know how they do their work. They are so wonderful. They keep their nose in the script and yet they notice everything you've done, exactly how you raised your hand when you said something, and where you crossed your legs. The whole thing is written down. It is extraordinary. It takes tremendous training. She was a great lady and a great pro— and still is. When I did an episode of VEGA$, Helen was the script lady and it was so good to see her."

Harris can always tell when LOST IN SPACE is going through a new re-run cycle somewhere because a new tide of mail starts coming in, "From a whole new generation of watchers, which delights me, I must say. Many of them are the children of the original viewers. The letters range from mature adults to kids who are having the time of their lives. They say lovely things like: 'My folks used to watch this and now they are watching it again with me .' The letter writers very often say how much they would like LOST IN SPACE to be redone and I refer them to Irwin Allen. Mostly they single out what I did and how much they hated me and loved me and my relationship with the robot. I thought that was rather unique to begin with and I dreamed up a lot of it myself. You may remember the alliteratives that I used to call him: Bumbling Booby, Neanderthal Ninny. I used to lie awake all night dreaming all this up. I had over a hundred of them. They were great fun.

"The fans ask many interesting questions, and I have always tried to answer them. It pleases me to get so much mail. It's nice to know that somebody out there is watching. You play in front of a black box and from time to time you wonder, 'Is there anybody watching? Is there anybody out there?' But there are people out there, all over the world. I have heard LOST IN SPACE dubbed in Spanish, Portuguese, Finnish, Swedish, Italian, French, Japanese and Thai. I receive mail from all over the world and I appreciate it.

"I was in Rio de Janeiro at a film festival for 20th Century Fox, and while there I was asked to go to Sao Paulo in Brazil and do a television interview. Before I went on they asked me whether I would like to see a bit of LOST IN SPACE with Portuguese dubbing. I did and it seemed to me that the man who was doing me really caught the flavor of Dr. Smith. He was a very good actor and I was just delighted. Then I went on the air and out came the man who had done the dubbing. He was very emotional and close to tears. We embraced and he said in Portuguese that he had dubbed Charles Laughton and Edward G. Robinson, but his greatest honor was dubbing Jonathan Harris. So we embraced again and cried a little bit and it was marvelous. Then of course I told him something that I really believed, that of all the dubbing I heard, he was the best. He was a lovely actor and it was quite obvious that he knew what he was doing. He was fulfilling the part, and that was very exciting."

When LOST IN SPACE was cancelled, it actually came as a surprise to the cast, and Harris still isn't actually sure what the reasons were for what he still regards as a premature demise.

"The network in its infinite wisdom cancels things. I think it was a mistake and that we had another year or two. From my own selfish point of view, I wish we had gone another year.

"But maybe it is just as well," Harris adds, looking at it from another point of view. "When you make an impact in a series, such as I did in LOST IN SPACE, you pay for it. This has nothing to do with modesty, this is the way it is. In the years to come, the audience tends to identify you only as Doctor Smith and you don't want to break their hearts by admitting that you have another name. When you are a character actor, people tend to remember the character you played rather than what your name is. It's something we all live with and it is okay. But if you make a strong impact, for years not only the audience but the industry decides that that's who you are and it costs you work."

Harris is surprised, though, at the longevity of the show in syndication. "I never thought that this would go on forever. I've been in show business for too many years to think that anything is forever. I know as soon as I start doing anything that one day quite soon it is going to close. I was brought up in the theatre, as I told you, and no matter how good the play was (and I was in wonderful plays that ran two and a half years) I knew that closing night was approaching. And so, with a series as well."

When asked to single out memorable episodes, Harris replies, "Favorite episodes, oh dear, it is hard to remember. One I particularly remember is called 'Cave of the Wizards.' I remember that because it involved a crazy makeup and costume. It also gave me a chance to really exercise the craft, so to speak. I had to find a tomb-like voice totally unlike my own, and I had to be a brand new character totally unlike Dr. Smith. I think all of it worked. I was pleased with the result.

"'His Majesty Smith,' I remember, was very fine and interesting. I haven't seen the show for years—I'd like to now."

Jonathan Harris with Bill Mumy, courageous as always.

Two Men and a Robot

The cast of LOST IN SPACE wasn't just humans. There was also the robot, perhaps the most humane and popular character in the series.

The original pilot didn't feature what was to become the series' most unique and popular character. But when Dr. Smith came on board, the robot was there to be his handy tool to undo the Robinsons' best laid plans to reach Alpha Centauri, the nearest star to our solar system. Their trip was cut short and they wound up in an unknown star system.

The robot was actually two men. Just like Robby the Robot in Forbidden Planet, upon which the LIS robot was obviously based, there was a man inside operating the robot with the voice later dubbed when the episode was edited. The men behind the robot were Bob May and Dick Tufeld.

The man who trudged around inside that "ridiculous rust pile," as Dr. Smith might have called him, is Bob May.

"I was at 20th Century Fox with Gordon Douglas and Red Buttons," May recalls, remembering the circumstances that led to his three year anonymous guest starring role. "I was there to work a deal with them for the picture STAGECOACH, which was the second re-make of that story. They wanted me to stunt-double Red Buttons. But I was called by the casting man on LOST IN SPACE asking me if I'd be interested in coming up and speaking to Irwin Allen for a show he was doing, a possible series, and I said I'd be glad to.

"I went up to Irwin's office and he remembered that I did a VOYAGE TO THE BOTTOM OF THE SEA. He told me that he was starting a new series and asked me if I would be interested in playing a robot. The next step was whether or not I would fit the suit which had already been made. They also needed someone who was strong because of the strenuous activities of the robot on an action show like this. But nobody really knew what the robot was going to be doing, so they wanted to be ready for anything. Irwin said that if I wasn't already signed for STAGECOACH he'd love to have me, so I went down and talked to Red Buttons and Gordon Douglas and Red said, 'Take it for God's sake!' and I said "Great!'"

So May went over to the prop shop, tried on the outfit and it fit fine. Allen came down and saw May with the Robot's designer, Bob Kinoshita, and said he had the series.

"It was weird because I was going out for a Western and I ended up in space!"

When he first joined the show, much of the labor of being a robot rested on May's broad shoulders.

"It was really an experimental time because they didn't have cables to pull the robot along with yet or an arrangement where I just carried the top section such as I did later on. I actually had to walk in that suit. It was tough. When they developed the cable which pulled me around it was much easier."

Since the robot's voice was dubbed in later, May would say the lines on the set to the actors while operating the panel lights from inside the suit. He also had other tricks, such as being able to make the robot's upper torso swing around.

"That's a secret that helped me to keep my job," he laughs. "I never told anyone how I did that, but I guess that now would be a good time. What I actually did was to turn my body as far as I could by leaving the arms out of the suit. Centrifugal force would keep them up as I'd spin the robot's body, but you still have to be strong to do it."

What wasn't so funny was the time May was in the full suit and it fell over.

"I didn't want to use the full outfit that time, just the top section, but Jerry (Nathan) Juran, the director of that episode, wanted me to use the full outfit because of the angle that the camera was being set up for. I thought it was a little too dangerous because there were so many of the cast near me as I was going up the ramp to the main hatch of the ship. Anyway, I was going up the ramp and one of the cast stepped on my power cable (which operated all of the lights on the robot). When they stepped off, the slack had to be taken up, and when it came up, I was just near the top of the ramp and it flipped me over. On a diving scale it would have been a ten!! I was out cold and the next thing I remember was June Lockhart cuddling me in her arms at the bottom of the ramp. They brought the paramedics there and Irwin came down to see if I was all right. I was pretty shook up and I remember June asking if I was all right. Sometimes strange things go through your mind, and you have to understand that I was not on a series contract at that point, but on week-to-week. So the first words out of my mouth were, 'Is the robot suit all right?' June said not to worry about it, but I was thinking, my god, if it's wrecked I'm out of a job!"

May's favorite LIS episode is "Junkyard in Space," the last episode of the series.

"There was a very emotional scene between the robot and Will Robinson at the conveyor belt when the robot was going to do himself in to help the family."

May says that he'd love to do LOST IN SPACE again if it was somehow ever brought back.

Dick Tufeld, the voice of the robot, met Irwin Allen years and years before LOST IN SPACE was even a glimmer in Allen's eye. Tufeld was eighteen and attending Northwestern University in Chicago.

"My home was in Los Angeles and I came back home one summer and got a job at KLAC radio working summer relief as an announcer. Part of our duties was to spin records and be engineers at the station. There was a guy there who had a Hollywood gossip type show and that was Irwin Allen! I used to spin his theme music and announce the opening of the show and that's when I first met him. He must have been in his late twenties then."

Years later their paths crossed again.

"I had a good friend named Emmet Lavery who was working in the business affairs department at 20th Century Fox. He knew Irwin and they were talking one day and Irwin mentioned to him that he was looking for a narrator for his new series, LOST IN

SPACE. Emmet suggested me and I think that Irwin vaguely remembered me. I was working at ABC at the time, but that's how I got called in for the show."

After trying out for the narrator, and being accepted for that position, Tufeld then tried out for the voice of the robot. Interestingly enough, Tufeld had also been the narrator on Guy Williams' previous TV series, ZORRO.

"After the first episode of LOST IN SPACE was being put together I got a call from my agent and he said that there was a robot character on the show now and Irwin was looking for a voice for it. I guess he wasn't satisfied with Bob May, who was inside the robot, so

he said that he'd like me to read for it. I showed up at the scheduled time at Fox, in one of the audio rooms, and I remember the first thing I said to Irwin was, 'This is a robot, so I presume what you're looking for is a kind of mechanical, robotian kind of sound?' Irwin recoiled and looked at me with horror and said, 'My dear boy, that is precisely and exactly what I do not want. What we have here is a very advanced, civilized culture and what I want is a low key, laid back Alexander Scourby kind of approach.' Well, that was a great New York narrator and actor who has since passed away and who did many wonderful documentary narrations and who was very cultured and laid back. So I started reading for him dong my best Alexander Scourby kind of imitation and he would say 'No, you're not getting it, try again.' After about ten minutes Irwin said, 'Well, this is not working. I appreciate your coming in, but you're still the narrator on the show and we'll see you later.' So I said, 'Irwin, let me try one more thing for you,' and I said something like 'WARNING! WARNING! DANGER! IT WILL NOT COMPUTE!' in my best mechanical, robotian kind of sound and Irwin said, 'My God! That's that Alexander Scourby approach I wanted! What the hell took you so long?' Honest, I had to turn away from him because I was afraid I was going to laugh in his face, and I couldn't have explained what I was laughing about! Like all of us, Irwin said what he wanted, but what he really wanted was what sounded right to his ear. He described what he wanted, but when I gave it to him it didn't sound right to his ear. When he heard a kind of mechanical robot sound, that sounded right in spite of what he said to me."

Since Dick Tufeld dubbed the robot's lines in later, he seldom saw the actors and came in after all of the footage for an episode had been filmed. Tufeld would match the recitation Bob May, while inside the robot suit, had said while pressing a button to light the robot's head in sync with each syllable he spoke.

"I always felt that what I did was not creative at all," Tufeld explains. "It was strictly a mechanical kind of a job in that what they did was make loops of Bob May's lines, a loop being one sentence, or maybe two sentences at a time. They showed me the picture and they would run Bob May's loop which belonged in that spot in the picture. I would have an earphone and I would hear Bob May's lines. What I had to do was be in exact sync with his lines. If I was in sync with his lines, I was therefore automatically in sync with the lights. I had anywhere from sixty to two hundred loops per show, depending on the show. But that's the way it worked. That's why I say I never considered anything that I did very creative on that show. The sound was certainly different. I had whatever sound I had, but in terms of speed, tempo, and that kind of thing, I had to read it exactly as May had uttered the line. I got pretty good at it after awhile as I got used to May's phraseology and the way he did things, so we did all the looping for a show in a rather short period, anywhere from 45 minutes to an hour and a half. Maybe two hours if I had a lot of lines."

And yet it was the voice which gave the robot the extra polish of personality.

The robot, perhaps the most human character. Bob May stood inside while Dick Tufeld provided the voice.

SEASON THREE

Introduction by Paul Monroe

LOST IN SPACE returned for its third season on September 6, 1967 with a new theme song, a new piece of equipment, new outfits, a smaller budget, and plans to "share" the scripts among the cast. During year two, Dr. Smith, Will, the robot and, to a lesser degree, Penny, had been at the center of almost every story while the rest of the cast delivered, at times, little more than cameo appearances. When Irwin Allen was finally approached by the "credited" leads concerning their minimal involvement, he promised the new season's stories would focus on a different character, or set of characters, each week. Indeed, the season's first episodes did, for the most part, involve everyone, and much of the drama that had been lost after the first year returned.

The animated credits were replaced with a new sequence of live-action clips of the cast from various third season episodes. Each episode's teaser would freeze-frame in a 7 to 1 countdown leading into an exciting, new theme song by a young John Williams. And yes, Jonathan Harris was still being billed as the "Special Guest Star" even after two full seasons. Gone, too, were the cliffhanger endings, dropped in favor of a preview of the next week's story narrated by Dick Tufeld.

A new vehicle called the Space Pod was also introduced in year three and was used frequently throughout the rest of the series. This one- or two-man craft, which greatly resembled NASA's Lunar Excursion Module, was capable of leaving the orbiting Jupiter II via a hatch on the bottom of the ship and landing on a planet either manually or remotely. The Jupiter's upper deck hatch located between the elevator and the freezing tubes was fitted with a window and now served as access to the Pod. No explanation of the Pod's sudden existence was ever given.

Highlights in the third season included returning to the Earth of 1947 in "A Visit To A Hostile Planet" which featured beautiful outdoor shots of the full Jupiter II mock-up, Guy Williams and Mark Goddard taking double roles as John, Don and their evil counterparts from a parallel universe in "The Anti-Matter Man," and Dr. Smith traveling to Earth on the night of the Jupiter's launch in "The Time Merchant." The last included footage from the pilot and "The Reluctant Stowaway," and an emotionless, monotone voiced robot reminiscent of the series' early episodes.

Unfortunately, this resurgence of more serious stories and a better use of the cast didn't last long. The character of Dr. Smith had been so outlandishly portrayed throughout the second season that it was now difficult to put him into any serious situations. Thus the latter half of year three slipped back into the Smith/Will/robot format. By June of 1968, the ratings had fallen lower than ever before, and it was hard to believe that this series had begun so seriously only two seasons before.

CAST AND CREDITS

CREATED AND PRODUCED BY: Irwin Allen
STORY EDITOR: Anthony Wilson
ASSOCIATE PRODUCER: William Faralla
MUSIC SUPERVISION: Lionel Newman
PRODUCTION SUPERVISOR: Jack Sonntag
PRODUCTION ASSOCIATE: Hal Herman
UNIT PRODUCTION MANAGER: Ted Butcher
DIRECTOR OF PHOTOGRAPHY: Frank Carson, A.S.C.
ART DIRECTORS: Jack Martin Smith, Roger Maus
SET DECORATORS: Walter M. Scott, James Hassinger
COSTUME DESIGNER: Paul Zastupnevich
SPECIAL PHOTOGRAPHIC EFFECTS: L.B. Abbott, A.S.C.
MAKE-UP SUPERVISION: Ben Nye
SUPERVISING SOUND EFFECTS EDITOR: Don Hall, Jr.
SOUND EFFECTS EDITOR: Robert Cornett
THEME: Johnny Williams
EXECUTIVE IN CHARGE OF PRODUCTION FOR VAN BERNARD:
Guy Della Cioppa

AN IRWIN ALLEN PRODUCTION IN ASSOCIATION WITH
Jodi Productions, Inc.
Van Bernard Productions, Inc.
Twentieth Century Fox Television, Inc.
CBS Television Network

IN CHARGE OF STUDIO PRODUCTION: William Self

EPISODE SIXTY:
"Condemned Of Space"

First telecast September 6, 1967
Writer: Peter Packer
Director: Nathan Juran
GUEST STAR: PHANZIG: Marcel Hillaire

The Jupiter II has finally been fully repaired and refueled and can take off soon. Their launch plans have to be accelerated, though, when the robot announces that a comet is approaching the planet on a collision course. The Robinsons prepare for an emergency take-off and launch just in time, leaving the planet just before it is destroyed by the comet.

The gravitational pull of the comet pulls it towards it, but the Jupiter II is able to avoid a collision and bypasses it.

As the Jupiter II resumes its course through space it detects an approaching supernova.

Amid all the confusion, Dr. Smith manages to accidentally eject the robot into space so that John Robinson has to make a spacewalk in order to retrieve it, but he's unable to recover the robot.

The Jupiter II is caught in the gravity pull of the supernova and even by overloading the engines their spacecraft cannot blast free of its influence. The ship is pulled into a void and manages to safely rendezvous with a space station.

While they are discussing what to do next, there is a knock at the door. It turns out to be the robot, which was pulled into the void on the same course as the Jupiter II.

Since the lower hatch of the Jupiter II is aligned with an entrance to the space station, John and Major West elect to go below in an attempt to get needed equipment for the Jupiter II.

The space station is filled with people in stasis tubes, frozen in suspended animation. It turns out that this is a prison ship where the inmates are to be freed after they have served their time. But the automatic clock on the vessel is inoperative so none of the inmates will ever be freed.

When they free one of the prisoners in hope of getting some useful information, he attacks them until they can ward him off and the robot is able to place the man in his stasis tube again.

Accompanying the robot to the station's control room, John and Major West find the spare parts they need for their ship.

Back aboard the Jupiter II, the robot reveals that there is a robot guard below in the prison ship, so Will and Smith go to warn John and Major West.

The robot explains that there are 9,874 prisoners aboard and Smith decides to release one who appears harmless enough. The prisoner, Phanzig, grabs Smith and holds him back because to step off the platform they're on would alert the guard-rob which would track the freed prisoner down again.

Phanzig shoves Smith into his stasis tube to replace him and then flees. But Smith gets off the platform and an alarm sounds.

The guard-rob encounters Major West first and immediately assumes that this must be the escaped prisoner and so freezes him.

When Phanzig runs into Smith again, the cowering Dr. Smith offers to help the prisoner escape aboard the Jupiter II. But when Smith reveals that the prison ship's clock has malfunctioned, Phanzig decides to stage a revolt.

The guard-rob takes Major West to the control room where the ship's computer mind accuses Major West of being Phanzig and freezes him again when Don attempts to deny the charge.

John and Will arrive in time to free Major West, but by this time Phanzig has freed other prisoners and staged his riot. The prisoners storm the control room to destroy the clock, but John gets them to hold off until he sees whether he can repair it.

John succeeds and the clock is reset. The master computer then announces that all of the prisoners have served their allotted time. The vessel, named the Vera Castle, will now transport all the former prisoners to their homeworld, Vera, where they'll be granted chances to start over again.

The Robinsons, Major West, Smith and the robot return to the Jupiter II where they can make their needed repairs with the spare parts they picked up and can resume their journey to attempt to return to Earth.

New uniforms are introduced for the Robinsons, West and Dr. Smith.
Plus, the Astrogator's spinning pendulum is now painted with a yellow curved pattern.
The comet effect used in this episode is borrowed from THE TIME TUNNEL.
The color stock footage of the Jupiter II take off is from the pilot, only it's run backwards to make it appear that the ship is leaving the planet.
But this episode also has the first new Jupiter II space footage shot since the second season.
Robby the Robot appears again in this episode.
Marcel Hillaire appears in this episode for the first time, but we'll see her again in the near future.

EPISODE SIXTY-ONE:
"Visit To A Hostile Planet"
First telecast September 13, 1967
Writer: Peter Packer
Director: Sobey Martin
Incidental Music: Cyril Mockridge
GUEST STARS: CRAGMIRE: Robert Foulk, GROVER: Pitt Herbert, STACEY: Clair Wilcox, CHARLIE: Norman Leavitt, CRAIG: Robert Pine

The Jupiter II is still traveling through space when the Robinsons discover impurities in the reserve fuel system. They decide to test the systems to see what problems this may cause when full power locks in and the thrust builds uncontrollably until the ship exceeds the speed of light.

Everyone aboard collapses from the shock of exceeding light speed, but when they awaken they find that the Jupiter II has apparently traversed a space-time vortex as the ship is approaching Earth.

John and Major West begin to prepare the ship for re-entry, but when they attempt to raise Alpha Control on the radio they receive no reply. The Jupiter II lands in the parking lot of a sawmill and they all split up to look for someone to contact as the place appears deserted.

Maureen, Penny and Judy enter a building where they find an old style telephone, but they can't call anyone on it and there's no one in the building.

John and Major West find an antique car which has a 1947 Michigan license plate on it. The car looks like it's in new condition and has a working radio in it.

Upon switching the radio on they pick up a news bulletin concerning a UFO sighted over Manitou Junction, and the report states that the spacecraft has landed in the parking lot of a sawmill. But according to the radio, the time is October 1947. They have apparently landed on Earth fifty years in the past.

In the parking lot by the saw mill, two locals named Charlie and Grover arrive, carrying guns. Grover reads science fiction stories and has decided that the people in the Jupiter II are just like the Voltons he's been reading about in one of his magazines.

Grover and Charlie prepare to arrest Will and Smith as dangerous alien invaders when the approach of the robot frightens them off. They try to blast the robot with their guns but it stuns the men with its electric bolts.

Everyone returns to the Jupiter II where Major West explains that they have to repair the inertial guidance systems before they can lift off. Although the repairs will take all night he's certain they'll be able to lift off by morning.

Dr. Smith has decided that with what he knows about future events he'd be able to profit handsomely by staying in the past, and perhaps even rule the world. But the Robinsons and Major West are determined to return to their own time.

Meanwhile, the deputy mayor, Captain Cragmire, forms a posse to capture the aliens.

Dr. Smith leaves the Jupiter II, determined to stay in the past, but Will and the robot follow him to try to talk him out of it. But Smith masquerades as the fire chief and when he sees Will and the robot he does his "civic duty" and turns them over to the mayor, deactivating the robot's power pack to keep it from making trouble.

Smith tells the townspeople that he's just arrived from out of town to help them, and his turning over of two of the aliens seems to back him up.

Judy is out picking apples when Craig, a young man who's a member of the posse, captures here. But John and Major West rescue her and tell Craig that they want Will returned, or else they'll level the town!

Will has been tied up in a barn when he's befriended by a young girl named Stacey. Smith wants Will to stay with him because he's lonely. When Smith goes off to lead the posse in a raid on the aliens he leaves the robot's power pack behind.

Will manages to get the power pack back on the robot and reactivate it so that the robot can release him.

Meanwhile the posse has dragged the cannon from the town square to the Jupiter II and sets it up, threatening to fire it at the Jupiter II if the aliens don't surrender.

Stacey likes Will and helps him get away by disguising him as a local boy, while the robot is made up to look like a mobile scarecrow.

The townspeople gather outside the ship and John goes outside in an attempt to reason with them, but they won't listen and instead they take him prisoner. Using John as a hostage, Smith forces the rest of the crew of the Jupiter II to surrender.

Captain Cragmire is preparing to fire the cannon and destroy the Jupiter II when Will comes running up. Will tells Dr. Smith that he'll remain on Earth with Smith if he lets the rest of them go. Smith agrees, but the deputy mayor doesn't agree and he fires the cannon, or should I say misfires it. The Jupiter II is untouched by the attack.

In the confusion, John grabs his laser back and holds the townspeople at bay so that the Robinsons can re-board their ship. At the last minute, Smith decides to board as well rather than be left behind with no friends. The Jupiter II lifts off, its mission to return to the future. It succeeds, but they are now far from Earth.

More new Jupiter II effects, including the descent into the planet's atmosphere and return to space. There's also rarely seen footage of the Jupiter II flying across a cloudy sky.

This episode has rare use of the full-size Jupiter II mock-up, including the landing gear.

Story influence:"Return From Outer Space."

EPISODE SIXTY-TWO:
"Kidnapped In Space"

First telecast September 20, 1967
Writer: Robert Hamner
Director: Don Richardson
GUEST STARS: 764: Grant Sullivan, 1220: Carol Williams, YOUNG SMITH: Joey Russo

A communications signal is received by the Jupiter II from a robot ship. The appeal for medical help is heard only by Will and Dr. Smith, and it comes from a Xenian Interspace Probe, and in particular android 764. The android's assistant is a female android, 1220.

The androids offer a reward for assistance, which piques Smith's interest. Smith enters an escape pod, determined to secure that reward. The robot attempts to halt Dr. Smith unauthorized use of the pod, but the robot's efforts and Smith resistance only result in the pod's accidental launch.

The pod is snatched up by a magnetic grapple from the Xenian ship which brings them aboard, where 764 and 1220 are on hand to greet them. Now Smith discovers that the nature of the medical emergency is that the leader of the androids needs brain surgery, and unless Smith performs it, they'll destroy him.

John and the others have finally noticed the missing Dr. Smith and the robot, as well as the missing escape pod. So the Jupiter II reverses course to try and pick up where the pod could have gone.

As the Jupiter II approaches the Xenian ship, the tractor beam grabs the ship and pulls it in. John and Major West exit the Jupiter II to discover where they are and what's happening, whereupon they are immediately taken captive by the androids.

In the meantime, Dr. Smith has been pretending that he knows how to perform brain surgery and has been preparing himself for the operation on the android's leader. Smith keeps stalling but is finally taken to his patient, which turns out to be a massive computer brain which, when repaired, plans to launch a conquest of the universe. The androids are all linked up to the computer and need it to function. Smith's bluff ends when it becomes obvious that he can't do anything to repair the computer brain.

But the robot does have the knowledge to repair the machine, but it refuses to do so because of the evil purpose his work would be put to.

Dr. Smith is ushered away and thrown into the same cell containing John and Major West, who demand to know what's happening.

Meanwhile, the androids sneak aboard the Jupiter II in order to find someone to hold as hostage to make the robot repair their master. They encounter Will and are trying to drag him off when Maureen is awakened by the disturbance and confronts the androids with a laser pistol. Android 764 reacts by activating a device it has which casts a green aura around Maureen. This causes Maureen to do everything backwards so that she returns to her quarters and goes back to sleep.

Will is taken to the robot, where the androids threaten to kill the boy unless the robot performs the operation on their leader.

--Will is put in the same cell with his father, where John and Major West soon manage a successful subterfuge to escape. But in so doing, John is fatally wounded. Using the android's time-reversal ray, Will is able to bring his father back to life.

Smith takes the device and turns it on himself, whereupon he becomes a nine year old boy.

Making their way to the main brain room, they find that the robot has finished repairing the android brain. The mechanical brain has been repaired and the androids are pursuing their prisoners.

Will pulls a control panel from the master brain which causes the androids to all freeze. The brain has indeed been repaired, though. In fact it isn't evil any longer. It restores Smith to normal and allows the humans to return to the Jupiter II and leave in peace.

This episode introduces the Space Pod, but doesn't explain where it's been hiding for the past two seasons.
Story influence:"Wreck Of The Robot."

EPISODE SIXTY-THREE:
"Hunter's Moon"
First telecast September 27, 1967
Writer: Jack Turley
Director: Don Richardson
GUEST STAR: MEGAZOR: Vincent Beck

The Jupiter II is undergoing problems with its propulsion system which must be repaired soon, but the repairs must be made soon and they can't be accomplished in space.

When a planet is detected nearby, John and the robot go to investigate it in one of the escape pods to search for a suitable place to land the Jupiter II. The escape pod passes through a force shield and lands on the planet without further incident.

But upon emerging from the pod, a hairy monster attacks them, and John is forced to slay it with his laser. Then a blue humanoid appears, proclaiming that his is a private hunting preserve and that John is poaching on it. The blue humanoid is named Megazor and he's destined to be the ruler of the planet Zarn. The creature John slew was one which Zarn had been hunting himself.

Zarn has his retainers bring John and the robot to an encampment where there are other strange creatures in cages. Because Zarn lost points due to John's interference, he plans to punish him. The hunters accumulate points. The winner needs 500 to be named king, but Zarn only has 50 so far.

Meanwhile, on the Jupiter II, when they can't establish communications with the escape pod, Major West decides to follow its path down to the planet's surface. But Dr. Smith panics and his interference causes the Jupiter II to crash land.

Don and Will go off to search for John, but they don't get far before they're attacked by a rock creature. They're saved by one of Megazor's guards, but he then takes the two before his master.

John's punishment is that he must battle an Invisio—an invisible creature against which he is given only a spear to defend himself. But John uses his head and by having the robot issue a cloud of steam, he's able to see where the Invisio is and slay it.

Now the hunting computer registers John Robinson as a target in the game worth 150 points. Now Megazor plans to hunt John to boost his score.

There are specific rules when a hunt begins. It lasts only one hour and both the hunter and his quarry are allowed one weapon each. The prey is given a five minute lead.

John is given his choice of weapons while Megazor prepares for the hunt. But John doesn't wait for the hunt to begin. Using a gas gun, his chosen weapon for the hunt, he knocks out his guard and then frees Don, Will and Smith. Unfortunately, Smith is recaptured due to his own stupidity.

Megazor is furious at the turn of events but feels that Smith is a valuable captive that he'll be able to use in John Robinson's place. When John learns of this, he surrenders in order to save Smith's miserable life. When Will tries to talk Megazor out of hunting his father, Will is taken captive as well by the single-minded hunter. Megazor reveals that he doesn't know who his parents were as he was raised in an incubator, and thus has no concept of familial love or other gentle human emotions such as compassion.

The hunt starts as it was originally planned to, with John wearing a protective suit. He can't even return to the escape pod as the area around it has been mined. The only alternative he feels that he has is to try to outrun Megazor for the allotted time of the hunt.

Megazor's weapon of choice is a Zarb destructor blade, a device shaped like a shield which shoots spinning discs with blades on the edge.

John's protective suit is ruined by a defect in it and then he tumbles into a quicksand pit. John escapes and when Megazor moves in to finish the hunt, John tricks him and knocks the hunter out.

As winner of the hunt, the game computer offers John a chance to try for the throne as well, but he refuses. He sees to it that Dr. Smith is released so that they can return to the Jupiter II to begin repairs on the propulsion system.

This episode makes extensive use of Fox's Malibu Ranch for its location shooting.

EPISODE SIXTY-FOUR:
"The Space Primevals"
First telecast October 4, 1967
Writer: Peter Packer
Director: Nathan Juran
Incidental Music: Fred Steiner
GUEST STAR: RANGAH: Arthur Batanides

The Jupiter II is in danger of being buried under lava from a nearby volcano which is threatening to erupt. Major West drags Dr. Smith along with him in the Chariot to help him plant the explosives which will hopefully cap the volcano and prevent a tragic eruption.

But their mission is cut short when they encounter savage natives who force the Chariot to halt. The leader of the primitives is a man with fantastic powers who is able to teleport the explosives to an undisclosed location. Smith and Don are then taken captive.

At the natives' encampment, Don and Major West observe that the primitives actually have a computer which they worship. When Major West attempts to explain the importance of their mission to the native leader, the man states, in English, that he doesn't understand their language.

The native leader, Rangah, is linked to the computer and states that they are only temporary life-forms evolving up the evolutionary ladder. He understand that Don wants to cap the volcano, but he forbids it because all of the machinery in their encampment derives its power from the volcano. Rangah condemns Smith and Major West to death for attempting to tamper with the sacred volcano and has them thrown into a cave to await their execution. Needless to say, Dr. Smith is beside himself with fear.

When Smith and Don are reported overdue, John Robinson takes an escape pod from the Jupiter II and goes in search of them, but he's unable to locate them. Since the volcano appears to be nearing an eruption, John cannot delay any longer and returns to the Jupiter II for another load of explosives.

Meanwhile, Will and the robot head out in search of Dr. Smith and Don themselves. They come upon the Chariot, which has been covered over with vines in an effort to hide it.

Major West and Dr. Smith have not been entirely idle while awaiting their execution as they've managed to dig through the floor of their prison into an underground passageway which leads beneath the holy computer which the natives worship. But this backfires as they end up trapped in the passage with their air running out. When Don stumbles and falls into a pit, Smith rescues him and Major West finally sees that Smith has another side to him.

When John arrives at the site of the abandoned Chariot, he meets up with Will who leads his father to the native encampment. The robot is there distracting the natives by amusing them with his dancing. While the natives stare in wonder at this strange machine, John sneaks up to the cavern where Don and Smith are trapped. But when a huge guardian monster suddenly blocks John's way, he has no choice but to blast it with his laser. Rangah suddenly sees that they have an intruder and orders his people to attack John.

The robot creates an electrical barrier between Rangah and the computer, effectively cutting off his powers. Rangah won't release his prisoners and so the robot is forced into a duel with Protinius, the computer. This strange spectacle occupies the natives so that John is able to complete his mission and free Smith and Major West.

Protinius uses its powers to shrink the robot down until it's only six inches tall. But when the volcano threatens to erupt, the computer realizes that they are all endangered unless it's capped. John and Will and allowed to take the explosives up there which John plants inside the lip of the crater. The explosives are detonated and the volcano is closed up. The robot is also returned to its normal height.

Protinius apologizes for all the trouble he and his people have caused and then it promptly vanishes along with all the natives.

They use the Fox backlot concrete cliff for the last time.

EPISODE SIXTY-FIVE:
"Space Destructors"
First telecast October 11, 1967
Writer: Robert Hamner
Director: Don Richardson
GUEST STAR: CYBORG: Tommy Farrell

Dr. Smith, Will and the robot are out and about when they're attracted to a cave which they find is filled with alien machinery. Will returns to the Jupiter II to reveal what he has found to the other.

Unable to control his curiosity, Dr. Smith begins pocking the machinery and pulling levers, which activates it. The machine releases a doughy substance which is seen to go through a process on a conveyor. When it comes out the other end a cyborg has been created which is distinctly unfriendly.

The cyborg attacks the robot, damaging it. When it heads towards Smith, he runs for his life, heading screaming back towards the Jupiter II, managing to stay just barely ahead of it.

John and Major West unleash an electrical net which is able to destroy the hostile cyborg.

When Dr. Smith returns to the cavern, he accidentally reactivates the machine. Knowing what will happen he tries to shut to down, but to no avail. When the hostile cyborg emerges, it comes after Smith. But he backs into what turns out to be the obedience circuits. The cyborg suddenly becomes Smith's slave, a situation that he cannot resist exploiting. Smith reactivates the machine to create additional servants for him, including soldiers, guard and even a cook.

Meanwhile, Will is worried about Smith's protracted absence and he goes searching for him. When Will reaches the cave, the first thing he encounters is a duplicate of Dr. Smith.

The real Dr. Smith has become power mad and is convinced that with this alien technology he'll be able to create an unstoppable army that he'll be able to use to conquer the universe. Smith demonstrates how easy it is to create a soldier, but when Will is clearly unsympathetic to Smith's plans, the boy is taken prisoner and help along with the robot.

Will works on repairing the robot, which is still damaged from its encounter with the first cyborg.

Dr. Smith returns to the Jupiter II with his cyborgs where he has one battle John and Major West. They manage to destroy the cyborg with a destructor capsule, but Smith has another which sneaks up on them. Having demonstrated his superiority, Smith demands that they turn the Jupiter II over to him, then leaves while they deliberate his demands.

Back at the cave, the robot lures their guard into the cave where it is being confined with Will. The robot grabs the guard and Will runs out, planning to warn the others back at the Jupiter II.

Dr. Smith is creating a general to command his troops. When he tries to sneak past Dr. Smith, he's caught by him. During his struggle to escape, Will falls into the cyborg machine and goes through the process to emerge at the other end, wearing a duplicate of Smith's face and programmed to be the perfect general.

The machinery now reveals that it had just been using Smith and by creating an army and a general, Smith has now served his purpose. Smith has the choice of leaving or being destroyed.

In a blind panic, Smith flees back to the Jupiter II and confesses to John and Major West what has happened, although doing his best to make it sound like it was less his fault than it really is. Grabbing destructor capsules, John and Major West head for the cave and the android army.

They encounter cyborgs along the way, which delays Major West while John makes it to the cave. John engages in a series of sword fights with cyborg musketeers until the machine exhausts its resources.

John frees the robot and then they search for Will. When they see what's happened to him, John orders the robot to destroy the cyborg machine. With that accomplished, Will reverts to normal.

Back at the Jupiter II, John plans to banish Dr. Smith for everything he did, but Smith manages to talk his way back in again and everyone has a good laugh at Smith's expense.

This episode is the famous one where hundreds of Smith androids were released.

During Prof. Robinson's swordfight with the androids, the set is dressed with molds for the mechanical men. Scattered about are molds for the robot's arms.

The Android's Machine's maw is a blood vessel salvaged from the Fox production of FANTASTIC VOYAGE.

EPISODE SIXTY-SIX:
"The Haunted Lighthouse"
First telecast October 18, 1967
Writer: Jackson Gillis
Director: Sobey Martin
Incidental Music
GUEST STARS: SILAS J. FOGEY: Woodrow Parfrey, J5: Lou Wagner, ZAYBO: Kenya Coburn

Heavy winds sweep in around the Jupiter II where it sits stranded on a planet. A space storm is apparently on its way. While everyone is preparing to get what they can inside the ship before the storm hits, Penny runs off after her scarf.

Meanwhile, Penny encounters an alien boy named J5. He has pointed ears, is the sole survivor of a failed colony and says he'd being hunted by a monster called Zaybo. When Penny sees a lion coming towards them, she runs back to the Jupiter II for help.

When Penny returns with her father, they find J5 lying on the ground where he appears to be dazed but is otherwise unhurt. Zaybo has turned invisible. When the Robinsons offer to return J5 to his home planet when they take off, J5 brings the invisible cat with him.

The Jupiter II lifts off and heads into space. Along the way they encounter something which looks like fog and which affects their instruments so that they are effectively trying to navigate blind. The Jupiter II collides with a space lighthouse, as Earth ship the F-12.

When John enters the space lighthouse, a computer aboard the craft correctly identifies him as John Robinson and even names what his mission is. John encounters a Col. Silas J. Fogey of the United States Air Force. He's a very old man and he leads John to the control room of the F-12, which is quite a mess. Fegey has been alone ever since the space lighthouse was established 11 years before. He explains that they are located in Galaxy 14-1.

Col. Fogey invites the rest of the Robinsons to be guests aboard the F-12, which he explains is a lightship which is there to survey space weather and be and aid in interplanetary navigation.

That night while they're all having dinner, the Colonel explains that he has galactic navigation charts which will help them find their way back to Earth. He also has spare fuel for the Jupiter II, but not enough to allow them to take J5 back to his home planet first.

When alarms go off indicating trouble on the bridge of the F-12, they go to investigate but nothing seems wrong. In fact, the alarms have even been switched off.

J5 places Zaybo, the invisible cat, in a cabinet in a room where Smith is. Later, Smith hears a woman calling to him, and when he opens the cabinet he finds a beautiful woman clad in jewels. She reveals that she's from J5's home world where jewels are common and lie about for anyone to pick up. She wants Smith to come to her, stating that she's just an illusion protected there by J5.

J5 turns up and tells Smith that he wants to know how to operate the Jupiter II so he can steal the ship and return home. Smith agrees, wanting to get a share of all those jewels, as well as meet the woman who spoke to him.

When the lightship starts drifting off course, Fogey is unable to do anything to correct it. He's not really a colonel after all, but just the ship's cook and handyman. The real colonel left years before and Fogey has been doing his best to learn how everything operates. But worse, he admits that he has no extra fuel or navigational charts.

Penny catches Smith and J5 attempting to steal the Jupiter II and gets into an argument with them.

Meanwhile, Will encounters Zaybo, who is now an invisible lion which attacks him. When Penny runs to save him, a concerned J5 accompanies her. Penny realizes that Zaybo is just a mental projection from J5, and when she confronts the boy with this, Zaybo disappears.

The lightship F-12 is pulled into a cosmic storm. They seem helpless in its grip since they can't get the F-12 out of its path. But then J5, who has a natural knack for machines, figures out the trouble in the stabilizers and fixes it. Once the stabilizers are repaired, things aren't as rough inside even though they're in a cosmic storm, and they're able to safely ride it out.

Once things have settled down, J5 accepts his situation and decides to stay behind with Silas Fogey and help him maintain the lightship. A relief ship is scheduled to rendezvous with the F-12 in three years, which would then return J5 either either to his homeworld, or anywhere else he wants to go, maybe even to Earth.

The Robinsons, Dr. Smith and Major West re-board the Jupiter II to resume their journey.

Lou Wagner's pointed ears were from Mr. Spock's ear molds.
The space lighthouse is actually stock footage from the second seasons episode "Wild Adventure."
The Lighthouse's automated voice gets the launch date of the Jupiter II wrong.

EPISODE SIXTY-SEVEN:
"Flight Into The Future"

First telecast October 25, 1967
Writer: Peter Packer
Director: Sobey Martin
GUEST STARS: COMMANDER FLETCHER: Lew Gallo, SERGEANT
SMITH: Don Eitner

The Jupiter II is approaching a verdant green world while Will and the robot are checking the systems in the escape pod. Smith accidentally activates the launch controls in the pod and all the pod is ejected into space with the three of them aboard where the gravity of the green world pulls it down, but the Jupiter II follows closely after it.

Although the Jupiter II lands in a rocky region only half a mile from the escape pod, when Will is contacted by radio, the boy states that the pod has landed in a rain forest.

John and Major West exit the Jupiter II and launch a search for the escape pod.

Meanwhile, Will, Dr. Smith and the robot exit the pod and observe the jungle into which they've fallen. Close by, some fruits which look somewhat like peaches suddenly burst open, emitting a fine spray which causes Will and Dr. Smith to pass out.

Will and Dr. Smith awake but find that the robot is now rusty and needs oiling. After getting the robot running again, they go to look for the Jupiter II but find that it is just an old hulk which is gutted and overgrown.

Outside the Jupiter II there is a statue of the robot which has a plaque on it declaring the device to be a cybernetic hero. The plaque indicates that it was erected in 2270 A.D., which should be 270 years in the Robinson's future.

Will and Dr. Smith start seeing strange visions. Will witnesses an Indian charge while Dr. Smith finds himself confronted by the cyclops which attacked them after the Jupiter II first crash-landed on another world long before.

Then they encounter to space explorers who state that they're part of an archaeological expedition from Earth. Their names are Commander Fletcher and Sergeant Smith, but Will doesn't buy their story and is suspicious of them.

When the two explorers give Dr. Smith some food, it turns out to be just an illusion. Meanwhile, Will and the robot go to investigate the ship which the Commander arrived in. Along the way they encounter a young woman who looks just like Judy, but she insists that she's actually Judy Robinson's great-great-great-granddaughter.

While Will goes to discuss things with "Judy," Dr. Smith gets into an altercation with Sergeant Smith and Smith is slapped with the Sergeant's glove. It turns out that this is Horatio Smith, and when he discovers who Dr. Smith is he challenges him because Zachary Smith was a notorious fifth columnist who forever blackened the family name.

Dr. Smith protests his innocence and will be given an opportunity to prove it when a hearing is held for him aboard the mothership, which is orbiting the planet right now. Since the mothership is scheduled to leave orbit in two hours, they have that much time to rendezvous with it in the escape pod from the Jupiter II.

Will doubts the reality of much of what they have been told, and things don't make any more logical sense when Commander Fletcher and "Judy" vanish. Now Will is really dead set against taking the pod up to the mothership.

If this isn't confounding enough, John and Major West locate the escape pod, but it's in a rocky area, is covered with moss and looks long abandoned. John suspects what is going on and so he and Major West concentrate on the pod, causing the illusion cast over it to waver and dissolve. Now they realize that illusions are being created all around them and they have to proceed carefully so as not to be tripped up by one.

Smith still believes what he's seen, but Will and the robot have decided to search for the origin of the illusions. John and Major West are also searching for the nexus of the hallucinations and as they get closer to it, more and more illusions are thrown into their path.

Finally they arrive at the source, which is a computer. The computer just wants to be left alone and creates the illusions to frighten away intruders. The computer creates something which is not an illusion, and which looks like some sort of cactus monster, which attacks Will. The robot zaps the computer and blows it up, thus ending its illusions forever.

When John and Major West arrive, they explain that Will has only been missing for an hour, not the 270 years which the illusions tried to make him believe.

Will, Dr. Smith and the robot happen upon a rusted, deteriorating Jupiter II, which is an interesting sight to behold.

The statue of the robot is actually the second robot costume treated to look like stone.

The space suits used by the Earth team also appeared in THE TIME TUNNEL.

EPISODE SIXTY-EIGHT:
"Collision Of Planets"

First telecast November 8, 1967
Writer: Peter Packer
Director: Don Richardson
Incidental Music: Gerald Fried
GUEST STARS: ILAN: Daniel J. Travanty, ALIEN GIRL: Linda Gaye Scott, ALIEN #3: Joey Tata

A group of interplanetary Hell's Angels are despatched to blow up the planet Chromo, an unstable world which is on a collision course for an inhabited world. This demolition team are the outcasts of their world and travel on space motorcycles.

Although they don't know it, the planet the Robinsons have just landed the Jupiter II on is none other than Chromo. They're supposed to be notified before the planet is destroyed.

On Chromo, a storm sweeps in and then the sunrise occurs at what they perceive to be the wrong time. They start running a systems check so that they can be ready to leave immediately, but a malfunction destroys their fuel supply and repairs to the Jupiter II will entail a week's worth of work.

Just then they receive the warning that Chromo is going to be destroyed and they have one day to evacuate the planet. When John and Major West detect the arrive of the demolition team, they go to meet with them to explain their situation.

Meanwhile, Will, Dr. Smith and the robot see a parachute attached to a box falling from the sky and they decide to investigate it. Arriving at the scene, Smith insists on opening the box, causing a gas to burst forth which seemingly kills him.

John and Major West discover a blasting site, and then find the hippie demolition team, who display no interest in the Robinson's problems. If the Robinsons are on the planet when it blows up, that's the way it goes.

Dr. Smith comes out of his trance with an enhanced physique but also bright green hair. The box was too heavy for the robot to carry, but the new Dr. Smith lifts it with ease and transports it back to the Jupiter II.

The box contains demolition materials needed by the hippie space-bikers, and when they realize that it's been taken, they're certain that the Robinsons stole it.

The bikers teleport to the Jupiter II and confront Dr. Smith, who suddenly becomes weak and cowardly so that the bikers have no trouble retrieving their explosives. But soon after Dr. Smith is able to regain is super-strength and goes in search of the hippies.

The space bikers are working at a drill site and John Robinson tries once again to reason with them. John gets into an argument with the bikers' leader, Ilan, and is knocked unconscious by the drill site. The hippies prime the explosives and leave with John unconscious close by. But John comes around just in time and escapes before the drill site is detonated.

Dr. Smith, Will and the robot arrive at the latest site occupied by the hippies. An alien girl gets friendly with Smith and then tricks him by cutting off his green hair, which was the real source of his super-strength.

Having the upper hand, the hippie bikers chain Will, Smith and the robot in a supply cave while another drilling site is worked on. But Smith's strength returns again and he frees them.

Back at the Jupiter II they make plans for an emergency liftoff. Since Will isn't around, John goes searching for the boy. Just as John finds his son with the robot and Dr. Smith, the hippie bikers catch up to them.

The bikers refuse to stop the drilling and planting of explosives, so John uses his later to disable their space bikes. It will take the hippies a day to repair their bikes, which will give the Robinsons a day to complete a week's worth of repairs on the Jupiter II.

The Jupiter II is just able to undergo its repairs and lift off before Chromo is detonated. They wonder if the bikers escaped as well, but they soon receive a message from them which makes it clear that they got away as well.

The Alien headquarters set is made from TIME TUNNEL miniatures.
The Alien biker is played by future HILL STREET BLUES star Daniel J. Travanty.

EPISODE SIXTY-NINE:
"Space Creature"
First telecast November 15, 1967
Writer: William Welch
Director: Sobey Martin

The Jupiter II approaches another planet but its gravity field is so strong that the spacecraft is unable to blast free. The atmosphere of the planet consists of methane and a substance that is actually an evil, hungry living organism.

A mist forms over the viewport and John and Major West are frozen into immobility as a large claw moves across the window. The airlock is opened from the outside, which allows some of the mist to enter the Jupiter II. Then all becomes normal again and no one realizes what just happened.

When the mist creature enters Will's room, it tries to tempt him with promises of power, but Will rejects it. But Dr. Smith is open to the space creature's promises and he states that he wishes the Robinsons would all just vanish.

The following morning, as Maureen is in the kitchen, she abruptly disappears. When Judy is on her way up in the elevator, she vanishes. Will searches the entire ship for them but he can't find a trace of his mother and sister.

Meanwhile, John, Major West and the robot hear a noise which sounds like something on the hull of the Jupiter II trying to get in. The robot explains that it believes that the space creature feeds on fear and is using things like this to generate terror to feed its lust for it.

When Penny vanishes, she reappears in a misty void. She sees Maureen and Judy there being taunted by the evil laughter of the space creature which kidnapped them.

Major West decides to descend to the planet in the escape pod in an attempt to locate the key to whatever is holding them in an unbreakable grip. But the electrical systems in the pod start to short out and he's forced to return to the Jupiter II. But when the pod is opened, Major West has disappeared.

Don is now in the same misty void with Judy, Penny and Maureen. The creature continues to provoke them and feed off of their resulting fear. The space creature admits that it is a young, growing creature that regards all of this as a game and an adventure.

Back on the Jupiter II, John and Will rope each other together in an attempt to prevent the other from disappearing. But Smith is not so lucky and soon he vanishes into the fearsome void as well.

John manages to figure out that each person who disappeared was standing near an oscillator. He decides to test this by reversing the polarity of an oscillator to see if it might bring the missing people back. John enters the pod to test his theory but suddenly vanishes, leaving only his end of the empty rope behind. When the robot vanishes as well, Will is left alone aboard the Jupiter II.

Smith is a perfect prisoner of the space creature because his fear is so boundless. The space creature is particularly happy with this prize, and the more Dr. Smith screams and pleads, the more the creature likes him.

Aboard the Jupiter II, Will hears a noise aboard the supposedly empty ship. When he checks the airlock, lo and behold there's Dr. Smith. Dr. Smith is acting quite different from normal, and is actually acting quite angry and behaving very coldly.

Will tries his father's experiment with the oscillator, which causes the robot to materialize. The robot immediately informs Will that the space creature has taken over Dr. Smith and is inside of him.

The Smith/creature chases Will, who retreats down into the power core of the Jupiter II. Suddenly John and Major West reappear from the void.

Will stands up to the creature, which reveals that it is the evil, inner self of Will Robinson from the future. Will realizes that it cannot really hurt him and so he stands up to the space creature in Dr. Smith's form.

The creature leaves Smith body and takes on a ghostly shape nearby. The creature wants to take Will's place in this time, but Will is able to trick it into getting too close to the ship's power core where it is destroyed. Upon the space creature's destruction, the rest of the missing crew reappear aboard the Jupiter II. Everyone gets a good laugh at Smith's expense, as usual, and they're now able to easily escape from orbit around the mysterious planet.

The first and last use of the Jupiter II's <u>third</u> lower level, containing the power core.
Story influence:"Ten Little Indians."

EPISODE SEVENTY:
"Deadliest Of The Species"

First telecast November 22, 1967
Writer: Robert Hamner
Director: Don Richardson
GUEST STARS: ALIEN LEADER: Ronald Gans, MECHANICAL MAN #1: Lyle Waggoner, MECHANICAL MAN #2: Ralph Lee, FEMALE ROBOT: Sue England

When the Jupiter II encounters trouble with its energizing module, it finds a nearby world and prepares to set down for repairs. On their way down they notice that something is following them, like a small satellite, but it doesn't appear to pose any threat to them.

Elsewhere, at the Bureau of Inter-Galactic Law Enforcement, two mechanical men are dispatched with orders to destroy the self-same capsule which happens to be following the Jupiter II. The Mechanical Men are told that if the Robinsons refuse to cooperate with them, that they are to be dispatched as well.

After the Jupiter II lands, Will and the robot exit and observe the capsule make a crash-landing. When Will runs back to tell his parents, the robot hears a woman's voice calling for help from the capsule and it goes to try to assist her.

The Mechanical Men arrive on the planet and go to the Robinsons and demand that the capsule be turned over to them. When John says he doesn't know what they're talking about, the robots become threatening, so the Robinsons erect their force field to hold the robots at bay.

That night the robot sneaks out of the Jupiter II and returns to the site where the capsule crash landed. In a nearby cave the robot has been reassembling the female robot which was in the capsule. The female robot is evil and has the Robinson's robot under her control.

At the Jupiter II, John drives off the Mechanical Men with his laser, but he's uncertain what they can do when those robots return.

Will discovers that their robot is missing and so goes off looking for it, not aware that it is under control of the evil robot. The evil robot needs an energizer to get more power, and the Robinsons just happen to have one which they use to power their force field.

When Will finds the two robots, the evil robot wants him killed immediately. But the Robinson's robot decides that it would be better to barter Will in exchange for the force field. When faced with this choice, John Robinson has no choice but to accept the trade, even though they'll be all but defenseless should the mechanical men attack again. John gives the robot the energizer and it promises to release Will as soon as it returns to where the boy is held captive.

Will is released and arrives back at the Jupiter II just as the Mechanical Men return with their alien leader. The Alien Leader explains that they are searching for a capsule which contains a female robot who is so evil and dangerous that she almost succeeded in destroying an entire planet. The robot had been disassembled and blasted into space to orbit forever, but now that she has landed they fear that she might be reassembled and become a menace once again.

When Will goes and tells their robot the truth, it is unmoved. So Will grabs the energizer and tries to run away with it, but the evil robot and the Robinson's robot follow close behind.

The two robots catch up to Will just as John, Major West, the Alien leader and the two Mechanical Men arrive on the scene. When the evil robot orders the Robinson's robot to kill the humans, it refuses. So the female robot slays the Alien Leader and the two mechanical men.

John, Major West, Will and their robot return to the Jupiter II, but the evil robot has the energizer and plans to kill them the next day after it has finished energizing itself.

John and Major West decide to set a trap for the evil robot by converting their ionic grid, but they need their robot to complete the circuit, but can it be trusted? When the female robot appears, they activate the grid, but their robot hesitates about completing the circuit. It believes it may well love this female robot. Finally it accepts the fact that this robot is evil and will kill the Robinsons and completes the circuit, causing her to be blown up. But it later rebuilds the female robot, wiping out her evil memory circuits.

Sue England returns as the voice of another evil, female robot.
Story influence:"The Ghost Planet."
CAROL BURNETT/WONDER WOMAN co-star Lyle Waggoner plays the silver-faced alien.

EPISODE SEVENTY-ONE:
"A Day At The Zoo"
First telecast November 29, 1967
Writer: Jackson Gillis
Director: Irvin Moore
Incidental Music: Alexander Courage
GUEST STARS: FARNUM: Leonard Stone, OGGO: Gary Tigerman, MORT: Ronald Weber

Penny is exploring the area near the Jupiter two when she encounters a primitive looking boy. He gestures and acts like he's trying to warn her about something, but Penny can't figure out what it is. She realizes what the boy is warning her about pretty quickly when she walks into a trap and is collected as a specimen for an inter-galactic zoo. Penny is taken to the trapper's ship, where things are dim and poorly illuminated.

The trapper wears a false head to try to appear more fearsome, but he's actual just an ordinary looking humanoid. He calls himself Farnum and he traps species for his private zoo. Farnum shows Penny other humans he has collected, including a knight in armor in one cell and Whistler's mother in another cage. Farnum ushers Penny into a room furnished to remind Penny of Earth. Then Farnum leaves to check another one of his traps which seems to have caught something.

The other trap has snared Judy and Major West, who had noted Penny's absence and gone searching for her. Major West puts up a struggle and Farnum has to summon his knight, Mort, to subdue him. Then Don and Judy and placed in another cell together.

Another alarm goes off, indicating that yet another of Farnum's traps have been sprung, and this one has snagged Dr. Smith, Will and the robot, who has been out hunting for Don, Judy and Penny.

When brought to Farnum's ship, Dr. Smith suggests a contest for their freedom, a battle between the robot and Mort the knight. Farnum agrees, but much to Smith's surprise, Mort slices up the robot. It's then revealed that the knight itself is a robot, and a superior piece of technology at that.

Farnum has decided that his menagerie is complete and he plans to take his leave of this planet.

Meanwhile, Will has managed to slip something into the lock of their cell door so that it doesn't shut all the way. He's been put in the same cell as Penny and they start exploring the ship, searching for some way to rescue their friends and escape from the zoo ship. When they discover that Farnum's "Whistler's Mother" is also a robot. They decide that Farnum has been misleading them.

Since the cave boy Penny met, Oggo, tried to warn her, she decides that he must be real. They encounter Oggo, who agrees to help Will get off the ship to go for help.

Dr. Smith is not at all adverse to being in a cell stocked with all the comforts of home, as these include champagne, caviar and even money.

An alarm sounds, warning Farnum that someone is trying to escape. Farnum catches Will near the world doors and during their struggle they fall through into a prehistoric world, which is where he obtained Oggo from. Farnum doesn't have his control box, which strands them both there, and the prehistoric planet is so dangerous that they'll be lucky to survive for 45 minutes.

Meanwhile, Dr. Smith finds Farnum's control box and determines that Oggo knows how to operate it. Smith decides that he'll take Farnum's place and profit from his human exhibits, which include Don, Judy and Penny.

They arrive at another planet and Smith has his zoo erected, with the robot acting as his barker, encouraging the aliens to purchase tickets to see the Earthlings perform.

But finally the robot is able to over-ride Smith's programming and frees Major West, who halts the performance. Penny talks Oggo into helping them, and the boy shows Don how to operate the control box so that they're able to pass through the world doors and save Will and Farnum from a fire-breathing dinosaur.

Back on the planet where the Jupiter II is, Farnum agrees to give up his idea of a zoo and will find some other business, with Oggo as his partner. Just before Farnum's ship takes off, he discovers Smith trying to stow away and throws him off, seeing that Smith is a bigger blowhard than Farnum ever was.

The first appearance by Leonard Stone as Farnum, whom we'd meet again.

EPISODE SEVENTY-TWO:
"Two Weeks In Space"
First telecast December 13, 1967
Writer: Robert Hamner
Director: Don Richardson
GUEST STARS: ZUMDISH: Fritz Feld, MXR: Richard Krishner, QZW: Eric Matthews, NON: Edy Williams, TAT: Carroll Roebke

A spaceship approaching the planet on which the Jupiter II is being repaired is a felon's spacecraft, fleeing from a bank robbery. On board the approaching ship are MXR, NON, QZW and TAT. They stole their spaceship from Mr. Zumdish and are being pursued by the Intergalactic Tribunal. Mr. Zumdish is still aboard but has been hypnotized into believing that he's a tour guide and the four criminals are the tourists he's guiding. The criminals disguise themselves by using a matter transformer to make their orange, tentacle-featured faces appear human.

The criminals detect the Jupiter II below and contact them for a landing beam they can follow in order to pass safely through the planet's radiation belt.

The rest of the Robinsons are out, leaving Dr. Smith in charge with Will and the robot. Upon discovering that they're about to have visitors, Dr. Smith decides that they (meaning him) can profit from the visit by making the Jupiter II over into "Smith's Happy Acres Hotel." Dr. Smith appoints himself manager, since the hotel was his idea, and the work has to be done by Will and the robot.

When the guests arrive, with Zumdish seemingly in charge, he demands that his guests be shown "fun, fun, fun!" Smith eagerly complies by having the robot teach the aliens such Earth games as badminton.

NON is a lovely young woman who pretends to be attracted to Smith. This is all part of their plot to foil the Space Patrol as MXR has decided that Smith would make the perfect dupe. Smith will be lured away and changed by the matter transformer to look like the aliens really do. Smith will then be killed and his body left in the wreckage of their spacecraft out in space, leading the Space Patrol to believe that they were all killed in some sort of space mishap. At night the alien resume their true forms, but at daybreak they resume their human guises.

NON gives Smith a ring, which she pretends is a symbol of her love. Actually, the ring is a matter transformer which will change Smith's appearance into that of an alien come nightfall. She makes arrangements to meet with Smith that night.

Come nightfall, the aliens revert to their true form and plan to kill all the humans, since they no longer need them to survive on this world.

Smith turns into an alien, but doesn't notice the change. But when he meets with NON and sees her in her true form, he's terrified and runs off.

The aliens are also searching for Will, but he spots them and eludes their deadly search.

At daybreak, Dr. Smith encounters the Chariot, which is returning to the Jupiter II with Major West and the rest of the Robinsons aboard. When Smith reveals what is going on, John and Major West run to the Jupiter II to check on Will and the ship. Will is there, all safe and sound, and he reveals that the aliens have gone.

Mr. Zumdish has come to his senses and explains that the aliens are criminals who had stolen his spacecraft. The aliens are now out hunting humans.

QZW and MXR encounter the Chariot and take Judy, Penny and Maureen prisoner. The two criminals take the women to a lava pool cave and prepare to hurl them in so that they'll be destroyed without a trace. But John and Major West track them down, and in the ensuing battle John blasts the two aliens out of existence.

The two male aliens were the worst threat, and with them gone Zumdish can handle NON and TAT himself. Before they leave, Smith gives NON back her ring, since he knows what she really looks like, although he never did figure out that for a time he looked that way too.

Fritz Delf returns in the role of Zomdish.
The alien ship stock footage is from the 50's Roger Corman film WAR OF THE SATELLITES.
Edy Williams plays the alien woman who toys with Smith. Williams is well known for her annual appearance at the Oscar ceremonies wearing as little as possible.

EPISODE SEVENTY-THREE:
"Castles In Space"

First telecast December 20, 1967
Writer: Peter Packer
Director: Sobey Martin
Incidental Music: Gerald Fried
GUEST STARS: CHAVO: Alberto Monte, REYKA: Corinna Tsopei

When Dr. Smith is attempting to teach Will the fine art of skeet shooting, all Smith manages to hit is the new radar station and Major West. Needless to say, Major West puts an end to the lesson very quickly.

Smith is attempting to clean up after himself when he presses a secret lever which causes a cave to open and a glowing, frozen block to emerge. Even more amazing is that the block of ice has a figure imprisoned in it frozen in suspended animation.

When Smith is left on guard by the block, the thermal blanket he's wearing doesn't keep him warm enough to his satisfaction, and so he tosses it over the block and returns to the Jupiter II to get a cup of coffee.

The thermal blanket causes the ice block to melt and a woman, Reyka the Ice Princess, emerges from it. When Smith returns to the site with Major West, Reyka threatens Smith with a spear, but Major West manages to get her to back off.

Just then a space ship lands, which gets Reyka upset all over again. Will dispatches the robot to investigate the new spacecraft. When the robot reaches the site it encounter a metallic being who looks somewhat like an old style Mexican bandito. This is Chavo, who makes friends with the robot. When Chavo manages to get the robot drunk, it reveals that the princess is awake.

As soon as Chavo hears this he returns to his ship to prepare. Will encounters the drunk robot and then continues to search for Chavo. He finds him and Chavo reveals that the King and Queen of her world hid Reyka on this world until the time arrived for her to assume the mantle of queen. But Chavo's intentions are anything but honorable and plans to hold the Ice Princess for a fabulous ransom. Since Will has found him out, Will is now his prisoner as well.

Chavo goes to the Jupiter II, where Major West makes it clear he doesn't trust him and forces Chavo to leave their encampment after he offers to exchange Will for the Ice Princess.

Don and Smith track Chavo back to his ship, but while they're gone, Reyko runs off to hide. With her gone, they need another plan and so the robot creates a decoy senorita to use on Chavo.

Chavo releases Will, but then takes Smith prisoner when he realizes that he's been tricked. Don arrives at the camp and confronts Chavo in a knife fight, but loses. Chavo is on the verge of slitting Don's throat when the robot rolls up and offers to fight Chavo in Don's place, which is what he'd wanted earlier.

The robot is to play the part of the bull with Chavo the matadore, but Chavo loses the bull fight and decides it's time he retired from the bull-fighting game. Chavo decides holding the princess for ransom would be too much trouble and leaves. Reyko also chooses now to return to her home world.

156

EPISODE SEVENTY-FOUR:
"The Anti-Matter Man"
First telecast December 27, 1967
Writer: K.C. Alison (actually Barney Slater and Robert Hamner)
Director: Sutton Roley

Two alien criminals who are imprisoned on an anti-matter world are virtual doubles for John Robinson and Major West (except the alien West has a beard). They are desperate to acquire an atomizing unit to serve as a focal point to enable them to escape to our universe.

Meanwhile, in our universe on the planet the Jupiter II is currently marooned on, John Robinson and the robot are running tests on the atomic motors of the Jupiter II. This creates the contact point between the two universes which the alternate John needs to make contact with his double and draw him across the contact point into the alternate universe.

Once John is snatched by his double, the double forced John to exchange clothes with him and then binds John so that he can't get away. The alternate universe John is cruel and cunning, and more than willing to kill to achieve his goals.

Back at the Jupiter II, the encampment is engulfed by an electrical storm. What they don't realize is that the magnetic disturbance is caused from the imbalance generated by the contact between the two universes. In the alternate universe a magnetic storm is also raging due to the imbalance created by there being two versions of John Robinson in that continuum.

In the Jupiter II, Will wants to find out what happened to his father, and so he and the robot reactivate the atomic motor and find themselves able to step into a realm between dimensions. They're able to trace John Robinson to the alternate universe. There they discover rocks which can move while people remain still. When Will and the robot encounter the alternate John Robinson, Will thinks that he's found his father.

Will, the robot and the alternate John return to the contact point between dimensions and return to the Jupiter II. As soon as they cross over, the magnetic storms cease as there is once more just one John Robinson in each continuum.

The alternate John wants repairs made on the Jupiter II immediately so that they can leave that world, and he's merciless in pushing to get the repairs completed.

Meanwhile, strange things are happening such as when Will and Don discover that their clocks are running backwards and Penny's tape recorder acts the same way.

When the robot detects things such as the fact that John Robinson casts no shadow, it deduces that this is not the real John that they know. When the robot convinces Will of this, the two plan to return to the alternate world and reactivate the atomic motor. Will passes through safely, but before the robot can follow, it is attacked by the alternate John, who then follows Will through the dimensional warp.

Major West and Dr. Smith aid the robot, and then West sends the robot and Smith through the gateway after the alternate John to save Will.

When the alternate John catches up with Will, he takes the boy captive and drags him to the cave where the real John is held captive. The alternate John states that he'll kill the boy's father if Will doesn't help him with his escape plans. Will feels that he has no choice except to agree to help the alternate John in his plans. The alternate John and Will leave the cave to return to the Jupiter II.

In the cave, the real John Robinson tricks the alternate Don West into attacking him so that John is able to overpower the man and knock him out. The creature which had been guarding the cave comes after John, but by this time the robot and Dr. Smith have arrived and the robot defeats the monster. The robot is suddenly surprised by discovering that it has an alternate as well which is imprisoned in the cave, but it is a lazy blowhard and the complete opposite of the real robot.

John Robinson is able to catch up to his doppelganger in the passageway between the universes and a battle ensues. The battle ends when the alternate John falls and vanishes in the realm between dimensions. The real John Robinson then returns through the gateway with Will, Dr. Smith and the robot. Once on the other side they make sure that the gateway cannot be reopened again.

Excellent direction by Sutton Roley. Great sets and camera work.
Look for cut-out horizon on stage wall when lightning strikes reveal the set dressing.
The second robot costume is used for the anti-matter robot.
Story influence:"Follow The Leader."

EPISODE SEVENTY-FIVE:
"Target: Earth"
First telecast January 3, 1968
Writer: Peter Packer
Director: Nathan Juran
GUEST STARS: GILT PROTO: James Gosa, PROTO: Brent Davis

The Jupiter II is once again space borne, but Dr. Smith is his usual arrogant, bumbling self and causes the escape pod to be accidentally launched when the bottom half of the robot is inside of it.

The pod is drawn down to the surface of a nearby planet, and the Robinsons are quite surprises when people on the planet contact them to come and reclaim their property.

The Jupiter II lands in what appears to be the town square of a city, but there's no sign of any of the inhabitants. As punishment for causing this situation, Dr. Smith is forced to go out and reconnoiter, but when he finds the pod and opens the door, he sees a monster inside of it. Dr. Smith runs screaming back to the Jupiter II, just ahead of the monster.

The creature is one of the planet's inhabitants. Named Gilt Proto, it freezes the crew of the Jupiter II and then takes the rest of the robot which it plans to use.

After Gilt Proto is gone, everyone comes back to normal. But Major West discovers that the ship's power has been drained and they're stranded.

Will wants to find the robot and begins searching in the nearest structure. He quickly encounters Gilt Proto. The creature reveals that his people have become stagnant because they all look alike and he's decided that by giving them differences he can make them adventurous again which will rejuvenate their society. To accomplish this, Gilt Proto has taken some of his people and made them over into duplicates of the Robinsons and Major West, and with them he'll take over the Jupiter II.

Gilt Proto intends to use the Jupiter II to invade Earth and duplicate the people they encounter. The robot has even been reprogrammed to serve the doubles created by Gilt Proto.

Will is allowed to leave and he reports what he's learned to his father. When John and Major West go to attempt to negotiate with the aliens, they encounter their doubles, which capture them. The real John and Major West are placed in stasis tubes and their duplicates take their place.

When Will and Dr. Smith are searching for John and Don, they discover the duplicate Robinsons and Major West preparing to take over the Jupiter II. Maureen, Penny and Judy are captured and placed in stasis, but Will and Dr. Smith overpower their own doubles and knock them out. Will and Smith then follow the doubles aboard the Jupiter II, but they're unaware that the duplicate Smith has revived and managed to stumble aboard before the ship lifts off.

While the Jupiter II is on its way to Earth, Will figures out that since the aliens had always been the same, that if they can be brought into conflict they'll be unable to function adequately, and so he tricks the John and Don duplicates into getting into an argument. Meanwhile, Will attempts to over-ride the alien programming in it, but is unsuccessful.

When Dr. Smith finds his double aboard, he tries to hide him, but the duplicate Maureen and Judy discover him and realize that they've been tricked.

Suddenly the Jupiter II encounters a meteor shower and it's Will's ability to think and reason as an individual which saves the ship. The duplicate John decides that the boy can be useful to them after all, even if he isn't a duplicate. But to keep Will in line, the duplicates hold Dr. Smith as a hostage.

The passage through the storm and the knocking around the robot endured has enabled it to over-ride the alien reprogramming. It reveals this to Will and offers to aid the boy in defeating the duplicates.

The Jupiter II approaches Earth and Will contacts Alpha Control on the ship's radio. Will warns them of the invasion attempt and Earth fires missiles at the Jupiter II, driving it off. The robot knocks out the duplicate John and Major West and they take the Jupiter II back to the planet they came from.

Back on the planet the duplicates vanish due to the failure of their mission and Gilt Proto sets the Robinsons free so that they can leave safely.

The alien building is the exterior of the Fox soundstage.
The meteor storm footage if the Jupiter II is from the pilot, but slightly tinted,
The Jupiter II actually lands in Earth in this episode, but Will takes off again.
Story influence:"Rocket To Earth."

EPISODE SEVENTY-SIX:
"Princess Of Space"
First telecast January 10, 1968
Writer: Jackson Gillis
Director: Don Richardson
GUEST STARS: CAPTAIN KRASPA: Robert Foulk, FEDOR: Arte Johnson,
AUNT GAMMA: Sheila Mathews

A reward has long been offered for the return of Princess Alpha, who was removed from her home on the planet Beta when just a child and left in an orphanage on Earth. The planet she is from is suffering from a revolt of the machines, and only someone of the royal family can quell the disturbance, which makes it even more imperative that she be found.

Searching for her is one Captain Kraspa, the stern commander of a vessel whose crew consists of computers. His only human aid is the meek Fedor.

When his ship passes near the planet which the Jupiter II is presently on, the computers inform Kraspa that there is a thirteen year old girl on that world, the same age that Princess Alpha would be.

Penny has been imagining what it would be like to be a princess when suddenly a red carpet and silver slippers magically appear. The carpet is intended to snatch up Penny, but somehow Will gets caught up in it instead and the carpet whisks Will off to Captain Kraspa's ship.

When he sees that his plan somehow failed, Kraspa decides to take things directly in hand himself. Kraspa goes down to the planet and when he encounters Penny, along with Smith and the robot, he wastes no time and just brings all of them back to his spacecraft. Kraspa neutralizes the robot and when Smith won't stop babbling about how harmless he is, the Captain reduces Smith to a piece of computer tape. This is a common technique employed by the Betans, who can restore people to normal just as easily.

Will asks Fedor for his help in saving his sister and his friends, and while the little man wants to help, he's terrified of Captain Kraspa. But Fedor says that he'll try to think of something to help Will and the others.

Although Captain Kraspa knows that Penny isn't really Princess Alpha, he plans to pass her off as the child princess anyway and so collect the reward.

Kraspa contacts Beta and communicates with the sole survivor of the royal family there, the Royal Aunt Gamma. Aunt Gamma announces that she'll soon arrive at Kraspa's ship to inspect the young girl whom he claims is the missing Princess.

Restoring Smith to human form, Captain Kraspa orders him to groom Penny so that she'll pass muster as a princess. Kraspa uses extortion to force Penny to go along with his plan by reducing Don and Judy to a strip of computer tape and threatening to burn it if Penny doesn't look like a princess when Aunt Gamma arrives.

Dr. Smith has the robot create a lavish gown for Penny to wear so that by the time Aunt Gamma appears, Penny really does look like a princess.

Aunt Gamma insists that everyone else leave the room, and when she's alone with Penny she starts studying the child to search for signs of royal lineage. Gamma explains that the Princess is the only one who can use the royal scepter to quell the revolt of the machines on Beta.

But Fedor chooses to betray Kraspa and slips Gamma a note which details the Captain's scheme. Gamma has Kraspa thrown into the brig and Fedor is promoted to Captain. But Gamma is starting to think that Penny might just be the missing Princess after all.

Will stumbles on the truth about Fedor, though, that he exposed Captain Kraspa in order to be made Captain because Fedor is really plotting with the machines. The machines want to get ahold of the royal scepter and thereby gain the final and absolute control of Beta. In fact, Fedor is really just a robot disguised as a man.

Going directly to Captain Kraspa, Will reveals what he's discovered and is able to help the Captain break out of the brig. They arrive on the scene just as Gamma is giving Penny the royal scepter. Kraspa lunges for Fedor and the machines attack.

In a blind panic, Smith causes the control to make Kraspa's ship veer wildly off course (he's good at that). Don and Judy have been restored to normal since Kraspa had been exposed, and Don gets the ship back on course. Don manages to discover that the real Princess had been reduced to a strip of computer tape and hidden in their robot!

The Robinson's robot uses the ship's machinery to restore the Princess and she uses the royal scepter to control the machines. She then reduces Fedor to a computer card.

With the revolt quelled, Aunt Gamma and Princess Alpha will return with Captain Kraspa to the planet Beta, while Penny and the others can return to the Jupiter II. But Penny did learn what it might be like to be a Princess, if only for a little while.

Sheila Mathews returns, this time playing a Queen.
Future LAUGH-IN star Arte Johnson appears as a lackey.

EPISODE SEVENTY-SEVEN:
"Time Merchant"

First telecast January 17, 1968
Writer: Bob and Wanda Duncan
Director: Ezra Stone
GUEST STARS: DR. CHRONOS: John Crawford, GENERAL SQUIRES: Byron Morrow, SGT. ROGER: Hoke Howell

When an approaching cosmic storm is detected, Will decides to try an experiment to trap cosmic particles. But instead of cosmic particles, Will's device traps a time merchant named Dr. Chronos. Chronos is most upset at being delayed by Will and in retaliation he takes the boy with him to his time factory where the boy can help him make up for lost time.

When the others realize what has happened, John, Dr. Smith and the robot follow Dr. Chronos through the dimensional passageway and come out the other end on the world of Chronos. This is a world with surreal landscapes with clocks all around.

Meanwhile, Dr. Chronos is busy observing a planet in the Omega galaxy where its inhabitants have been wasting time and thereby have caused their time to run out. Dr. Chronos passes judgment and casually destroys that planet.

Dr. Chronos encounters Smith, who wants to purchase some time from the merchant, more specifically his youth. When Dr. Chronos shows Smith a recording of his past, Smith asks to see October 16, 1997, the day the Jupiter II left Earth. Smith then sneaks into a transporter device which will return him to that moment in time.

Dr. Chronos is angry because Smith left without paying for the service and so he demands that John and Will make good on Smith's purchase. But the only payment that Dr. Chronos will deal in is time and wants a certain number of years off a person's life. On top of this, Smith might well alter time. In fact, Dr. Chronos states that if Smith fails to board the Jupiter II and sabotage the mission that the spacecraft will collide with an uncharted asteroid four months into its journey, destroying everyone aboard. So Dr. Smith must be prevented from altering the past.

Dr. Smith is back on time on Earth in Alpha Control, relaxing and watching television. General Squires is puzzled by Smith's off behavior towards both the mission and the way he treated the robot which was just taken aboard.

Meanwhile, John Robinson suggests that the robot be sent back in order to force Smith to board the Jupiter II, a suggestion Dr. Chronos accepts, along with the payment of five years of John's life.

But when the robot arrives in 1997, it doesn't remember its mission until Dr. Smith characteristically insults it. But before the robot can insure things are set right, General Squires has Smith arrested due to how suspicious he has been acting.

The robot reveals what will happen if time is changed and helps Smith escape. Smith's friendship for the Robinsons overcomes his fear and he sneaks aboard the Jupiter II along with the robot. Thus time resumes its natural course.

But John and Will don't trust Chronos, and Dr. Chronos confirms their fears when he tears up John's contract and tries to extort even more years of John's life in payment for services rendered.

John overpowers Dr. Chronos and forces him into submission by threatening the time merchant with his scythe device. John forces Dr. Chronos to return Smith and the robot to the present, but this causes the time factory to begin to explode. They are all able to escape through the dimensional rift and back to the Jupiter II just in time.

A semi-classic episode where Smith returns to the launch date of the Jupiter II. Black and white footage from the pilot is seen on Smith's TV set in Alpha Control.

The robot actually speaks in his old, monotone voice from the early first season.

EPISODE SEVENTY-EIGHT:
"The Promised Planet"
First telecast January 24, 1968
Writer: Peter Packer
Director: Ezra Stone
GUEST STARS: BARTHOLOMEW: Gil Rogers, EDGAR: Keith Taylor

The Jupiter II seems to be approaching Alpha Centauri and the robot confirms this observation. Signals are received from someone named Bartholomew from the planet Delta. The Jupiter II follows the signal down and comes in for a safe landing.

When the Robinsons emerge from the ship, they encounter a group of youths who know exactly who the Robinsons are and what their mission is. The kids claim that Delta has been colonized for three years by Americans. The youngsters claim that the main colony is on the nearby planet Gamma, and that this station on Delta is just a preparation point.

Penny and Will are led away by the uniformed youths and explains how they'll be indoctrinated into the colony. Bartholomew starts disparaging their parents, calling them "olders" and themselves "youngers."

Bartholomew leads Will and Penny into a room which appears to be a discotheque where other youths are dancing to "modern" music amid flashing lights. Will and Penny are led to interrogation booths where they are quizzed while the music blares in the background. They find it difficult to concentrate under those conditions and they are unable to correctly answer most of the questions they're barraged with.

Penny is taken away and undergoes a conversion process which turns her into one of the hip talking "youngers," and her regular clothes are exchanged for the same style clothes the other "youngers" wear. But Will resists this indoctrination and is taken to a different room.

When Edgar takes Will for further indoctrination, the boy encounters his sister dancing in the disco and she demonstrates that she's been converted by putting down the "olders" and extolling the virtues of the "youngers."

In order to break down Will's resistance, he's given memory cubes to burn. Meanwhile, Bartholomew turns some kind of suspension gas on John, Maureen,

Judy and Don and uses a hypnosis process to make them forget that Will and Penny are the Robinson's children.

Dr. Smith is nosing around and his snooping causes a screen to become activated which shows what the so-called "youngers" of Delta really look like. They're not Earth colonists at all, but aliens with green skin and pointed ears. Smith is confronted by the "youngers" who threaten him unless they aid in breaking down Will's resistance and converting him. They make Smith look like a "younger" by having him wear a pendant and a long hair wig.

Will forces Penny to come with him back to the Jupiter II, but when they arrive they're treated like strangers. In tears, they watch as the Jupiter II takes off, leaving Will and Penny behind.

But once the ship is space borne, the robot breaks through the illusion and reveals that this is not Alpha Centauri and the colonists are actually aliens.

Before they left, Will had given John the memory cubes, which when burned cause the Robinsons to remember Will and Penny. They reverse course and return the Jupiter II to Delta.

The aliens detect the ship returning and attempt to repel it with an electromagnetic barrier. Bartholomew tells Will and Penny that if they want to save the Jupiter II, they have to agree to give themselves over to them as "youngers" and not resist any longer. Will sees no other way out and contacts John Robinson on the radio, claiming that he doesn't want them to come back and that they should leave them alone because they like it there.

John realizes what is happening and says that he'll follow Will's command and reverses course so that the Jupiter II heads back out into space, but only for five minutes.

Will and Penny find the converted Dr. Smith and convince him to help them pull off a robbery. They send Smith into the communications room, and Smith's bungling causes the communications center to blow up. Edgar attempts to make repairs, but without success. Bartholomew realizes that Will and Penny must be behind this and take them off for an operation, which will insure their final indoctrination into the "youngers."

Although the aliens never age, they believe that the aging properties in human blood will enable them to become adults. They are preparing a blood transfusion from Will and Penny when the Jupiter II returns and lands.

John and Don overpower Edgar and force him to take them to Will and Penny. Dr. Smith activates the music so that the "youngers" begin dancing as they're programmed to. This enables Smith, Will, Penny, John and Don to escape to the Jupiter II and leave the planet, although Smith discards his long hair and pendant and rejoins the crew of the Jupiter II.

Keith Taylor also appeared in the first season episode "Return To Earth."

EPISODE SEVENTY-NINE:
"Fugitives In Space"
First telecast January 31, 1968
Writer: Robert Hamner
Director: Ezra Stone
GUEST STARS: CREECH: Michael Conrad, WARDEN: Tol Avery, GUARD #1: Charles Horvath

On the prison planet Destruction, in quadrant 5, Creech makes good his escape by overpowering a guard and stealing a space cycle, which when activated vanisnes immediately. The space cycle takes Creech to the planet which the Jupiter II is presently on.

Dr. Smith finds the alien seemingly unconscious, although Smith is so badly frightened that he believes the ape-like Creech is dead. Before Smith can run off, Creech jumps him and changes coats with Smith. When the guards from Destruction trace the space cycle, they see Smith wearing Creech's coat and assume that he's their escaped prisoner.

The warden arrives and when Don and Smith try to explain about the mix-up, the warden agrees that Smith is not Creech, but he accuses the pair of conspiring to help Creech escape. Don and Smith are taken into custody for an immediate trial.

They are taken to the Jupiter II where Will and the robot are. The computer-run court soon arrives to hold the trial. The Warden makes it clear that no one has ever escaped from him before.

The Robinson's robot states that it will defend Don and Smith. It states that the computer-controlled court is a model 781E, which literally interprets the letter of the law. The robot states that they must locate Creech, the escaped prisoner, and sets off to do so itself.

In the robot's absence the trial is held anyway with Don and Dr. Smith found guilty of helping Creech to escape. When the robot brings in Creech, the prisoner claims that Don and Smith did help him, so that he won't be going back to Destruction without taking someone with him, and thus having a measure of revenge. Don, Smith and Creech are sentenced to life in prison and sent to quadrant 5 for hard labor where they are chained together.

The three have to break rocks in the broiling heat or else they won't be given any ice, and without the water from ice they'll quickly die.

Creech insists that the only way to survive is to escape as no one is ever paroled. Don West dismisses this but when Creech promises Smith a share of his loot if he'll help him escape, Smith is tempted.

Meanwhile, the robot makes a cake lined with plastic explosives and it delivers the cake when the robot and Will come to Destruction during visiting hours. But Smith screws up again and the cake is prematurely detonated, foiling the escape plan.

When the guard takes Will and the robot to the Warden, Creech uses this as an opportunity to escape. He needs to take Don with him, since they're chained together, and so Creech stuns Don and carries him over his shoulder so that he can flee and rendezvous with his gang.

The Warden reveals to Will that he knows that Don and Smith were framed, but he wants Creech to escape again so that he can lead the authorities to his gang and recover his everything that he's stole and hid.

Will is furious that the Warden would use Don and Smith so heartlessly and sets off with the robot to try to find his friends first.

Creech is trying to make his way across a minefield by forcing Smith to go ahead of him to see if any mines are in his path.

Don comes around and attacks Creech, but just gets knocked out again.

When Will and the robot come upon the minefield, the robot detonates the mines electronically so that they can safely traverse the area.

When Creech finally reaches the Devil's Quadrant where his gang is hiding out, he manages to break the chain holding them all together and offers to take Smith with him, but Dr. Smith isn't interested any more. Smith wants to help Don, who Creech worked over pretty well.

But when Creech tries to leave he's disintegrated as the Warden tracked Creech to the area and captured his gang and the hidden spoils of their crimes. The Warden grants pardons to Dr. Smith and Major West and releases them so that they can return to the Jupiter II.

Excellent makeup for future HILL STREET BLUES star Michael Conrad. Use of latex appliances foreshadowed PLANET OF THE APES.

EPISODE EIGHTY:
"Space Beauty"
First telecast February 14, 1968
Writer: Jackson Gillis
Director: Irving J. Moore
GUEST STARS: FARNUM: Leonard Stone, NANCY PI SQUARED: Dee Hartford, MISS TEUTONIUM: Miriam Schiller

Two mysterious aliens, wearing helmets and long black cloaks, enter the Jupiter II. When Don and the robot encounter them, the aliens stun Major West and neutralize the robot before heading to the lower deck. From a place of concealment the aliens secretly observe Penny and Judy.

But by the next morning, Don and the robot are back to normal with no memory of the strange events of the previous evening.

Will and Major West are attempting to build a cloud seeding device, but they aren't having any success in making rain.

Meanwhile, Judy and Penny encounter Farnum B, the ex-circus owner they'd met previously. This time he has an assistant named Nancy Pi Squared. Farnum explains that a mysterious employer hired them to search for contestants for a planned Miss Galaxy beauty contest. Although they've never met their employer, they know that he's the dictator of a world referred to as the dark planet.

Farnum isn't looking for humans to be in the contest, but is interested in unusual creatures such as Miss Teutonium, an ape-like being, or even a woman with a fish's head. Farnum doesn't know what the dictator would consider beautiful, so he doesn't want to take any chances.

Shortly thereafter, the two cloaked aliens appear and command that Farnum include Judy among his selections after all. Since Nancy sold Farnum's soul to seal the pact with the dictator, Farnum feels that he has no choice but to obey. Hell-fire threatens should he break the pact. Unfortunately, when asked, Judy rejects the offer as beauty pageants don't interest her. This creates an unfortunate dilemma for Farnum.

When Farnum wants to interest a lady dragon in the contest, Will comes up with an idea whereby they place a mirror in her path. When the dragon stops to admire herself, Farnum knows that the creature believes herself to be attractive. Farnum has no trouble then enlisting the dragon in the contest.

Since Farnum gets a thousand gold squandros for each contestant who signs up, Dr. Smith suddenly becomes very interested in this contest. When he learns that Farnum very much wants to sign up Judy, Smith agrees to help, for a percentage, of course. But Smith, failing to interest Judy on his own, decides to just forger her signature on the contract and collect the reward. But his deception is quickly revealed and Smith is gassed as punishment for his attempted deception.

Reduced to dealing honestly, Smith attempts to talk Judy into signing up. Smith finally settles on reverse psychology and says that it's just as well she doesn't enter since she'd be terribly disappointed when she lost. When Don tells Judy that she shouldn't sign, Judy becomes annoyed at both Don and Smith and signs the contract to spite them.

Once he's paid, Smith is so pleased with himself that he finds another contestant to sign up—the robot. Smith has reprogrammed the robot to have the voice and affections of Nancy Pi.

Meanwhile, Major West decides he should read this contract Judy signed. When he does he discovers that the fine print states that the winner of the contest must like with the great dictator forever!

The dictator arrives on the planet. He's dressed in armor and chooses Judy as the winner out of the assembled contestants. But when the dictator raises the faceplate of his armor, instead of a face there's a mass of flame.

Judy is amazed and doesn't know what to do. Farnum is given ten minutes to prepare the winner to go off with the dictator. They retreat to the Jupiter II and erect the force field, but it cannot hold back the dictator.

Don tells Smith that he's got to stall the dictator while he and Will try to get the rain-maker operating.

Smith does his oily best, but the dictator just ignores him and uses the contract to hypnotically attract Judy towards him.

Don and Will work frantically on the machine and it finally pays off, causing snow and rain to fall just before Judy reaches the dictator. Being just a flame being, the dictator is extinguished by the precipitation, along with his retainers and guards.

With the dictator destroyed, Farnum's soul is once more his own and he's able to safely leave with Nancy Pi.

Rare story featuring Judy Robinson.
Leonard Stone returns as Farnum.
Dee Hartford returns, but plays a different character—Farnum's assistant.
Smith actually tunes the robot's voice to sound female.

EPISODE EIGHTY-ONE:
"The Flaming Planet"
First telecast February 21, 1968
Writer: Barney Slater
Director: Don Richardson
GUEST STAR: SOBRAM: Abraham Sofaer

Although John Robinson has forbidden any plantlife being brought aboard the Jupiter II, Dr. Smith thinks that it would be harmless to have one little houseplant, which he's growing in his cabin. When the Jupiter II passes through a strange radiation belt, the entire vessel is affected, particular Smith's plant.

The plant metamorphosizes into a thinking being that feels affection for Smith, whom it regards as its mother.

Will convinces Smith that the plant could become dangerous, and since it has already become annoying to him, Dr. Smith agree to eject the plant through the waste disposal chute.

But cast into space, the plant survives and settles on the top of the Jupiter II where it expands in size and blocks the air intake system, which interferes with the ship's life support. Because of this, the Jupiter II only has enough air left for half an hour.

When they detect a nearby planet they decide to head into the atmosphere so that the heat on the hull caused by the friction of entry will burn the plant off the ship. But a voice received on their radio warns them off, stating that they are in a restricted zone. When they attempt to explain their dilemma to the mystery voice, they are ignore and missiles are fired to warn them off.

They successfully enter the atmosphere and burn the plant away, but a beam from the planet below drains their power. They're in orbit now and it will take them twenty hours to recharge so that they can leave orbit, but before that time can elapse they'll pass over the restricted zone in eleven hours.

Don takes the escape pod down in order to try to make contact with the aliens. Since Smith's plant got them into this trouble, Don orders Smith at gunpoint to accompany him into the pod.

The escape pod lands, but unnoticed by them a tendril of Smith's plant has survived and come down on the pod with them.

Don and Smith discover a cave containing old style cannons, suits of armor and a large book. The book reveals that this is the mobile world of the Sobrams, a long dead race of great warriors.

The escape pod returns to the Jupiter II, so John, Will and the robot decide to take it down and see what's happening.

When Don and Smith find the missile launchers which were used to attack them, they also find the alien who warned them off. It's an old, green-skinned man who is the last of the Sobram race.

The Sobram says that he'll allow the Jupiter II to pass overhead peacefully if one of them agrees to remain behind and take his place when he dies and guard the planet. Major West agrees for the good of the ship, but the Sobram rejects him when he tests out as too ethical to be a good warrior. Don isn't heartless enough.

When John, Will and the robot arrive from the escape pod, the robot reveals that Sobram doesn't want a replacement—he wants an opponent. Sobram wants his opponent to man another missile station so that they can battle it out and die a warrior's death by having the planet blasted into an inferno.

The Sobram finally agrees that the robot should be his opponent. Don and Will return to the escape pod and the Jupiter II, but John and Smith remain behind and encounter the regenerated plant creature. Since the plant creature is an excellent survivor type, John and Smith hatch a plan in which it can prove useful.

John runs up to Sobram and warns that his planet is being invaded by intelligent plants. Smith has given the plant a laser, and when the Sobram fires on it, the plant splits into two separate creatures. Sobram is fascinated, and while he's engaged in his final, seemingly endless, battle, John, Smith and the robot leave to return to the Jupiter II.

EPISODE EIGHTY-TWO:
"The Great Vegetable Rebellion"
First Telecast February 28, 1968
Writer: Peter Packer
Director: Don Richardson
GUEST STARS: TYBO: Stanley Adams, WILLOUGHBY: James Millholin

It's the robot's birthday. We all know robots have birthdays. It's the day the last bolt was tightened and when it was first juiced up and ready to go. Since the Jupiter II is orbiting a planet rich in plant life, Dr. Smith decides to take the pod down and collect some posies for the occasion. After all, it's not every day that a robot celebrates its birth pangs.

Dr. Smith lands the pod and emerges on the planet. He sights some likely vegetation and begins clipping away, only as he does so he hears tiny screams. Now where could they be coming from? Before Smith can piece the obvious together, a giant carrot man emerges from the overgrowth and, with its mastery of languages, accuses Smith in English of slaughtering helpless plants. The punishment for such a crime is execution, possibly by being stir-fried.

Shrieking in his finest falsetto, Smith runs for his life. Smith blunders into a human named Willoughby. He was stranded on the planet and his life was saved by Tybo (Mr. Carrot) when he was given a vegetable heart. When Smith is cornered by Tybo, it's decided that instead of killing him, they'll just transform him into a vegetable.

The robot's party is in full swing and it's getting crocked on 3-in-1 oil when everyone notices that Smith isn't around being obnoxious. They notice the pod is missing and when John contacts it, Dr. Smith's replies are strange and he refuses to return to the ship. Although Major West argues against it, John decides that they'll take the Jupiter II down to the surface. They have to at least retrieve the pod.

Since there is thick vegetation around, John, Maureen, Penny and Major West have to hack their way through to where they detect the pod is parked. Funny thing, though, they keep hearing these little screams. . .

The four are captured in one of Tybo's man-traps. Meanwhile, back at the Jupiter II, the robot is on guard but finds itself besieged by creeping vines which crawl over over the robot to immobilize it. Judy and Will manage to pull the vines off the robot, whereupon the robot declares that the jungle has declared war on all human life. It's jungle warfare at its most primitive.

Judy, Will and the robot are really concerned about the others now and decide that they'd better try to find them.

First they encounter Dr. Smith, who is slowly changing into a plant, and they're quickly captured themselves by vines before they can accomplish anything further.

But then Willoughby arrives on the scene and talks the plants into releasing Will and Judy. He then reveals that their family is being held prisoner in something resembling a hot house surrounded by a force field. Although Willoughby doesn't dare help them directly, he reveals that Tybo's hydrostatic system is located underneath the hot house.

Penny is already starting to turn into a plant in the hot house, so John decides that they've got to try entering Tybo's hydrostatic system. He and Major West unearth a trap door and descend into the system. They're able to find the water supply and shut it down because the system is neatly labeled so that they can read it.

Will and Judy are still trying to find their parents but stumble into another trap, this one being a pit where a huge plant attacks them. But then the robot rolls up and helps to pull them out of the pit. They then go to where Smith is still undergoing his vegetable metamorphosis.

Will wants to free his parents and so finds Tybo and tries to explain that this is all just a horrible misunderstanding, but the carrot man doesn't care what Will has to say.

Meanwhile, Judy convinces Willoughby that Smith shouldn't be changed into a human stalk of celery and he relents, changing Smith back to his normal, craven self.

John's shut down of the water supply has had a profound affect as Tybo soon collapses from the lack of water. The family breaks out of the hot house, but they take pity on Tybo and give him enough water to save his life. Willoughby, with his vegetable heart, wants to remain on this world while the Robinsons, Smith and Major West and the robot return to the pod and the Jupiter II and take their leave of this planet of talking plants.

This is LIS's most infamous episode.
Stanley Adams, who plays Tybo, guest-starred in the classic STAR TREK episode "The Trouble With Tribbles."
In an ironic reverse, this story seems to have influenced SPACE: 1999, which did a similar theme in the episode "Rules Of Luton."

EPISODE EIGHTY-THREE:
"Junkyard In Space"
First telecast March 6, 1968
Writer: Barney Slater
Director: Ezra Stone
GUEST STAR: THE JUNK MAN: Marcel Hillaire

The Jupiter II is approaching a cosmic cloud when a fire in the port fuel cells disables the long-range sensors. They'll have to investigate it from the pod, and although Dr. Smith is appointed for the task, Smith manages to talk the robot into taking his place.

The pod is launched into the cosmic cloud where the robot reports that there is no danger from it. But then the pod is gripped by a mysterious force which pulls it to the surface of a nearby planet. When the pod crashes, the robot becomes imprisoned by an electromagnetic force in what appears to be a junk yard.

The Jupiter II goes down to the planet's surface so that they can retrieve the robot and the pod. While John Robinson remains behind to repair the damage to the long-range sensors, Major West, Will and a reluctant Dr. Smith go in search of the missing robot. Unbeknownst to them, they are under observation by a strange metallic looking alien being.

They come upon the junk yard and manage to free the robot. When they go to make their way back to the ship, they encounter an alien junk man. He explains that he collects scrap metal to melt down in his huge blast furnace and offers to buy the Jupiter II from them for this purpose, but they turn the junk man down.

Maureen discovers that somehow the ship's entire food supply has been contaminated and so they'll have to locate some food on this junk world before they can take off again.

When Smith and the robot encounter the junk man, he offers to trade food for parts of the robot. The junk man claims he needs these parts to repair himself. Dr. Smith readily agrees and convinces the robot that by sacrificing parts of himself, he'll be able to acquire food to save the starving Robinsons.

With the new parts, the Junk Man is able to improve his appearance dramatically. His next step in his plan is to gain possession of the Jupiter II.

The robot collapses back at the ship due to its missing parts. When Smith goes back to the new improved Junk Man, the alien offers Smith more food in exchange for taking him off the planet on the Jupiter II.

Dr. Smith sneaks the alien aboard the ship, but then the Junk Man sneakily locks everyone except Smith out of the Jupiter II. Since it possesses the robot's memory banks, it knows how to operate the ship's controls.

The alien takes off in the Jupiter II, ignoring Smith's please to not leave the Robinsons behind.

Don goes back to the pod and takes it up, giving chase, but the alien fires missiles to turn the pod back.

The robot blames itself and decides to place itself on the conveyor belt leading to the blast furnace.

Will believes that he can somehow appear to the alien and takes the pod up himself to contact the Junk Man with. Will plays on the emotions in the robot's memory banks of its friendship with the Robinsons. The Junk Man decides to allow the pod to space dock with the Jupiter II to hear what else he has to say. But all the Junk Man really plans to do is allow Will to stay and send Smith back down in the pod.

Will appeals to the Junk Man to be kind, like the robot was, and the alien relents, taking the Jupiter II back down to the surface.

The Junk Man then races to the furnace with Will, realizing that the robot is attempting to destroy itself. But the robot goes into the furnace on the conveyor just before they arrive.

But the robot has heard their cries and emerges from the flames, scorched but functioning.

Will is able to repair the robot, with the Junk Man's help, and they leave the alien on his junk world while the Jupiter II once again blasts off into space.

Marcel Hillaire returns, this time playing a Galactic junk man.
Smith again sells parts of the robot in exchange for food.
The junk man repels the Space Pod with missiles fired from the Jupiter II. This is the first, and only, mention of the offensive capabilities of the ship.
Story influence: "The Trader."

The Phantom
The Green Hornet
The Shadow
The Batman

Each issue of Serials Adventures Presents offers 100 or more pages of pure nostalgic fun for $16.95

SERIALS ADVENTURES MAGAZINE

Flash Gordon Part One
Flash Gordon Part Two
Blackhawk

Each issue of Serials Adventures Presents features a chapter by chapter review of a rare serial combined with biographies of the stars and behind-the-scenes information. Plus rare photos. See the videotapes and read the books!

THE U.N.C.L.E. TECHNICAL MANUAL
Every technical device completely detailed and blueprinted, including weapons, communications, weaponry, organization, facitilites... 80 pages, 2 volumes...$9.95 each

NUMBER SIX: THE COMPLEAT PRISONER
The most unique and intelligent television series ever aired! Patrick McGoohan's tour-de-force of spies and mental mazes finally explained episode by episode, including an interview with the McGoohan and the complete layout of the real village!...160 pages...$14.95

THE GREEN HORNET
Daring action adventure with the Green Hornet and Kato. This show appeared before Bruce Lee had achieved popularity but delivered fun, superheroic action. Episode guide and character profiles combine to tell the whole story...120 pages...$14.95

WILD, WILD, WEST
Is it a Western or a Spy show? We couldn't decide so we're listing it twice. Fantastic adventure, convoluted plots, incredible devices...all set in the wild, wild west! Details of fantastic devices, character profiles and an episode-by-episode guide...120 pages...$17.95